FAMILY LAW DICTIONARY

FAMILY LAW DICTIONARY

marriage, divorce, children & living together

By Robin D. Leonard & Stephen R. Elias

NOLO PRESS • 950 Parker St. • Berkeley, CA • 94710

IMPORTANT

Nolo Press is committed to keeping its books up-to-date. Each new printing, whether or not it is called a new edition, has been revised to reflect the latest law changes. This book was printed and updated on the last date indicated below. Before you rely on information in it, you might wish to call Nolo Press (415) 549-1976 to check whether a later printing or edition has been issued.

PRINTING HISTORY

New "**Printing**" means there have been some minor changes, but usually not enough so that people will need to trade in or discard an earlier printing of the same edition. Obviously, this is a judgment call and any change, no matter how minor, might affect you.

New "**Edition**" means one or more major, or a number of minor, law changes since the previous edition.

FIRST EDITION	April 1988
ILLUSTRATIONS	Linda Allison
	Mari Stein
PRODUCTION	Stephanie Harolde
BOOK DESIGN & LAYOUT	Jackie Clark
	Toni Ihara
	Amy Ihara
PRINTING	Delta Lithograph

ISBN 0-87337-061-9
Library of Congress Catalog Card Number: 88-60701
Copyright © 1988 by Robin D. Leonard and Stephen R. Elias

ACKNOWLEDGMENTS

No project that is years in the making is ever done alone (or in this case, by two people). This certainly is true of this dictionary, which has been read, re-read and re-read again by many wonderfully insightful people. Also needing thanks are all those people who played "stump the authors" by calling with messages something like:

"Have you included 'Et Ux?'"

"What about 'Siblings?'"

"Okay—I've got one for you. How about 'Conjugal?'"

"Do you define 'Rehabilitative Alimony?'"

Specific thanks go to:

Mary Randolph (and her father, Judge William Randolph of Macomb, Illinois) and Albin Renauer, whose editorial skills, humor and patience made this dictionary a reality. Thanks especially for suggesting "a rare type of pasta" as an alternative definition of "Vinculo Matrimonii," for insisting that we find, and then supplying, an entry for "X," and for suggesting "Living in the Sun (California)" as the entry following "Living in Sin."

Carol Bohmer, Robin's Family Law professor at Cornell University, who spent cold, wintery, Ithaca days reading the manuscript so that those terms not commonly used in California would be accurate and understandable.

Janice Kosel, Mary Jane Foran and Ellen Lyons, who made important contributions to the dictionary early in its development.

Jake Warner who plopped down at least 50 family-law books on our desks for sources of words for the dictionary, who waited (most patiently) for Robin to finish up the dictionary before editing her next project, and who was the favorite player of "stump the authors."

Jackie Clark, Toni Ihara, Amy Ihara and Stephanie Harolde, who anxiously awaited the raw text, charts, cross-references, and marginalia, and then turned it all into an attractive and useful dictionary.

David Cole, who knocked us back to reality when we suggested ponderous and lawyerly titles for the dictionary ("The Vocabulary of the Law Affecting. . .").

Because everyone at Nolo is ultimately vital to the success of every project, our thanks to Janet Bergen, Karen Chambers, Susan Cornell, Jack Devaney, John O'Donnell, Leili Eghbal (who valiantly tried to come up with an "X" entry), Sue Fox, Ann Heron (especially for helping with the non-traditional family entries), Barbara Hodovan, Toshiro Ihara, Kate Thill, and Alison Towle.

DEDICATIONS

To Lee, who has helped me broaden the definition of "family," and to the memory of Cheryl, one of the first people to tell me it was okay to stop practicing law.

—RDL

To Rubin, who patiently suffered the loss of his father from time to time during the writing of this dictionary.

—SRE

ABOUT THE AUTHORS

Robin D. Leonard survived Ithaca, New York winters and graduated from Cornell Law School in 1985. She came to Nolo after unhappily practicing family law in San Francisco for a year and a half. Since joining Nolo, Robin has edited Nolo's *California Marriage and Divorce Law* and *Billpayers' Rights*.

Stephen R. Elias received a law degree from Hastings College of Law in 1969. He practiced in California, New York and Vermont until 1983 when he decided to make a full-time career of helping non-lawyers understand the law. Since 1982, Steve has authored or edited a number of Nolo Books. At present, Steve teaches legal research for the Nolo Press Seminar series, and is working on several new Nolo-related enterprises.

NOLO'S OTHER FAMILY LAW BOOKS

California Marriage and Divorce Law
Warner, Ihara & Elias

How to Adopt Your Stepchild
Zagone & Randolph

How to Change Your Name
Loeb & Brown

How to Do Your Own Divorce in California
Sherman

How to Modify and Collect Child Support in California
Matthews, Segal & Willis

A Legal Guide for Lesbian and Gay Couples
Curry & Clifford

The Living Together Kit
Ihara & Warner

Plan Your Estate: Wills, Probate Avoidance, Trusts and Taxes
Clifford

The Power of Attorney Book
Clifford

Social Security, Medicare & Pensions: A Sourcebook for Older Americans
Matthews & Berman

Your Family Records: How to Preserve Personal, Financial and Legal History
Pladsen & Clifford

INTRODUCTION

The *Family Law Dictionary: Marriage, Divorce, Children and Living Together* is a dictionary of words and phrases used in the legal area referred to as "family law." The dictionary includes terms relating to marriage, divorce, adoption, support, custody, guardianship, living together, paternity, abortion and the like. Although Nolo hopes someday to publish a comprehensive legal dictionary for use by your family, similar to "Your Family Medical Dictionary," this is not that endeavor. Or, to put it another way, read the title as "FamilyLaw Dictionary," not "Family LawDictionary."

The Family Law Dictionary differs from other legal dictionaries in several important ways.

First, the definitions are written in plain English, not legalese. If you doubt that other law dictionaries are incomprehensible, take a look at this comparison between a definition from our dictionary and a definition from *Black's Law Dictionary*, the best selling legal dictionary in the United States:

Condonation (Nolo). Condonation is someone's approval of another's activities. For example, a wife who does not object to her husband's adultery may be said to condone it. In states with fault divorce, condonation may constitute a defense to divorce. If the wife sues her husband for divorce, claiming he has committed adultery, the husband may argue as a defense that she condoned his behavior.

Condonation (Black's). The conditional remission or forgiveness, by means of continuance or resumption of marital cohabitation, by one of the married parties, of a known matrimonial offense committed by the other, that would constitute a cause of divorce; the condition being that the offense shall not be repeated.

Second, we define not only legal terms, but also commonly used non-legal terms, such as "extended family," "marriage of convenience," and "same-sex marriage."

Third, we include both the terms and the context in which the terms are used. Many entries contain examples, and others include two or three paragraph discussions.

Fourth, the dictionary features extensive cross-referencing. Terms used in one definition that are themselves defined in another entry appear in boldface. Or, if the entry you've chosen just whets your appetite and you want to know more, turn to one of the related terms listed after many entries.

Fifth, we've provided charts to help you visualize what you're reading, especially when the law differs substantially among the states. For instance, one chart lists the grounds for divorce in all 50 states (and Washington, D.C.) while another shows incest and marital prohibitions. Did you know, for example, that in Iowa, you can't marry your grandchild's spouse and in Kentucky you can't marry your first cousin once removed? (In case you're wondering who exactly your first cousin once removed is, that's in the chart called "Who is Your Kin.")

Sixth, because dictionaries don't always make the most entertaining reading, we've included some lesser known international comparisons in margin notes (marginalia). Examples include:

• In the Conja state of Ghana, a married woman is given a plot in her husband's land to plant beans, peppers and okra.

• In Yugoslavia, an adoption may be dissolved by reason of the ingratitude of the adopted child.

• In 1984, a Swedish government commission recommended that lesbian and gay couples be granted legal status similar to that granted married couples.

• One ground for divorce in Mexico is a husband's suggestion that his wife engage in prostitution.

And now for a brief and but important comment. Family law, probably more than any other area of law, differs among states tremendously. What is called "visitation" in one state, is called "parental contact" in another. Some states have done away with the term "divorce," and now use "dissolution."

"Alimony" is gone in number of states, and has been replace by either "spousal support" or "maintenance." And some states call parental sharing of custody "joint custody," while other states call it "shared custody."

Terminology isn't the only thing that differs. The laws themselves do as well. For example, when it is necessary to determine how a married couple's property is divided at divorce, eight states follow community property principles, one follows a modified community property principle, 40 use a system known as "equitable distribution of property" and one uses traditional common law property principles. Also, some states have made laws preferring joint custody whenever possible; other states have laws rejecting joint custody.

What does all this mean? Where terminology differs, we have defined the concept at one entry and have cross-referenced the others. Thus, the money paid to a divorced spouse for support by his or her ex is under "alimony." "Maintenance" and "spousal support" simply say "See Alimony." Where laws differ, we have tried to be as specific and as inclusive as possible, but out of necessity, some definitions are broadly written and refer you to other terms.

How to Use This Dictionary: The Family Law Dictionary is easy to use. All words and phrases, whether defined entries or those providing cross-references to other entires, appear in straight alphabetical order. There are no sections, sub-sections or parts.

If you are not sure how to look up a word, phrase or concept (for example, you want to know what it means to serve someone with an order to show cause for a contempt of court hearing), your best bet is to look up any of the words with which you are unfamiliar. In this example, "show cause" refers you to "order to show cause," and "serve," "contempt of court," "hearing," and "order to show cause" are defined. If you look up a phrase and it's neither included nor cross-referenced, don't stop searching. Look at the entries before and after it. Because words come in different tenses and forms, we've had to limit ourselves to only one entry per word. For example, you won't find "adopt," "adopting," "adopted" or "adoptable" in the Family Law Dictionary; you will, however, find "adoption." "Emancipation" isn't there either, but "emancipated minor" is. Although we have undoubtedly missed some terms, we have gone to great effort to be comprehensive. So don't give up if you fail on your first try.

The best way to explain the organization of each entry is by way of an example:

Debts Incurred Between Separation and Divorce: State law varies on who is responsible for **debts** incurred after a **married** couple permanently **separates** but before the **divorce** is final. In some states, each spouse is responsible for his own debts. In many states, however, creditors may sue both the husband and the wife for a debt incurred by either one of them before the official divorce. If a creditor obtains payment from the wife, but the husband incurred the debt, the wife must request the court to order her husband to **reimburse** her.

In a few states, debts incurred between separation and divorce for **necessaries** (food, housing, clothing and health care) for the spouse or children (unless there is a **child support order** stating who must pay) are considered joint debts. A creditor may obtain payment from either spouse. If the wife pays, but the husband incurred the debt, the wife will not be entitled to reimbursement.

EXAMPLE

George and Fran separated in October and planned to divorce. In December, George was in a car accident, and was billed $250 for fixing the car and $100 toward his medical costs. In March, when George and Fran drafted their divorce agreement, George requested that Fran contribute toward the bills. Fran refused, and so they brought the question before a judge. The judge ordered George to pay the full car bill, but ordered Fran to help with the medical costs (a necessary of life).

See also *Community Debts; Debts: Effect on Alimony and Child Support; Debts Incurred Before Marriage;* and *Debts Incurred During Marriage.*

The main entry is **Debts Incurred Between Separation and Divorce**. All main entries are in **slightly larger boldface print**. All words appearing in an entry defined elsewhere are in **boldface**. Related words and phrases are in *boldface italics*. Most related words and phrases are at the end of entries, following the words "see also," (or occasionally "related terms"). Many entries have examples. Short examples are incorporated into the text; longer ones are in boxes.

The dictionary may be used as a vocabulary builder, as well as a reference tool. Although each definition stands alone, the boldface terms give you an opportunity to learn more about a given subject.

Any omission is unintentional. We encourage feedback; if you think we've left something out, please write and tell us.

OFFER

Here is your opportunity to play "stump the authors." If you think a word or phrase has been omitted from the dictionary, send it to us with a *brief* definition. If we include it in the next edition, your name will appear in the acknowledgments.

WORD OR PHRASE: _____

BRIEF DEFINITION: _____

_____

YOUR NAME AND ADDRESS: _____

_____

THANKS,

ROBIN LEONARD & STEVE ELIAS
Nolo Press • 950 Parker Street • Berkeley CA 94710

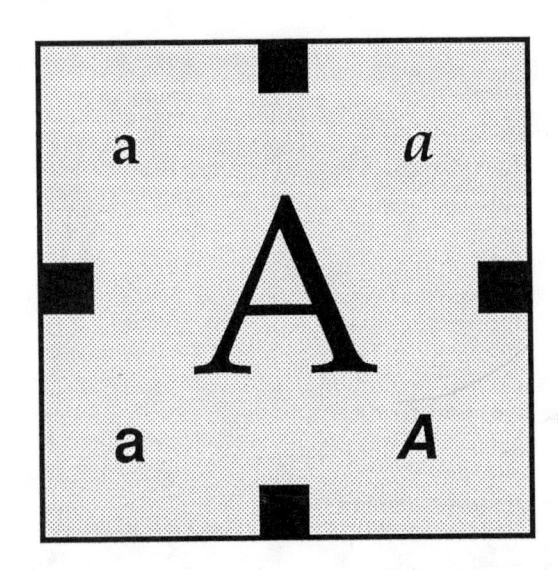

Abandonment of Child: When a parent fails to provide any financial assistance to, and/or communicate with, his child over a period of time, a court may deem the child legally abandoned by that parent. Two important consequences of a court finding of abandonment are that the parent's rights are terminated and the child may be **adopted** through court proceedings without the parent's permission. This determination is made at a court **hearing**. Abandonment actions are often initiated by **stepparents** or **foster parents** who want to adopt but cannot get permission from one or both of the **natural parents**.

Abandonment also describes situations where a child is physically abandoned: left on a doorstep, delivered to a hospital or placed in a trash can, for example. These children are usually placed in **orphanages** or **foster homes** and made available for adoption. Parents who abandon their children in this way may be criminally prosecuted.

Ability to be Self-Supporting: The ability of an ex-spouse to support herself is normally considered by a court when setting the amount and duration of **alimony** to be paid to that spouse. A court looks to whether the ex-spouse possesses marketable skills and whether she is able to work outside the home (having **custody** of preschool children and not having access to **day care** could make this impossible). The ability to be self-supporting differs from actually being self-supporting. If a spouse has marketable skills and is able to work outside the home, but has chosen not to look for work, the court is very likely to limit the amount and **length of alimony**.

In many states, no alimony is awarded if both spouses are able to support themselves. If, however, one spouse was dependent on the other for support during the **marriage**, the dependent spouse is often awarded alimony for a specified period or until she becomes self-supporting. If a spouse receiving alimony becomes self-supporting before the time set by the court for the alimony to end, the paying spouse can go to court and file a **request for modification** or a request for **termination of alimony**. Conversely, if at the end of the support period the supported spouse does not have the ability to support herself, she may request an **extension of alimony**, which, however, is difficult to obtain.

Ability to Earn: When a court computes the amount of **alimony** or **child support** to be paid by a spouse or parent, both **parties'** ability to earn is usually taken into account. Actual **earnings** are an important factor in determining a person's ability to earn, but are not conclusive where there is **evidence** that a person could earn more if she chose to do so. Some states, however, set alimony or child support payments based only on actual earnings—that is, the actual **ability to pay**.

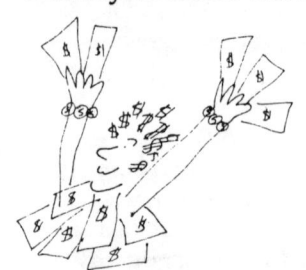

> **EXAMPLE**
>
> Jane Doctor, who has earned $100,000 a year for the past three years while married, quit her job when she and her husband **separated** in order to become a TV repairperson with an annual income of approximately $20,000. During the **divorce trial**, Jane's husband, Lionel, requested alimony and child support for himself and Lionel Jr. Because Jane abruptly changed her income, which has affected her **family**, the court imposed a larger alimony and child support obligation on Jane than she can afford earning $20,000 a year. The court has reasoned that Jane can return to the world of medicine if she needs to and that her ex-husband and son should not be penalized because of her employment decision. In some states, however, the court would reason that ability to earn is too speculative and would set alimony and child support on the basis of Jane's $20,000 income.

Ability to Pay: Courts always consider a person's ability to pay when setting his **alimony** and **child support** obligations. A court looks at the payor's gross income from all sources (wages, public benefits, interest and dividends on investments, rents from **real property**, profits from patents and the like, and any other sources of income), less any **mandatory deductions** (income taxes, social security, health care, mandatory union dues, etc.). In some states, the court also looks beyond actual **earnings** if there is **evidence** that a person's **ability to earn** is much greater than his actual earnings, and he is earning the lesser amount in order to minimize his support obligation.

Also when setting support obligations, the court takes into account the reasonable expenses incurred by the paying spouse for his own basic **necessaries** of life (such as rent or mortgage, food, clothing and health care). Courts, however, typically do not allow expenses such as school expenses, dining outside the home and entertainment to influence their support determination on the theory that family support should come before these types of personal expenses.

Abortion: Abortion is the voluntary termination of pregnancy. It is the absolute legal right of all adult women in consultation with their doctors during the first three months (called the first trimester) of their pregnancy, under a U.S. Supreme Court **case** known as *Roe v. Wade*, 410 U.S. 113 (1973). *Roe v. Wade* also held that a state may impose restrictions on abortion during the the period following the first trimester until viability (when the fetus may survive outside the mother's womb) if those restrictions are reasonably related to protecting the mother's health, and that a state may ban abortion altogether after viability.

U.S. Supreme Court cases decided after *Roe v. Wade* have held that during the first trimester, a state cannot:
• require a woman to obtain her husband's consent before obtaining an abortion
• require the abortion to be performed in a hospital
• require a woman to obtain approval from any doctor other than her own personal physician
• or require a woman to reside in the state where the abortion is to be performed.

Twenty-three states have enacted laws requiring a woman under the **age of majority** to either notify her parent or obtain her parent's consent before having an abortion. States which have enacted parental consent laws, however, must also provide a procedure whereby a minor unable to obtain her parent's permission has the opportunity to either be declared **emancipated** by a court and therefore able to make the decision herself, or have a judge declare her mature enough to undergo the abortion. The constitutionality of parental consent and notification statutes has been challenged, and in twelve states the courts have ruled the laws unenforceable because of constitutional problems.•

Above Captioned Cause: The "above captioned cause" is a phrase used in **court papers** meaning the particular **case**. It allows the writer to refer to the case without restating its name. It is not necessary, however, to use this form.

EXAMPLE

Assume Fred Johnson is representing himself in his **divorce** and files a **request for a modification of child support**. In court papers, he may refer to his own case of *Johnson v. Johnson* as "the above captioned cause."

Absent Parent: For purposes of **enforcement of child support**, an absent parent is any adult legally responsible for providing monetary support for a child, who is absent from the home.

Abuse of Discretion: See *Discretion of Judge*.

Accepting Service of Court Papers: When one person sues another, the **party** who is sued (called the **defendant** or respondent) is entitled to receive formal **notice** of the lawsuit. The least expensive and most convenient way to satisfy this notice requirement is for someone on behalf of the **plaintiff** (the person who initiated the **case**) to mail the **court papers** (usually a **summons** and **complaint**) to the defendant and ask her to sign, date and return a form acknowledging that she received them. This voluntary acceptance of court papers is called "accepting service" or "acknowledgment of service," and saves the plaintiff from having to pay someone to locate and hand deliver the papers to the defendant (called personal service), which is otherwise required if the defendant doesn't cooperate. In some states, the failure to accept service voluntarily makes the defendant responsible for the cost of service even if he otherwise wins the case.

Once the defendant has been **served** with the summons and complaint, service of most subsequent court papers may be done by mailing them, without the need for an acknowledgment of service form. Some papers, however, such as **contempt of court** hearing notices and **temporary restraining orders** must still be served formally. The party being served, however, may voluntarily accept these papers.

See also *Process and Process Server; Quashing Service of Process* and *Service of Court Papers*.

Acknowledged Father: An acknowledged father is any biological father of a child born to unmarried parents for whom **paternity** has been established by either the admission of the father or the agreement of the parents.

Acknowledgment of Service: See *Accepting Service of Court Papers*.

Action: Action is another word for lawsuit, case, legal matter or **litigation**. "Cause of action" refers to a set of facts that make up the grounds for filing a lawsuit.

EXAMPLE

Janis is the victim of **domestic violence** by her husband James. This violence constitutes the cause of action known as **battery**, and any lawsuit Janis files against James may be generally referred to as an action.

Active Military Duty: A person on active military duty is a person who has enlisted in the armed services and is serving out the term of his enlistment, or is an officer in the armed services who has not transferred to the Reserves, resigned, retired or been dismissed. A person on active military duty is prohibited by a federal law (Soldiers and Sailors Civil Relief Act, 50 U.S.C. § 501 et seq.) from being subjected to any civil court **action**, including a **divorce**, unless he consents to the power of the court (called the court's **jurisdiction**) to hear the case. A plaintiff who wants to sue someone on active military duty must wait until he leaves active duty. The reasons for this rule are:

• it would not be fair to proceed in court against a serviceperson who is prevented from attending because of his military duty; and

• it would be too disruptive and expensive for the military to have its members coming and going long distances just because they have been sued.

The Soldiers and Sailors Civil Relief Act does not apply to criminal prosecutions—that is, a person on active military duty may be charged with and prosecuted for criminal offenses.

When a **minor** goes on active military duty, he is usually considered **emancipated**. This means his parents no longer have a duty to support him and any **child support** payments to the emancipated child's **custodial parent** are cancelled.

Actual Damages: When damages, which have been suffered by someone as a result of another's wrongdoing, can be precisely measured, they are called actual damages.

Examples of actual damages are:
• Loss of income because of an injury
• Medical expenses
• Costs of repairing damaged **property**
• Specific business losses occurring because of a breach of a contract.

Actual damages are rarely awarded in **family law** cases, although some states now allow a parent to recover from his child's other parent the actual damages suffered if thwarted when trying to exercise **visitation** rights (e.g., the visiting parent buys a non-refundable plane ticket to have his child visit him, only to find out that the child has suddenly been shipped off to his grandmother's).

Additional Financial Burden: When a **child support** or **alimony** obligation is temporarily made more difficult by an additional financial burden (for example, a **medical emergency**), a court may order a **temporary modification of alimony or child support**, reducing the amount to be paid. Likewise, a person to whom alimony or child support is owed may sometimes obtain a temporary increase in support if she faces a temporary additional economic **hardship**.

Additional Income From Remarriage: If a parent with **child support** obligations **remarries** and has some of his new spouse's income available for living expenses, the parent receiving the support may be able to get an increase by filing a **request for modification**. This is because the paying parent now has a greater share of his own income available to fund the increase. On the other hand, if a paying parent assumes a **new support obligation** (through **adoption** or a child by a second marriage) he may be able to obtain a corresponding reduction in child support. Courts, however, do not usually look favorably on parents who seek to reduce one familial obligation to support another.

When a parent receiving child support remarries, the paying parent is still usually required to pay the full amount of court-ordered child support, even if the recipient parent and the children have the benefit of the new spouse's income. This is because the **stepparent** has no legal obligation to support the child, and because the child's needs have not changed just because the parent she lives with has remarried.

When an **alimony** recipient remarries, there is usually a **termination of alimony** on the theory that the recipient is now obtaining additional income from the remarriage.

When the alimony payor remarries, the recipient is unlikely to be able to obtain an increase in alimony unless she can show an increased need which happened to coincide with or predate the payor's remarriage.

Adjudicate:
When a judge decides a **case**, she is said to adjudicate the matter.

Ad Litem:
"Ad litem" means "for the purpose of the litigation." See *Guardian Ad Litem*.

Administrative Hearing:
Administrative law is the body of law governing administrative agencies, i.e., those agencies created by Congress or state legislatures such as the Social Security Administration, state Unemployment Insurance Boards, state Welfare Commissions, and the Occupational Safety and Health Administration. The authority these agencies possess is delegated to them by the bodies which created them; the Social Security Administration's power comes from Congress.

Administrative agencies administer law through the creation and enforcement of regulations; most of these regulations pertain to providing some type of benefit to applicants. Frequently, an applicant objects to an agency's decision to deny, limit or terminate the benefits provided and seeks to have the decision reviewed. This review is called an administrative hearing and is held before an administrative law judge (A.L.J.).

Administrative hearings are informal, yet very important. Usually, the A.L.J. meets with representatives from the agency and the applicant seeking benefits. The applicant may choose to be or not be represented by an attorney and in fact, many administrative agencies permit paralegals, law students or law clerks to appear on behalf of applicants. Each side presents its **evidence** and elicits testimony from its witnesses. The hearing is often tape recorded, as opposed to taken down by a **court reporter**. The A.L.J. renders a decision called an administrative **order**, which may be reviewed by either a higher level within the agency or by a court.

Admissible Evidence:
Anything a judge allows a jury (or himself) to consider in reaching a decision during the **trial** is called admissible evidence because it is "admitted" into evidence. Many types of **evidence** are not admissible because they don't satisfy legal standards of reliability or fairness.

These standards have developed over hundreds of years and are constantly subject to change.

EXAMPLE

Laura is six years old, and there is evidence that she has been abused by her father. Under traditional evidence rules, any statements Laura made outside of the courtroom to a counselor, parent or other person concerning the abuse would be considered inadmissible evidence (see **hearsay**). Only her statements made in court in front of her father would be admissible. Because of the difficulty in having a child speak freely in a court, many states are now experimenting with allowing children to testify on videotape outside the courtroom and then showing the tape in court.

Admission: An admission is any statement made by a **party** to a lawsuit (either before a court **action** or during it) which tends to support the position of the other side or diminish his own position. For example, if a husband sues his wife for **divorce** on the grounds of **adultery,** and she states out of court that she has had affairs, her statement is an admission. Any admission made by a party is **admissible evidence** in a court proceeding, even though it is technically considered **hearsay** (which is normally inadmissible). Attorneys tell their clients not to talk to anyone about their **case** or about the events leading up to it in order to prevent their clients from making admissions.

Adoption: Adoption is a legal method of creating a parent-child relationship that is recognized for all purposes—including **child support** obligations, **inheritance** rights, and **custody**—as equivalent to the biological relationship. While in most cases adults adopt **minors**, it is possible in most states for one adult to adopt another. (Only Alabama, Arizona, Hawaii, Michigan, Nebraska and Ohio prohibit adult adoptions.)

Adoptions are categorized by courts and social service agencies into three basic types: **stepparent adoptions** (the child is living with a **natural parent** who has remarried, and the new spouse wants to adopt); **agency adoptions** (the child is under the care of a charity or publicly funded agency and is put up for adoption); and **private adoptions** (non-government agencies or individuals arrange adoptions).

Regardless of type, adoptions can be granted only by a court and are allowed only when the court declares the adoption to be in the **best interests of the child**. To assist the court in making this determination, the state (or local) welfare department conducts an investigation into the home maintained by the prospective adopting parents. The court looks at:

• the occupations, earnings and stability of the prospective parents
• the medical, emotional and physical needs of the child
• religious and racial compatibility (religion and race need not be the same, but the court looks at the potential societal difficulties if they are not)
• whether the prospective parent has any criminal record or history of child abuse
• and the age of the child.

In addition, most states require the consent of the person being adopted if she is over a certain age, usually about twelve. Most states give preference to married people in granting adoptions, although in many states anyone capable of being a good parent may adopt, including single people. In fact, to encourage adoption of hard-to-place children (see unado*ptable children*), increased numbers of single people, including lesbians and gay men are being allowed to adopt. A few states, however, including Florida and New Hampshire, expressly prohibit lesbians and gay men from adopting.

An adoption results in a **termination of parental rights** and responsibilities of the natural parents of the adopted child. A few states, however, have allowed **grandparents** to obtain **visitation** rights in certain types of adoptions, even though the natural parent loses all of his rights.

See also *Abandonment of Child; Adoption Record* and *Birth Certificate*.

Adoption Record: Because of the potential psychological trauma to both the **adopted** child and the natural parents, nearly all states have laws denying adopted persons access to court information containing the identities of the natural parents, or other information which would lead to the discovery of their identities (e.g., the location of the adoption, the persons who arranged the adoption, etc.). A growing number of states, however, including Alabama, Kansas, South Dakota and Virginia, allow adoptees who have reached adulthood access to this information. California and a few other states allow an adult adoptee access to the records only if the natural parent consents.

Adulterine Bastard: Adulterine bastard, though not used in many places, is a term used to describe a child born to a married woman when the woman's husband is not the father of the child. This may occur if a woman becomes pregnant by someone other than her husband during the **marriage**; if a woman enters the marriage already pregnant (by someone other than her husband); or if a woman, without her husband's consent, becomes pregnant through **artificial insemination** by donor.

In the past, **divorcing** husbands attempted to evade paying **child support** for children born as a result of artificial insemination during the marriage by claiming that the children were adulterine bastards and therefore not "theirs." Where the husband had consented to artificial insemination, the argument was not successful. In fact, many states have laws which irrebuttably **presume** (i.e., the presumption cannot be disproved) that a child born during a marriage is the child of the husband, regardless of who the biological father is.

Adultery: Sexual intercourse by a **married** person with somebody other than her spouse is called adultery. In many states, adultery is technically a crime, but rarely is anyone prosecuted for it. In states which still permit **fault divorce**, adultery is virtually always a ground for obtaining a **divorce**. In states where **marital misconduct** affects the **division of property** and/or **alimony**, an adulterous spouse may be awarded less **property** or alimony (or ordered to pay more alimony) than she would have been granted (or ordered to pay) had there been no accusation. In addition, a parent accused by her spouse of adultery may, in some states, find judges hostile to granting her **custody** of children of the marriage.

Adversary System: The American legal system is based on the philosophy that the true facts of a given situation—and hence justice—will emerge if the **parties** to a court **action** act as adversaries rather than as cooperative participants. The theory is that if each side vigorously advances its own version of the facts, an impartial third person or group of persons (judge or jury) will sift out the truth. Critics point out that this system depends on equality of representation (assuming the parties are proceeding through advocates). If one advocate is better than the other, or has more money to prepare the case, the truth may not emerge. The adversary system's use has been especially criticized in **family law cases** on the ground that it intensifies divisions within a **family** rather than ameliorates them. Because cooperation between former spouses is necessary if children are involved, the adversary system seems particularly inappropriate in these instances. Accordingly, many family law courts and practitioners are beginning to emphasize **conciliation services** and **mediation** techniques instead of traditional **divorce** litigation.

AFDC: See *Aid to Families with Dependent Children.*

Affidavit: An affidavit is a written statement made by a person who signs the statement in front of a **notary public** and swears to its truth. Affidavits are used in place of live testimony in many circumstances (for example when a **motion** is filed, a supporting affidavit may be filed with it). Because it is sometimes inconvenient to find a notary public, some states now allow **declarations** (written statements made under penalty of perjury but not signed in front of a notary public) to be used in lieu of affidavits.

Affinity: Affinity is the term used to describe any relationship created by **marriage**. A husband, for example, is related to his wife's sister by affinity. Direct affinity is the relationship of a spouse to his mate's blood relatives, such as the example of the husband and his wife's sister. Secondary affinity describes the relationship of a spouse to his mate's marital relatives, such as a husband and his wife's sister's husband. Collateral affinity is the relationship between a spouse's relatives and his mate's relatives, such as a husband's brother and a wife's sister.

See also *Consanguinity* and *Kin.*

Affirm: The act of an **appellate court** upholding a decision of a **trial court** or a lower appellate court is called affirming the decision.

After-Born Child: An after-born child is one born after his parent signs a **will**. Even if the will is not changed to mention or provide for the child before the parent dies, the laws of most states allow the child to inherit a portion of the parent's **property**. The law assumes the parent would have wanted the child to inherit. If, however, the **evidence** shows that the parent did intend that the child receive nothing, the after-born child will probably get nothing. The legal term for any child omitted from a parent's will (either after-born or living at the time the will was executed) is **pretermitted heir**.

Age of Consent: Every state sets an age under which people must obtain the consent of a parent or **guardian** in order to **marry**. The age at which no parental consent is needed is called the age of consent and is 18 in most states (a few states allow younger persons to marry without a parent's consent). Some states require professional counseling and the approval of a judge instead of parental consent if a person under 18 want to get married.

The age of consent also refers to the age at which an unmarried person may legally consent to engage in sexual intercourse. For this purpose, the age of consent varies among the states and is usually 14 to 18. An adult over the age of consent who has sexual intercourse with someone under the age of consent may be prosecuted for **statutory rape**, regardless of who initiated the encounter or whether the over-age person actually knew the other's age.

Age of Majority: The age of majority is the age at which a **minor**, in the eyes of the law, becomes an adult. This age is 18 in most states. Once a person reaches the age of majority, she may vote, sign a **will**, enter into a binding contract, buy **property**, and generally act without parental consent. A growing number of states, however, require a person to be 21 before buying alcoholic beverages. A state may not have one age of majority for men and a different one for women.

Agency Adoption: **Adoptions** arranged by charities or publicly-funded social services agencies are called agency adoptions (also called county adoptions or public adoptions). Agency adoptions involve more court or welfare department involvement than do **private adoptions**. Agency adoptions usually occur when a child lives at an **orphanage** or in a **foster home,** or when a mother simply places an infant "up for adoption."

Agreed Interlocutory Judgment: See *Integrated Property Settlement Agreement.*

Agreement Before Marriage: Before a couple marries, they may make an agreement concerning certain aspects of their relationship, including how they will **characterize** their **property** during **marriage**, whether **alimony** will be paid in the event the couple later **divorces**, and other issues. A spouse, however, cannot agree to give up **child support** in the event of divorce. These agreements are also called ante-nuptial, pre-nuptial or pre-marital agreementss. They are usually upheld by courts unless one person shows that the agreement is likely to promote divorce (e.g., by including a large alimony amount in the event of divorce), was written and signed with the intention of divorcing, or was unfairly entered into (e.g., a spouse giving up all of his rights in his spouse's future **earnings** without the advice of an attorney). Eleven states limit these agreements to issues of property ownership only, and refuse to enforce any provisions which force or encourage one spouse to give up alimony.

See also *Uniform Premarital Agreement Act*.

Agreement During Marriage: Contracts made between a husband and wife during their **marriage** are interchangeably called post-nuptial, marital and post-marital agreements. Usually these agreements involve how **property** ownership is to be handled during the marriage and upon **divorce**, but occasionally they also cover matters such as chore division, child responsibility, etc. A spouse, however, cannot agree to give up **child support** in the event of divorce. In most states, it is legal for a couple to transfer property from one to the other, from one to both or from both to one, or to agree that **earnings** will be solely or jointly owned, even though the state's law would treat the earnings or property differently in the agreement's absence. Courts usually enforce legally executed property agreements which are fair to both spouses, but will not enforce agreements where a spouse has been deceived. In addition, courts do not want to get involved with personal matters (such as the division of chores), and it is wise to keep personal agreements separate from property agreements.

Agreement to Modify Alimony, Child Support, Custody or Visitation: After a **final decree** of **divorce** is filed with a court, former spouses may agree to modify the **alimony, child support, custody, visitation** or even **property** division terms. This modified agreement (also called a "stipulated modification") may be made without court approval. If one person, however, later reneges on the agreement, the other person may not be able to enforce it unless the court has approved the modification. Thus, it is advisable in most situations to obtain court approval before relying on such agreements. Courts routinely approve agreed upon modifications as long as child support is adequate.

EXAMPLE

Assume that Gloria and John's **divorce agreement** provides that John is to pay 75% of the debts (and Gloria 25%) in exchange for John keeping the Jaguar. After the divorce, Gloria's company transfers her 50 miles from her home, and she can no longer take mass transit. She and John therefore agree for her to take the Jaguar and also to pay 75% of the debts. Gloria and John wisely put their agreement in writing and have the court approve it.

Aid to Families with Dependent Children (AFDC): AFDC is a federally funded but state administered welfare program which provides financial assistance to the parent, **stepparent**, grandparent, sibling, aunt, uncle, niece, nephew or first cousin of a **minor** dependent child. A child qualifies for aid if she is economically needy and has been deprived of parental support or care because of the death, continued absence or incapacity of a parent, or in some states, the unemployment of a father. Financial eligibility requirements vary from state to state. In some states, AFDC is available to anyone in need who has a minor child; in others, it is only available if a parent is unemployed. Thus, a family with both parents where one works full-time may be ineligible even if the wage earner's income is so low that the family remains in need.

The overwhelming majority of people who receive AFDC are single women with children. When a woman applies for AFDC, the state is required to seek the identity and location of the father of the child, and then to look to him for **reimbursement** of the benefits paid to the woman. The failure of the woman to cooperate with the welfare department in locating the father may reduce or even negate her eligibility for benefits.

Alienation of Affection: When a person intentionally "came between" a husband and wife, he was technically guilty of "alienation of affection." At one time, courts in all states but Louisiana allowed the injured spouse to sue the interloper for the harm done to the marriage. Most states have eliminated alienation of affection lawsuits. They still exist in a few states, however, including Hawaii, Kansas, Rhode Island and Tennessee.

See also *Heart-Balm Lawsuits*.

Alimony: Alimony is money paid by one ex-spouse to the other for her support. Until the 1970's, alimony was a natural extension of the financial arrangement in "traditional" **marriages**, where the husband was the breadwinner and the wife stayed home, caring for the house and children but not earning any income; alimony was paid only by the husband to the wife. The amount of alimony was determined by a number of factors—the needs of the **parties**, their status in life, their wealth, and their relative **marital misconduct**; if a husband was committing **adultery**, or treating his wife with **cruelty**, he would pay a relatively large amount. If, however, the wife was having an affair or treating her husband cruelly, she would receive little or no alimony.

Today, alimony (now often called maintenance or spousal support) is based on fault in only about 20 states. (See chart, **FACTORS IN SETTING AND TERMINATING ALIMONY**.) Increasingly, alimony is determined by the following factors:

• needs of the recipient
• **ability to pay** of the payor
• age and health of the parties
• **length of the marriage**
• **standard of living** of the parties
• each party's **ability to earn**
• the **division of property**
• the recipient's **non-monetary contributions** to the marriage
• the recipient's **ability to be self-supporting**
• **tax consequences** to the parties

FACTORS IN SETTING AND TERMINATING ALIMONY

Although no-fault divorce is available in every state, many states bar or limit alimony if one spouse shows the other's marital fault (e.g., adultery, mental cruelty, desertion). In addition, some states reduce or terminate alimony if the recipient cohabits.

Fault has No Bearing on Alimony	Fault May Bar or Limit Alimony	Cohabitation May End or Reduce Alimony
Alaska	Alabama	Alabama
Arizona	Arkansas	California
California	Connecticut	Connecticut
Colorado	Florida	Georgia
Delaware	Georgia	Illinois
Illinois	Hawaii	Louisiana
Indiana	Idaho	Maryland
Iowa	Louisiana	New York
Kansas	Maryland	Ohio
Kentucky	Massachusetts	Oklahoma
Maine	Missouri	Pennsylvania
Michigan	North Carolina	Tennessee
Minnesota	Pennsylvania	Utah
Mississippi	Rhode Island	Wisconsin
Montana	South Carolina	
Nebraska	South Dakota	
Nevada	Tennessee	
New Hampshire	Texas	
New Jersey	Utah	
New Mexico	Virginia	
New York	West Virginia	
North Dakota	Washington, DC	
Ohio		
Oklahoma		
Oregon		
Vermont		
Washington		
Wisconsin		
Wyoming		

• any **agreement before marriage** or any **agreement during marriage**.

Except in marriages of long duration (10 years or more) or in the case of an ill or ailing spouse, alimony today usually lasts for a set period of time (and in a few states can only be for a set period), with the expectation that the recipient spouse will become self-supporting.

In addition, alimony is not available in Texas.

RELATED TERMS

Additional Financial Burden
Additional Income from Remarriage
Agreement to Modify Alimony, Child Support, Custody or Visitation
Change of Job: Effect on Alimony and Child Support
Changed Circumstance
Cost of Living Increase
Debts: Effect on Alimony and Child Support
Decrease in Income
Decreased Need for Alimony
Disability
Due and Payable
Enforcement of Alimony
Extension of Alimony
Financial Emergency
Guidelines for Temporary Alimony and Child Support
Hardship
Integrated Property Settlement Agreement
Length of Alimony
Lump Sum Support
Marital Misconduct as Defense to Alimony
Medical Emergencies
New Support Obligations
Periodic Support
Permanent Alimony, Child Support, Custody or Visitation
Presumption of Decreased Need Caused by Cohabitation
Professional Degree or License
Rehabilitative Alimony
Relative Income and Assets
Request for Modification of Alimony, Child Support, Custody or Visitation
Retroactive Modification of Alimony or Child Support
Temporary Modification of Alimony or Child Support
Temporary Provision for Alimony, Child Support, Custody, Visitation and Property Division
Termination of Alimony
Transition Period

Alimony in Gross: See *Lump Sum Support*.

Allegation: An allegation is a statement made in **court papers** that sets forth a **party's** belief as to what the facts are in a given case. Referring to statements made in court papers as allegations serves as a reminder that they may or may not be true.

Thus, when a party has alleged something, she has made charges which remain to be proven.

Allege: See *Allegation*.

Alleged Father: See *Putative Father*.

All Fours: An already decided **case** which decided issues very similar to those in a case being **litigated** is sometimes said to be on "all fours" with it.

Alternative Dispute Resolution (ADR): Until recently, the court system was often the only way disputing people could resolve their disagreement. Now, however, there are many ways to settle differences, collectively known as alternative dispute resolution.
See *Dispute Resolution*.

A Mensa et Thoro: A mensa et thoro is a Latin term meaning "from table and bed" which became used in English as "from bed and board." A separation a mensa et thoro—that is, a separation from bed and board—is another term for a **legal separation**.

Annulment: Annulment is a court procedure that dissolves a **marriage** and treats it as though it never happened. Annulments may be obtained for one of the following reasons:

• misrepresentation (e.g., a spouse lied about the capacity to have children, stated that she had reached the **age of consent**, or failed to say that she was still married to someone else)
• misunderstanding (e.g., one person wanted children and the other did not)
• inability to consummate the marriage (i.e., one spouse cannot have sex).

In the past, when **divorces** were difficult to obtain because **fault** had to be proved (for example, until 1966, **adultery** was the only **ground for divorce** in New York), judges often interpreted annulment **statutes** liberally in order to make annulments readily available. Today, however, when it is relatively easy to obtain a divorce in most states, annulments are rare. Where an annulment occurs after children have been born, those children are not considered **illegitimate**, even though the parents were "never married."

(**Note:** This discussion is limited to civil annulments; within the Roman Catholic church, a couple may obtain a religious annulment, after obtaining a civil divorce, in order for one or both spouses to **remarry**.)

Answer: An answer is a formal response to **allegations** made in a **complaint** (or petition). Normally, the answer either admits or denies the allegations, although some states allow an answer to state a lack of knowledge as to whether a particular allegation is true or false. If a **party** who is sued (the **defendant**) fails to file an answer, the party bringing the lawsuit (the **plaintiff**) usually wins by default. In a **divorce**, failure to file an answer may result in a **default divorce**.

> **EXAMPLE**
>
> Martin is sued for **paternity** by his former lover, Rhoda. Martin will be served with a complaint (or petition) containing the allegation that Rhoda believes he is the father of her child. He must answer within a certain period of time (usually about 30 days) or lose by **default**. In his answer, he must either admit or deny each of the complaint's allegations. In some states, Martin may respond that he doesn't know whether or not an allegation is true.

Antenuptial Agreement: See *Agreement Before Marriage.*

Appeal: When one or both **parties** to a lawsuit disagree with the result in the **trial court**, it is usually possible to get a higher court (called an **appellate court**) to review the decision. Normally, an appellate court reviews only whether the trial court followed the correct law and procedures, and no **evidence** is presented. Some states have two levels of appeals courts; an appeal is usually first considered by an intermediate court (often called a court of appeals). If a party is still unhappy with the result, it is sometimes possible to get the state's highest court (usually called supreme court) to review the **case**.

To appeal the trial court's decision, a notice must usually be filed with the trial court within a short period of time (usually about 30 days) after the **entry of judgment** by the **court clerk**.

See also *Appellant* and *Appellee.*

Appellant: The person who objects to the **trial court** decision and asks the **appellate court** to review the decision by filing an **appeal** is called an appellant (also called petitioner in some states).
See also *Appellee.*

Appellate Court: An appellate court is one which decides **appeals** of lower court decisions.

Appellee: The **party** against whom an **appeal** is filed is called the appellee or the respondent. Sometimes the appellee will also appeal certain aspects of the lower court's decision; he then becomes a cross-appellant as well as an appellee. In this situation, the **appellant** (the one who filed the appeal) becomes a cross-appellee or cross-respondent.

Appraisal: An appraisal is the process of determining the fair market value of an **asset**. Appraisals of **real property** and automobiles are common when the item is to be sold or divided. One common method of appraising real property is to compare the property in question to similar property recently sold. Another common method, especially with vehicles, is to start with the purchase price and then to adjust the value based on inflation, appreciation and depreciation. To obtain an appraisal, it is usually necessary to consult an expert in the field (e.g., real estate broker, art dealer or actuary).
See also *Valuation of Property.*

Arbitrary and Capricious: When a judge or government administrator makes a decision without reasonable grounds or adequate consideration of the circumstances, it is said to be arbitrary and capricious and can be invalidated by a court on that ground. There is, however, no set standard for what constitutes an arbitrary and capricious decision; what appears arbitrary to one judge may seem perfectly reasonable to another.

EXAMPLE

Paul and Myra, both in their mid-30's, are involved in a disputed **custody case**. Both parents are fit to have custody of the child, so the judge must review all relevant information and decide what is in the **best interests of the child**. Myra raised the fact that when Paul was 16, he pleaded guilty to possessing marijuana. Based solely on Paul's conviction, the judge awarded custody to Myra. Paul **appealed**, arguing that the judge's decision was arbitrary and capricious, that his conviction nearly 20 years earlier was irrelevant, and that there is no reasonable basis to support the decision. The **appellate court** judges will make the decision.

Arbitration: Arbitration is the submission of a dispute to an impartial third person or persons. The arbitrator or arbitrators are directly selected by the **parties** or under a contract in which the parties have agreed to use a court ordered arbitrator or an arbitrator from the American Arbitration Association. If there is no contract, usually each party chooses an arbitrator and the two arbitrators select a third. When parties submit to arbitration, they agree to be bound by and comply with the arbitrators' decision. The arbitrators' decision is given after an informal proceeding where each side presents **evidence** and witnesses.

Some arbitration proceedings are mandatory (enforced by **statute**), such as many labor disputes. Other arbitration proceedings are selected in advance and written into contracts. In fact, many couples who sign **cohabitation agreements** or **divorce agreements** include a clause agreeing to go to arbitration if any dispute should arise, thereby avoiding the delay, expense, bitterness and formality of **litigation**. Other arbitration proceedings are chosen by the disputing parties after the conflict arises, but also to avoid the delay, expense, bitterness and formality of courts.

Arrearage: Arrearage (also called arrears) is a general term for accumulated past due payments on a debt. In **family law**, an arrearage occurs when a parent or ex-spouse falls behind in **alimony** or **child support** payments. While the person with an arrearage can ask a court for a modification of future payments, the court will usually insist that the arrearage be paid in full, either immediately or in installments. For this reason, if a spouse with a support obligation starts falling behind because his income has decreased or his debts have increased, he should immediately seek a **temporary modification**.

Artificial Insemination: Artificial insemination is a procedure by which a woman is inseminated by a means other than sexual intercourse. If the semen came from her husband, (sometimes called homologous artificial insemination), the law considers this father-child relationship the same as any father-child relationship where the child is born during **marriage**. If the semen is from a man other than her husband, the procedure is termed "artificial insemination by donor" or heterologous artificial insemination.

If the woman is married when the insemination and birth occur, and her husband consented to the insemination, the husband, and not the donor, is considered the father. If the woman is unmarried when the insemination occurs, whether the donor is considered the father depends on a number of factors, including the details of the procedure and the state. In Oregon and New Jersey, for example, the woman and the donor may enter into an agreement outlining their intentions, including declaring the donor not to be the father. In California, if the insemination procedure for an unmarried woman is performed by a doctor, the donor is not considered the father. If no doctor is used, the donor may be considered the father.

Assault: See *Battery*.

Asset: Asset is a general term for **property** of all kinds. Property includes tangible things such as real estate, an art collection and motorcycles, but also includes intangible items such as **business good will**, the right to receive future **pensions**, patents, stocks and money owed to a person by others. **Debts** are considered "negative assets."

Assignment of Property: See *Division of Property*.

Assignment of Wages: See *Wage Attachment*.

Attachment of Wages: See *Wage Attachment*.

Attorneys' Fees: Attorneys' fees are the fees an attorney charges to represent a client in a particular matter. In certain types of **cases**, such as those involving personal injuries, where the client may or may not recover money from the **defendant**, the attorney's fee is often a contingency fee, meaning the attorney gets paid only if the client recovers any money. (The attorney's fee is contingent on the client winning the case.) In **divorces** and other **family law** cases, contingency fees are normally prohibited. Instead, the client works out a payment arrangement with the attorney, such as an hourly rate or a flat fee. (Hourly or flat fees may also be used in personal injury cases, though they are less common than contingency fees.) In some states, if one **party** to a divorce is in a better economic position than the other, the court may order that spouse to pay all or some of the other's attorney's fees so that she has equal access to an attorney.

Note: Some states, notably California, require written fee agreements if the attorney expects to charge more than a certain amount (in California, $1000) for her services.

Authentication of Evidence: When a document or other physical item is offered into **evidence** at trial, it is necessary to show that the item is genuine. This process is called authentication. One way to authenticate a document is by the testimony of the person who wrote or signed it; another is by the testimony of an **expert witness** such as a document examiner or handwriting analyst.

Authority of Court Case: See *Precedent* and *All Fours*.

Automatic Termination of Alimony: See *Termination of Alimony*.

Automatic Termination of Child Support: See *Termination of Child Support*.

Award: Award means the amount and/or form of a **judgment** a judge or jury gives the successful **party** in a lawsuit. It is often, but not always, an amount of money.

EXAMPLE

In a **divorce** case, one party might be awarded the divorce, $300 per month in **alimony**, **custody** of the children, $600 per month in **child support** and the **family home**. The other party might be awarded the family business.

In order for authorities in the Soviet Union to verify that people are marrying of their own accord, they must appear before the authorities twice—once to declare an intent to marry, and once to register the marriage.

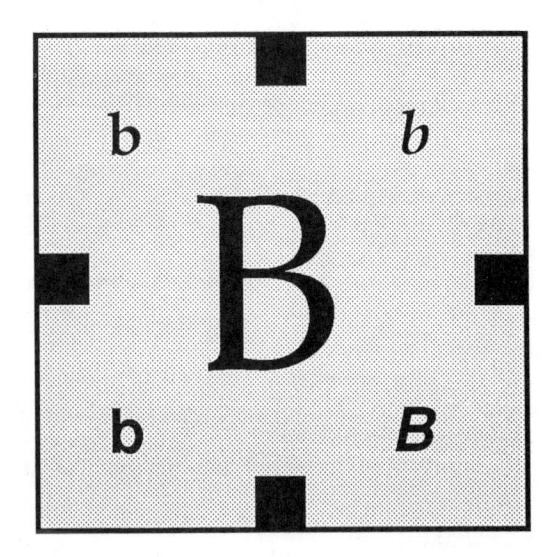

Baby M. Case: See *Surrogate Mother*.

Back Support: See *Arrearage*.

Bailiff: A bailiff is a law enforcement officer, usually a sheriff, marshal or constable, assigned to a courtroom to keep peace and assist the judge, courtroom **clerks**, witnesses and jury.

Bankruptcy: Bankruptcy is a federal court proceeding in which a person unable to pay her **debts** asks the court to either cancel them (Chapter 7 bankruptcy) or allow their payment—often in less than the full amount—in an orderly manner over a three year period (Chapter 13 bankruptcy). For **married** couples, either or both spouses may file for bankruptcy; if both wish to file, each must make a separate request to the court, although the bankruptcy court will allow the couple to use one set of forms. It is usually a good idea for both spouses to file for bankruptcy when a couple is having debt problems. Otherwise, if only one declares bankruptcy, a creditor may still go after the other for payment of any debts attributable to the marriage.

Bastardy Statute: Bastardy statutes were criminal laws which allowed states to punish **unwed fathers** who did not support their children. Because bastardy statutes did not punish **unwed mothers**, the statutes have been declared unconstitutional and are therefore unenforceable.

Battered Women: Women who are the victims of **domestic violence** are often called "battered women."

Battered Women's Shelters: Many areas have temporary homes called battered women shelters where women (and their children) who are victims of **domestic violence** may stay until the crisis passes or until they are able to find a permanent place to relocate. The best way to find these shelters is to consult the local police, phone book, welfare department, neighborhood resource center or women's center. In California, the police must provide an apparent battering victim a list of referrals for emergency housing, legal services, and counseling services.

Battery: "Battery" is the crime of physically injuring someone intentionally. "Assault" is the crime of threatening to use unlawful force against another. Assault is a part of battery, thus the phrase "assault and battery."
See also *Domestic Violence.*

Behind on Alimony or Child Support: See *Arrearage.*

Bench: The furniture on which the judge sits is called the bench. When something is done "from the bench," it means it was done by a **trial** judge.
See also *Bench Trial* and *Bench Warrent.*

Bench Trial: A **trial** conducted by a judge without a jury is termed a bench trial or a court trial.

Bench Warrant: If a person fails to appear in court when she has been properly ordered to do so, the judge is authorized to issue a warrant (a court **order** authorizing a law enforcement officer to arrest someone) for her arrest. A warrant issued this way is called a **bench** warrant.

EXAMPLE

Joe has fallen behind on his court-ordered **child support**. Joe's former wife, Jill, has served (see *service of court papers*) Joe with an **order to show cause** why he should not be held in **contempt of court** for not complying. Joe failed to appear at the scheduled **hearing**; the judge issued a bench warrant authorizing the police to arrest Joe and bring him before the judge to answer the charge of contempt.

Best Interests of the Child: When deciding **custody** and **visitation** rights, or when deciding whether to approve **adoptions** and **guardianships**, a court gives the best interests of the child the highest priority. What the best interests of the child are in a given situation depends upon many factors, including:
• the love and emotional ties between the parent or guardian and the child
• the ability of the parent or guardian to give the child love and guidance
• the ability of the parent or guardian to provide the child with food, shelter, clothing and medical care (called "**necessaries**")
• any **established living pattern**

• the health of the parent or guardian;
• the child's home, school, community and religious ties
• the **child's preference**, if the child is old enough to have an opinion
• the ability of the parent to foster healthy communication and contact between the child and the other parent.

EXAMPLE

Larry and Tanya **divorced** after 15 years of **marriage** and two children. Both requested custody. The judge was faced with a hard decision because both Larry and Tanya were able, loving parents. After the divorce, however, Tanya moved 100 miles from where the **family** lived; Larry stayed in the same town. Because both parents would provide the children with love, guidance and financial support, the judge awarded custody to Larry, emphasizing that the children's home, school and community ties were established and that there was no reason to further disrupt them.

Betrothal: An agreement or promise to **marry** is called a betrothal. A betrothal may be an informal promise between a man and woman, or, in some cultures, it may be a formal arrangement made between the man's and woman's parents. Nowadays, couples who plan to marry are usually called engaged instead of betrothed.
See also *Breach of Promise to Marry*.

In China, a man may not request a divorce if his wife is pregnant or the couple has a child under a year old.

Bias: Any mental condition that would prevent a judge or juror from being fair and impartial is called bias. It may be ground for disqualification of the judge or juror in question. Bias also affects witnesses in a **trial** or **hearing**. Lawyers spend much time trying to prove that the other side's witnesses are biased so that the judge or jury will discredit the witnesses' testimony.

Bifurcation: Bifurcation is the act of dividing a **trial** into two parts. Murder trials are commonly bifurcated; one trial is held to determine the defendant's guilt or innocence, and if the defendant is found guilty, another trial is held to determine the penalty. In **family law**, bifurcation occurs when the **divorce** itself is determined separately from the related issues of **custody** and **visitation**, **child support**, **alimony**, and **property** division.
See also *Divisible Divorce*.

In Israel, under rabbinical law, a man must marry his brother's widow if she has children, even if he is already married. He doesn't divorce his first wife, but stays married to both. If either woman objects, she can request a divorce.

Bigamy: A person who knows he is already legally **married** and marries another person is guilty of the crime of bigamy in every state. Prosecution for this crime may occur when the already married person enters into the second marriage and harms his new spouse (for example, by using his new wife's or his own marital property on the first wife). There is no crime if one person makes a legitimate mistake (for example, **remarrying** when one mistakenly believes that his **divorce** has been finalized).

See also *Polygamy; Putative Marriage;* and *Putative Spouse.*

Bills Incurred Before Marriage: See *Debts Incurred Before Marriage.*

Bills Incurred Between Separation and Divorce: See *Debts Incurred Between Separation and Divorce.*

Bills Incurred During Marriage: See *Debts Incurred During Marriage.*

Bird's Nest Custody: Bird's nest custody is a **joint custody** arrangement where the children remain in the **family home** and the parents take turns moving in and out.

Birth Certificate: A birth certificate is a document executed by a county official or by a person delivering a baby, and then filed with the county shortly after a baby is born. Its purpose is to record the birth. A birth certificate cannot normally be modified except to reflect an **adoption** (the new parents' names are inserted) or to correct clerical errors (such as a misspelling or wrong date). A **change of name** proceeding, while valid to legally change a person's name for all practical purposes, does not normally change the name on the birth certificate. A person may obtain a certified copy of her birth certificate from the county where she was born.

Birth Control: Birth control is any procedure used by persons engaging in sexual intercourse to minimize the chances of the woman getting pregnant.

See also *Griswold v. Connecticut.*

Blood Test Before Marriage: All states but Maryland, Minnesota, Nevada, South Carolina and Washington require a couple planning to **marry** to take blood tests to find out whether either is afflicted with venereal disease or with rubella (measles). Some states, including Illinois, also require testing for the presence of AIDS virus antibodies. These tests may also disclose the existence of other communicable diseases or genetic defects. Couples who marry under California's **confidential marriage statute** do not have to have blood tests.

Bodily Heirs: See *Issue*.

Breach of Promise to Marry: Under traditional **common law**, a broken engagement could be treated as a breach of promise to marry which would support a lawsuit for money damages against the person who broke the engagement. Today, most states have done away with this type of lawsuit. It may be possible, however, for the giver of an engagement ring or other gift made in contemplation of **marriage** to get the gift back if the other person broke off the engagement and the couple understood that the ring or other gift was a precursor to marriage.

See also *Heart-Balm Lawsuits*.

Brief: When a **party** (either through her lawyer or in **pro per**) submits a written legal argument to a court, the document is often called a brief. It typically consists of a statement of the facts relevant to the **case** and arguments supported by references to legal authority (**statutes**, regulations, or earlier court decisions). Many briefs are quite lengthy; the label brief is an infamous misnomer celebrated by Franz Kafka who defined a lawyer as "a person who writes a 10,000 word document and calls it a brief."

See also *Points and Authorities* and *Trial Brief*.

Burden of Proof: The burden of proof refers to the obligation of a **party** to prove his **allegations** during a trial. Typically, the **plaintiff** must prove whatever allegations he included in his **complaint** in order to win his case. The **defendant** is given the opportunity to submit evidence to **rebut** the plaintiff's case.

See also *Standard of Proof*.

Business Good Will: Any established business has a name and reputation which by themselves can be expected to generate a certain amount of income in the future. A shorthand name for the value of a business's name and reputation is good will. The good will of a business depends on a number of factors including its name recognition, length of existence, and revenues. IBM, for example, has a significant good will based on name recognition alone.

In virtually all states, a business owned by one or both spouses is treated like any other item of **marital property** in a **divorce**, that is, it is **appraised** to determine its value and then divided between the spouses. Most states require that the business good will be included as part of the overall appraisal of the business. A few states, however, have expressly rejected the argument that business good will is a part of the business appraised during divorce.

See also *Valuation of Property*.

Business Value as Divisible Asset Upon Divorce: In a divorce, the value of a business owned by one or both spouses is often divided by the court to reflect the portion that belongs to each spouse. How much of a business will be considered **marital** or **community property** subject to division by a court depends on whose money went into the business, the amount of time spent by each spouse in making the business grow, and the law of the state where the divorce occurs. When the business has been run or managed by one spouse only, that spouse will most likely be awarded the business, and the other spouse will be given his share in other marital or community property. If both spouses have run or managed the business, one spouse often will purchase the other's share.

See also *Business Good Will* and *Valuation of Property.*

EXAMPLE

Judy and Roy owned and operated a gasoline station during their **marriage**. Roy put down an initial $30,000 of his own **property** while Judy contributed $15,000 of hers. Judy, however, ran the business alone for its first three years; Roy worked there only during the last two. All **improvements** to the business were paid for out of marital property. At divorce, the court divides the business evenly (for example, Judy buying Roy's share from him, or Roy given the gas station and Judy given different marital property equal in value to her share of the business), because although Roy contributed twice as much money, Judy has contributed significantly more time.

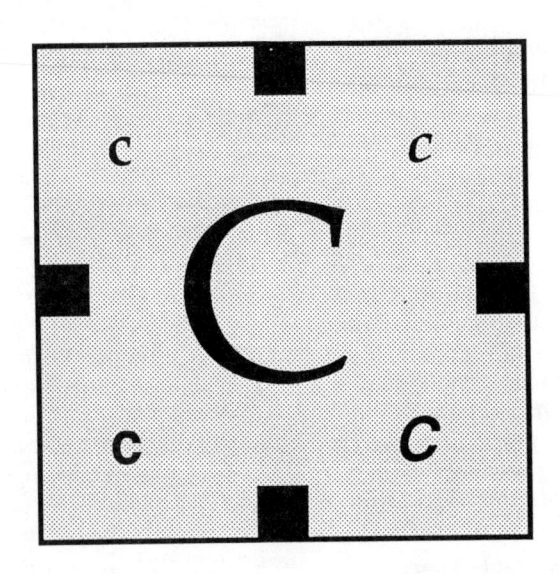

Calendar: When used as a verb, the word "calendar" is slang for scheduling a trial (for example, "the Murphy divorce case is calendared for September 3rd"). When used as a noun, it refers to a master list kept by a court, called the civil calendar, which shows cases that are ready for or in trial. Some states do not allow cases to be placed on a court calendar until all preliminary procedures, such as **discovery** and **motions**, have been completed. Unless the **plaintiff** or **defendant** (or one of their lawyers) requests that a case be placed on this calendar, it will never be scheduled for trial. In fact, many cases are dismissed every year because attorneys fail to take this vitally important step.

Capricious: See *Arbitrary and Capricious*.

Caption: The caption refers to the heading which appears on all **court papers**. The caption contains the names of the **parties** to the lawsuit (e.g., Susan Roe, **Plaintiff**, v. Robert Roe, **Defendant**), the name of the court (e.g., Federal District Court for the Eastern District of Pennsylvania), the **case number** which has been assigned by the court **clerk**, and the title of the **court paper** (e.g., **Complaint** for **Annulment**).

Case: When a dispute is taken to court, it becomes a case. An **appellate court** decision published in a book of such decisions is also called a case and may be used as guidance or **precedent** by other courts. A person doing

-27-

legal research will commonly say that he has to "look up a case" to see if its ruling on a point should be followed by other courts. A published case is found by referring to its **citation**.

See also *Case Law*.

Case Law: There are two major ways in which we develop law. One is through the passage of **statutes**, regulations, and **ordinances** by voters and legislative bodies (e.g., legislatures, city councils). The other is through **appellate court** decisions in individual cases. The latter is called case law or **precedent**, and these decisions serve as guidance (sometimes binding, other times merely persuasive) for courts that are faced with the same or similar issues later.

Case Number: The number given by the court **clerk** to a lawsuit when it is filed is called the case number. Each case in a county has a unique number so that it may be distinguished from all other cases in that county.

Case Record: All papers filed with the court during a lawsuit and the transcripts of all **hearings** and **trials** (made by a **court reporter**) become part of the official case record. If a **party** appeals from a **trial court judgment**, the **appellate court** normally considers only information contained in the case record. It is therefore important for a party during the trial to get all of her **evidence** and objections into the case record in the event she later decides to appeal.

Cause of Action: See *Action*.

Ceremony of Marriage: See *Wedding*.

Certificate of Marriage: See *Marriage Certificate*.

Chambers: A judge's office is referred to as her chambers. **Settlement conferences** and **adoptions** are usually held in her chambers. During a **trial**, when the judge wants to examine documents, speak with witnesses or speak with the attorneys outside the jury's presence, the judge presides "in camera," the Latin term for in chambers, and holds a conference either in the chambers or at the **bench** (where the attorneys and judge whisper so the jury can't hear).

Change in Law as Changed Circumstance: When a law affecting **alimony** or **child support** is amended or a new law enacted, this by itself can sometimes constitute the **changed circumstance** necessary to file a **request for modification** of a prior alimony or child support **order**.

Change of Alimony or Child Support: See *Request for Modification of Alimony, Child Support, Custody or Visitation*.

Change of Custody or Visitation: See *Request for Modification of Alimony, Child Support, Custody or Visitation*.

Change of Job: Effect on Alimony and Child Support: When a person paying **alimony** or **child support** changes jobs and earns less income, he may be able to obtain a reduction in the alimony or child support payments by filing an appropriate request for modification. The change, however, must be in reasonable furtherance of his career development and future increased income opportunities. If the court believes that the decrease in income is for the purpose of lessening or avoiding support obligations, the request for modification will probably be denied.

If a person paying alimony or child support changes jobs and receives an increase in pay, the recipient may be able to obtain a corresponding increase in support, but only if the current support is inadequate.

Change of Job: Effect on Custody and Visitation: See *Geographic Move: Effect on Custody and Visitation.*

Change of Name: In most states, an adult can change his name by either getting a court **order** or simply adopting a new name and using it consistently. If the second method is used, it is important for the person to notify everyone who has an interest in knowing (e.g., the IRS, his creditors), to show that his name change is not being done for a fraudulent reason. Although the usage method is legally valid, it is easier to change certain official documents, such as passports, if one obtains a court-ordered name change. In a **divorce**, a woman who has taken her husband's name has the option of returning to her prior **name**. If she chooses to, her name will be changed by order of the divorce **decree**. No state requires a woman to change her name when she marries.

See also *Changing Child's Name* and *Maiden Name*.

Changed Circumstances: When a party files a **request for modification of alimony, child support, custody, or visitation,** she must usually show that circumstances have changed substantially since the time of the previously issued **order**. This rule encourages stability of arrangements and helps prevent the court from becoming overburdened with frequent and repetitive modification requests.

RELATED TERMS

Ability to Earn
Ability to Pay
Additional Financial Burden
Additional Income from Remarriage
Best Interests of the Child
Cohabitation
Cost of Living Increase
Decrease in Income
Decreased Need for Alimony
Destabilized Household
Disability
Due and Payable
Escalator Clause
Established Living Pattern
Extension of Alimony
Gay and Lesbian Lifestyle: Effect on Custody
Geographic Move: Effect on Custody and Visitation
Hardship

Increase in Income
Lifestyle and Social Factors: Effect on Custody and Visitation
Needs of Child
New Support Obligation
Presumption of Decreased Need Caused by Cohabitation
Standards for Custody
Unfitness of Parent

Changing Child's Name: When a parent seeks to change either a child's given name (first name) or surname (last name), the change is permitted in most states as long as the court determines it to be in the **best interests of the child.** A child's name cannot legally be changed without a court **order,** however. In some states, courts refuse to grant a name change if one parent objects.

In Czechoslovakia, before a couple marries the partners must choose what surname their children will have.

Character Evidence: Evidence introduced in a trial which bears on the truth and honesty of a witness or **party** is termed character evidence. Character evidence includes criminal convictions and reputation in the community for honesty. Character evidence is usually permitted when a person's honesty is an issue, such as when a criminal defendant testifies or has been charged with perjury or fraud. It is not permitted when the defendant does not testify and the crime he is charged with doesn't involve the defendant's truthfulness (e.g., the defendant is charged with illegal possession of drugs). Although used infrequently in civil cases, character evidence may be given in **custody** cases where the honesty of a party arguably affects her ability to be a good parent (e.g., in the case of a habitual liar), or in cases of **fault divorce.**

Characterization of Property Acquired During Marriage: In a divorce where the **parties** cannot agree on how to divide their **property,** the court must classify the the disputed items as either **marital property** or **separate property** in order to decide who gets what. In the **community property states, earnings** and other property received by either spouse during marriage are jointly owned under **community property** principles and are divided equally. In most other states, earnings and property obtained by a couple during the **marriage** are marital property and are divided equitably (equally or near equally). In virtually all states, **inheritances** and gifts made to one spouse only are considered the separate property of the recipient spouse and are accordingly distributed to that spouse.

A couple may sign an **agreement during marriage** to change the nature of any property from marital to separate or from separate to marital if they follow the rules of their state for doing this. If they divorce, the property will be divided according to the agreement if a judge finds the agreement valid. While these agreements may sometimes be legal if made orally, they are easier to refer to and to prove if they are in writing.

Chattel: Any item of **personal property** is a chattel.

Child Abduction: See *Childnapping*.

Child Abuse: Physical, emotional, or sexual mistreatment of a child is child abuse. In some situations, an abused child is removed from the home by a court and placed in the care of the state. Many are placed in **foster homes**. In addition, the abuser may be criminally prosecuted.

What legally constitutes child abuse varies from situation to situation, although severe physical punishment, restraint, or deprivation usually qualifies, as does virtually any sexual act inflicted on the child. A few states have adopted laws requiring any person with knowledge of an instance of child abuse to report it to the local police or welfare department. Some other states penalize health care providers or teachers who fail to report suspected abuse. Child abuse by a parent is normally an important factor in awarding or limiting **custody** and **visitation** rights in the event of a **divorce**. A past act of child abuse may also disqualify a person seeking to an **adopt** a child.

See also *Child Neglect* and *Domestic Violence*.

Child Custody: See *Custody*.

Childnapping: When a parent without **physical custody** (who may or may not have **visitation** rights) removes a child from, or refuses to return a child to, the parent with physical custody, it is called childnapping. A federal law, the **Parental Kidnapping Prevention Act**, and many state laws have been passed to prosecute and punish parents guilty of childnapping, which is a felony in over 40 states.

Child Neglect: When a parent or **guardian** fails to provide a child with adequate **necessaries**, education, supervision, or general guidance, the adult may be guilty of child neglect. If child neglect is suspected, the local welfare department will conduct an investigation. In severe cases, the child will be removed from the home after a court **hearing** and placed in a **foster home**. If the parents do not improve their situation within a reasonable time (usually between six months and two years, depending on the state) the child may be taken away permanently and placed for **adoption**. In especially severe cases, the parents or guardian may be criminally prosecuted.

In some situations, parents may be unable to properly care for their children by themselves but may have the ability to perform their responsibilities with appropriate outside help. In these instances, courts often allow the children to stay with the parents as long as the parents accept help, usually from a social service agency.

See also *Child Abuse* and *Termination of Parental Rights*.

Child's Decreased or Increased Need for Support: See *Needs of Child*.

Child's Preference in Custody:
Over 35 states have laws authorizing courts to consider a child's preference concerning which parent she wants to live with following a **divorce** or **separation**, provided the child is over a certain age (about 10). Generally, the older the child, the more weight the desire is given. In a few states, the court must grant the child's wish if the child is at least a certain age (usually 12 to 14).

Child Support:
All states require **natural parents** and **adoptive** parents to support their children until the children reach the **age of majority** (and sometimes longer), are declared **emancipated** by a court, or until

In New Zealand, a custodial parent receives child support from the government. The other parent reimburses the government, making child support enforcement the responsibility of the government and not the custodial parent.

there is a **termination of parental rights** and responsibilities (as in the case where a child is adopted). In a **divorce**, this means that the **non-custodial parent** is often required to pay some kind of child support while the **custodial parent** is deemed to be meeting his support duty through the **custody** itself. In states that have **joint custody**, the support obligation of each parent is often based on the ratio of each parent's income to their combined incomes, and the percentage of time the child spends with each parent.

While divorcing spouses are permitted to decide virtually all other terms of their divorce without court intervention, the court often insists on reviewing the child support arrangement. If the court approves of the arrangement, the court will include it in the divorce **decree**.

Some of the factors evaluated by courts in setting child support include:

- **needs of the child**
- **standard of living** of the child before the divorce or **separation**
- the non-custodial parent's **ability to earn** and **ability to pay**
- **relative income and assets** of the parent
- **tax consequences of alimony and child support**.

Unfortunately, a large percentage of parents ordered to pay child support do not. Society has become less tolerant of these parents, and the federal government and most state governments have passed laws to facilitate **enforcement of child support orders**; these laws work to some extent, but still far from adequate.

RELATED TERMS

Additional Financial Burden
Additional Income from Remarriage
Aid to Families with Dependent Children (AFDC)
Arrearage
Best Interests of the Child
Change in Job: Effect on Alimony and Child Support
Changed Circumstance
Continuing Duty to Support
Cost of Living Increase
Decrease in Income
Disability
Due and Payable
Fair Amount of Child Support
Financial Emergency
Guidelines for Temporary Alimony and Child Support
Hardship
Medical Emergencies
Net Income
New Support Obligations
Permanent Alimony, Child Support, Custody or Visitation
Request for Modification of Alimony, Child Support, Custody or Visitation
Retroactive Modification of Alimony or Child Support
Revised Uniform Reciprocal Enforcement of Support Act (RURESA)
Temporary Modification of Alimony or Child Support
Temporary Provisions for Alimony, Child Support, Custody, Visitation and Property Division
Termination of Child Support

Child Support Enforcement Act of 1984: See *Enforcement of Child Support*.

Child Support Order for Delinquent Child: When a child has been declared delinquent by a **juvenile court** and placed outside his home (e.g., **foster home** or reform school), many states require the parents to meet part or all of the cost of the placement through a support order. In California, however, this practice was struck down as unconstitutional.

Circumstantial Evidence: Circumstantial evidence is best explained by saying what it is not—it is not **direct evidence** from a witness who saw or heard something. Circumstantial evidence is a fact that can be used to infer another fact.

> **EXAMPLE**
>
> Bart is suing his wife Pam for a **divorce**, claiming she is having an affair with Tony, and Tony's fingerprints are found on a book in Bart and Pam's bedroom. A judge or jury may infer that Tony was in the bedroom. The fingerprints are circumstantial evidence of Tony's presence in the bedroom. Circumstantial evidence is usually not as good as direct evidence (an eyewitness saw Tony in the bedroom) because it is easy to make the wrong inference—Pam may have loaned Tony the book and then carried it back to the bedroom herself after getting it back.

Circumstantial evidence is generally **admissible** in court unless the connection between the fact and the inference is too weak to be of help in deciding the **case**.

Citation: The proper reference (as established by the legal profession) to a **case**, constitution, **statute**, legal encyclopedia or legal treatise is called a citation. A citation contains the name of the case or other authority, the name of the book in which it is found, the volume in which it appears, its page or section number, and the year decided or enacted. Citations allow any reader to find the source and read it.

> **EXAMPLE**
>
> The proper citation for the case allowing women to have an **abortion** is *Roe v. Wade*, 410 U.S. 133 (1973). The name of the case includes the name of the **plaintiff** (Roe) followed by a v. (meaning versus) followed by the **defendant's** name (Wade). 410 is the volume number where the case is found in the series called United States Reports (abbreviated by U.S.) at page 133. The case was decided in 1973.

Civil Clerk: See *Clerk*.

Civil Contempt: See *Contempt of Court*.

Civil Procedure: Civil procedure refers to those laws (usually **statutes**) which tell how (the methods, procedures and practices) to go to court and get **judicial relief** in non-criminal **cases**.

See also *Court Rules* and *Substantive Law*.

Clean Hands Doctrine: Under the "clean hands" doctrine, a person who has acted wrongly, either morally or legally (i.e., who has "unclean hands") will not be helped by a court when complaining about the actions of someone else.

In **family law**, the doctrine is invoked most often in two situations. First, a parent who **childnaps** and then later requests **custody** will often be denied custody unless the child is in danger of harm from the other parent. Second, a spouse who conceals **assets** or otherwise misappropriates **marital property** during the **marriage** or **separation** will often be penalized in the **division of property** at the **divorce** by being awarded less than her fair share. This, of course, requires that the "innocent" spouse learn of the concealment or misappropriation.

Clerk: Within our judicial system, there are many types of clerks. Court clerks (frequently called county clerks) keep track of documents filed with courts; these clerks may also be called civil or criminal clerks, depending on the court in which they work. Courtroom clerks are assigned to particular judges to handle the paper flow in the courtroom; law clerks (usually law students or lawyers) assist judges (and sometimes attorneys) in legal research and writing. **Calendar** clerks handle the scheduling of **trials** and **hearings**.

Closing Argument: After all the **evidence** has been introduced in a **trial**, each **party** is permitted to present a closing argument (also called a final argument) to the jury (or judge if there is no jury) summarizing the evidence in a light most favorable to his position.

Codes: Most state **statutes** are organized by subject matter and published in books referred to as codes. Typically, a state has a civil code (where the **divorce** laws are usually contained), a criminal code (where **incest, bigamy** and **domestic violence** laws are often found), welfare code (which contains laws related to public benefits), probate code (where laws about **wills**, trusts and probate proceedings are collected) and many other codes dealing with a wide variety of topics. Federal statutes are organized into subject matter titles within the United States Code (e.g., Title 18 for crimes and Title 11 for bankruptcy). Local **ordinances** and regulations are commonly found in the building, fire, planning, and administrative codes of each city.

Cohabitation: Cohabitation generally refers to when a man and a woman live together in an intimate sexual relationship without **marrying**. In some states, cohabitation by a person receiving **alimony** is a ground for termination of alimony. Also, in some states, a parent who cohabits may have difficulty obtaining **custody** of her children. Cohabitation is still a crime in some places, though rarely is anyone prosecuted for it. Some people describe a cohabitating couple's relationship as a **meretricious relationship**.

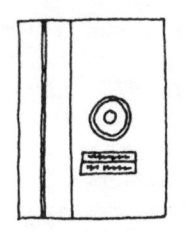

See also *Cohabitation Agreement; Common Law Marriage; Marvin v. Marvin; Palimony; Presumption of Decreased Need Caused by Cohabitation; Putative Marriage; Putative Spouse* and *Same-Sex Marriage*.

See chart, **FACTORS IN SETTING AND TERMINATING ALIMONY** under *Alimony*.

Cohabitation Agreement: A cohabitation agreement is a contract entered into by a couple (heterosexual, lesbian or gay) living together to arrange **property** rights, and in some cases, **custody, child support** and **alimony**-like support arrangements in the event the couple breaks up or one partner dies. Until 1977, courts generally did not enforce cohabitation agreements because they reasoned that the underlying sexual relationship formed the basis of the contractual relationship and that the agreement therefore improperly arranged an exchange of sex for money (i.e., prostitution). In 1977, however, the California Supreme Court ruled in *Marvin v. Marvin* that cohabitating couples in California could execute written or oral contracts, and where no contract existed, the court could imply one based on the **parties'** behavior. Since 1977, a number of other states including Alaska, Arizona, Connecticut, Florida, Indiana, Maryland, Michigan, Minnesota, Nebraska, New Hampshire, New Jersey, New Mexico, New York, Oregon, Pennsylvania, Washington, Wisconsin and Wyoming have enforced cohabitation agreements.

EXAMPLE

Rose and Ted have lived together for four years. They've never had any written agreement, but their behavior has been consistent: they've purchased a car, an oak table, and a china set, with each one paying half. If they split up, a court is likely to imply an agreement and equally divide the items purchased together.

EXAMPLE

Jon and Steve plan to buy a fixer-upper house and move in together. Jon is a carpenter; Steve is a university professor who makes nearly twice as much as Jon. Jon and Steve plan to own their home equally, so they agree in writing as follows: Steve will pay two-thirds of the mortgage, and Jon will pay one-third. Steve and Jon will equally pay for the materials to fix up the house, and Jon will contribute all the labor. Steve and Jon also agree to equally own all the property, furniture and fixtures they buy once they move in together.

Collateral Attack: When a lawsuit is filed to challenge some aspect of an earlier and separate **case**, it is called a collateral attack on the earlier case.

EXAMPLE

Sam obtains a **divorce** in Nevada without properly notifying his wife Laurie. Laurie files a later lawsuit seeking to set aside the divorce and start the divorce proceedings over. Laurie's case is a collateral attack on the divorce.

The law wants **judgments** to be final whenever possible, and thus collateral attacks are discouraged. Many are filed, but usually only succeed when an obvious injustice or unconstitutional treatment occurred in the earlier case.

See also *Appeal*.

Collusion: Collusion is the secret cooperation of two people in order to mislead or deceive a third person. Before **no-fault divorces**, many couples wanted to **divorce**, but neither spouse had a legal basis (ground) for the divorce. They would therefore pretend that one of them was committing **adultery** or was otherwise at fault in order to manufacture a **ground for divorce**. This was collusion because they were cooperating in order to mislead the judge. If, before the divorce, the **defendant** decided he no longer wanted a divorce, he could raise the collusion as a **defense to the divorce**.

Comity: Comity is the legal doctrine under which countries recognize and enforce each others' legal **decrees**. Comity usually arises in two situations in **family law**. The first is where a **divorce** is granted by another country. If both parties were present and consented to the divorce, there is usually no problem with the United States recognizing the **foreign divorce** decree. The second situation arises in child **custody** cases. The **Uniform Child Custody Jurisdiction Act** requires that state courts recognize properly entered custody decrees of other nations; in turn, many other countries are beginning to recognize United States custody **orders**.

See also *Dominican Divorces*.

Commingling: Commingling is the mixing together by spouses of their **marital property** with the **separate property** of one spouse, or one spouse's separate property with the other spouse's separate property. For instance, if cash belonging separately to one spouse is put in a bank account containing marital property, the separate property is commingled with the marital property. Upon **divorce**, commingled funds are often treated as marital property, and property purchased from commingled funds is treated as marital unless very careful records have been kept tracking the separate property funds from the time they were deposited until the time they were spent on the property in question. This is referred to as the **tracing of funds**.

Common Law: Legal principles that are developed by **appellate courts** when deciding **appeals** are collectively termed the common law. Since the twelfth century, the common law was England's primary system of law. When the United States became independent, states adopted the English common law as their law. Since that time, decisions by American courts have developed a body of American common law which has superseded English common law in most areas. It is not proper, however, to say that America is a "common law" country. Rather, under the United States and state constitutions, Congress and state legislatures create the primary source of law (see *statute*), and the "common law" applies when there is no statutory law. Thus, today the term "common law" usually means any legal principle developed by the courts.

In 18th Century England common law, one method of terminating marriage was wife-selling.

Common Law Marriage: In Alabama, Colorado, Georgia, Idaho, Iowa, Kansas, Montana, Ohio, Oklahoma, Pennsylvania, Rhode Island, South Carolina, Texas and Washington, D.C., couples can become legally **married** by living together for a long period of time and either holding themselves out to others as husband and wife or intending to be married. These are called common law marriages. Contrary to popular belief, however, even if two people **cohabit** for a certain number of years, if they don't intend to be married or don't hold themselves out as married, there is no common law marriage—even in those states which recognize such marriages.

When a common law marriage does exist, the spouses are entitled to the same legal treatment received by other married couples, including the necessity of going through a formal **divorce** to end the marriage.

Common Law Property: Under the traditional **common law** as developed in England and later adopted by the United States, **property** acquired during **marriage** was divided upon **divorce** according to who had legal **title to the property**, that is, who owned it. This property division system was also sometimes referred to as "title division." Only property jointly owned by the couple could be divided by the court. Virtually all states that originally followed this common law rule have since adopted **equitable distribution** rules, which provide that property acquired during marriage is equitably divided at divorce, regardless of who has legal title. Mississippi remains the only state which still strictly follows the common law property scheme of dividing **marital property**.

Community Debts: Community debts are **debts incurred during marriage** by a couple living in a **community property state**. Both partners are responsible for community debts. If a creditor was specifically looking for payment from the **separate property** of one spouse, however, the debt is not a community debt, and only the spouse to whom the creditor looked is responsible for the debt. In addition, most community property states require that the debt "benefit the community" (the couple), i.e., not promote the breakdown of the **marriage**. If the debt does not benefit the community, the spouse who does benefit by the debt will be solely responsible for it.

EXAMPLE

Lee buys herself a motorcycle; that is a community debt because the community benefits by Lee's enjoying the motorcycle, even if her husband never uses the motorcycle. If Lee takes a trip to the Caribbean with her lover, however, that debt will be her separate debt because the community of Lee and her husband does not benefit by Lee and her lover's trip.

Community Estate: In the eight **community property states**, the total of **assets** and **debts** qualifying as **community property** is called the community estate. At **divorce**, a court first **appraises** and then, under most circumstances, divides the community estate equally between the **parties**.

Community Property: Community property is a method of defining the ownership of **property** acquired (including **earnings**) during a **marriage** and the responsibility for **debts** incurred during marriage. It is used in eight states. Generally, all **earnings during marriage** and all property acquired with those earnings are considered community property. This includes wages, stock options, **pensions** and other employment compensation, family business profits, **business good will**, household goods, motor vehicles, bank accounts, life **insurance** policies, **tax refunds**, **real property**, art collections, copyrights and inventions. Additionally, all **debts** incurred during marriage, unless the creditor was specifically looking for payment from the **separate property** of one spouse, are community property debts.

The major exceptions to these rules are that gifts and **inheritances** specifically made to one spouse during marriage, personal injury **awards** received by one spouse during marriage and the proceeds of a pension which had already vested (i.e., the pensioner is legally entitled to receive it) before marriage are separate property.

Property purchased with the separate funds of a spouse remains that spouse's separate property. A business owned by one spouse before the marriage remains his separate property during the marriage, although a portion of the value of the business may be attributed to the community if it increased in value during the marriage or both spouses worked at it. Property purchased partially with separate funds and partially with community property funds is part community and part separate property.

Upon **divorce**, community property is generally divided equally between the spouses. (In many community property states, for purpose of divorce, property held in **joint tenancy** is **presumed** to be community property.) A spouse who contributed separate property to a community asset may be entitled to **reimbursement** for that contribution. Conversely, the **community estate** may be reimbursed for community property contributions to a spouse's separate property.

On death, one-half of each item of community property automatically goes to the remaining spouse. (This discussion does not apply to property held in joint tenancy.) The other half goes to the remaining spouse if the deceased person died without a **will**, or left it to her husband in her will. Otherwise, the half goes to whomever the deceased person left it to in her will. (This could result in the surviving spouse owning half of an item and the deceased's brother, aunt, friend or lover owning the other half.)

In most community property states, a court has the discretion to divide the property "equitably," if dividing the property equally would result in unfairness to one **party**. Additionally, in some community property states which still have **fault divorce**, a spouse deemed at fault in ending the marriage may be awarded less than 50% of the community property. (These exceptions do not apply in California, the biggest community property state.)

EXAMPLE

Aaron and Rachel have: Rachel's boat purchased before their marriage; oil paintings Rachel inherited; Aaron's photo equipment from before their marriage; Aaron's stamp collection, part of which was acquired before they married and part acquired during the marriage; a VCR Aaron purchased during the marriage with money he had earned before the marriage; a jointly purchased house and household furniture; a Mercedes they won in a raffle; and various record albums, some acquired by each before the marriage and some acquired during the marriage.

Their property is characterized as:

Rachel's	Aaron's	Community
boat	photo equipment	house
oil paintings	stamp collection (part)	stamp collection (part)
records (some)	records (some)	records (some)
	VCR	Mercedes
		furniture

If a court divides their property, Rachel and Aaron each would keep what they owned before they married. The house, furniture, Mercedes and stamp collection would be **appraised** and, along with the remaining records, divided equally. One way to divide the community property would be to sell it all and split the proceeds. Another way would be to sell the house, split the rest of the property, and divide the house proceeds, evening up the balance. If Rachel and Aaron divide their property without court intervention, they can agree on whatever division they want.

Community Property States: Arizona, California, Idaho, Louisiana, Nevada, New Mexico, Texas and Washington follow **community property** legal traditions from Spain. Wisconsin has adopted a system virtually identical to community property, but does not call it community property.

See also *Common Law Property* and *Equitable Distribution States*.

Comparative Rectitude: Comparative rectitude is a doctrine used in states with **fault divorce**. Under comparative rectitude, a court will grant the spouse least at fault a **divorce** when both **parties** have shown **grounds for divorce**. The doctrine is often invoked when the **plaintiff** alleges that the **defendant** is at fault and the defendant raises the plaintiff's **marital misconduct** as a defense. Under **common law**, when both parties were at fault, neither was entitled to a divorce. The absurdity of this result gave rise to the doctrine of comparative rectitude.

Compensatory Damages: See *Actual Damages*.

Complaint: The complaint is the first **court paper** filed in a lawsuit. It briefly states the **plaintiff's** view of the crux of the legal dispute and asks the court to resolve the dispute. In some types of **cases** and in certain states, a complaint is called a petition or a libel.

Concealing Child from Custodial Parent: See *Childnapping*.

Concealment as Grounds for Annulment: Concealing a very important fact from a spouse before **marriage** may constitute grounds for an **annulment**. Examples of important facts include addiction to alcohol or drugs, conviction of a felony, children from a prior relationship, a sexually transmitted disease, or impotency.

Conciliation Service: In many states, persons contemplating divorce can get help from court-provided services that attempt to bring the parties back together (conciliation) or help them work out some disputed issues (**mediation**). Many states also offer conciliation services and mediation to divorcing spouses to help resolve disputes over **child support**, **alimony**, **custody**, **visitation** and division of property through negotiation rather than adversarial court proceedings.

Conclusions of Law: See *Findings of Fact and Conclusions of Law*.

Conclusive Presumption: A fact assumed to be true under the law is called a **presumption**. When the law does not allow a presumption to be attacked, it is called an irrebuttable or conclusive presumption. A common conclusive presumption, which sometimes produce arbitrary results, is that a husband is the father of any child born to his wife during the **marriage**. Because of the absurd result this presumption can sometimes lead to, some states now allow it to be rebutted (disproved) under certain circumstances.

Condonation: Condonation is someone's approval of another's activities. For example, a wife who does not object to her husband's **adultery** may be said to condone it. In states with **fault divorce**, condonation may constitute a **defense to divorce**. If the wife sues her husband for **divorce**, claiming he has committed adultery, the husband may argue as a defense that she condoned his behavior.

Confidential Marriage: In California, couples may undergo a **marriage** in which only the two **parties** and the official performing the marriage are present. This is called a confidential marriage. Confidential marriages are not witnessed, nor are they entered into public county records. (They are entered into "non-public" records.) Although they are rarely performed, they are legally binding. In order to obtain a confidential marriage, the parties must:
- each be at least 18
- be a man and a woman (i.e., no **same-sex marriages**)
- and have lived together "for a long period of time."

Confidential Relationship: A confidential relationship is one between two people where each has gained the confidence of the other, purports to act or advise with the other's interest in mind, and therefore has a duty to act toward the other with good faith and honesty (sometimes termed a "fiduciary duty"). The most common confidential relationship is between spouses. People in confidential relationships have a duty not to conceal or misappropriate **property** from one another, not to incur **debts** holding the other liable without authorization, and to be open and honest with each other even during **divorce**. If a spouse breaches any of these duties, in virtually all states she will be awarded less than her share of the **marital property** on divorce. Other confidential relationships commonly recognized are between parents and children, and sometimes between **non-marital partners**.

Conjugal: Conjugal means relating to **marriage**. Conjugal rights are a husband and wife's rights to mutual love, affection, comfort, companionship and sex.

Connivance: Connivance is the setting up of a situation so that the other person commits a wrongdoing. For example, a wife who invites her husband's **co-respondent** to the house and then leaves for the weekend may be said to have connived his adultery. In states with **fault divorce**, connivance may constitute a **defense to divorce**. If the wife sues her husband for divorce, claiming he has committed adultery, the husband may argue as a defense that she connived—that is, set up—his actions.

Consanguinity: Consanguinity describes any blood relationship, such as between parent and child, brother and sister, grandparent and grandchild, and uncle and nephew.

See also *Affinity* and *Kin*.

Conservator: When an adult cannot manage his own affairs, a court has the power to appoint someone to take charge of him. The appointed person is now frequently called a conservator, although she is still called a **guardian** in many places. The relationship between the disabled adult and the conservator is called a conservatorship. Conservators are often appointed when the disabled adult has sizable **assets** or a large income. The court must hold a **hearing** to determine whether there is a need for a conservator before one can be appointed.

To avoid court involvement in the event of incompetency, more and more people prepare a document called a **durable power of attorney**. This document allows the person preparing it to select the person he wants to manage his assets and make other decisions should he become incapacitated, rather than leave that decision to a court.

Constructive Abandonment: When a spouse refuses to both recognize a **marriage** and act married, he is said to have constructively (that is, not actually, but for all practical purposes) abandoned the marriage and the spouse. In states which still have **fault divorce**, abandonment of a spouse often constitutes **grounds for divorce**.

Constructive Desertion: See *Constructive Abandonment* and *Desertion*.

Consummation of Marriage: Consummation of **marriage** refers to the first time a married couple has sexual intercourse. A spouse's refusal to consummate the marriage is usually ground for an **annulment**.

Contempt of Court: A judge who feels someone is improperly challenging or ignoring the court's authority has the power to declare the defiant person (called the "contemnor") in contempt of court. There are two types of contempt—criminal and civil. Criminal contempt occurs when the contemnor actually interferes with the ability of the court to function properly, for example, by yelling at the judge. (This is also called direct contempt because it occurs directly in front of the judge.) A criminal contemnor may be fined, jailed or both as punishment for his act.

Civil contempt occurs when the contemnor willfully disobeys a court **order**. (This is also called indirect contempt because it occurs outside the judge's immediate realm and **evidence** must be presented to the judge to prove the contempt.) A civil contemnor, too, may be fined, jailed or both, however, the fine or jailing is meant to coerce the contemnor into obeying the court, not to punish him, and the contemnor will be released from jail just as soon as he complies with the court order. In **divorce** proceedings, civil contempt is one way the court enforces **alimony, child support, custody** and **visitation** orders which have been ignored.

Contested Hearing: When one **party** objects either in person or in writing, to the other party's request for a court **order**, the court **hearing** on the request is called contested. On the other hand, when both parties agree to what is being requested, or one of the parties does not respond at the hearing, the hearing is uncontested.

> **EXAMPLE**
>
> Joe and Mary's **divorce** has been declared **final**. Sometime later, Joe files a **request for a modification** of the **custody** order giving Mary **sole custody**. If Mary attends the hearing to voice her objection to Joe's request, the hearing is contested. If Mary calls Joe and they work out an agreement, or if Mary simply fails to attend the hearing or file a written objection, it is uncontested. In the latter case, Joe will most likely be granted his request.

Continuance: When a court postpones a **hearing, trial** or other scheduled appointment (such as a **settlement conference**), it is called a continuance. If one **party** is not prepared for a hearing or trial, the court may grant a continuance to allow the party to get a lawyer or otherwise prepare so as not to be at a disadvantage. While continuances are often called for on the ground of fairness, they also are commonly sought by attorneys solely for the purpose of delaying the proceeding or harassing the other side.

Continuing Duty to Support: Absent a court **order** to the contrary, a parent has a continuing duty to support his biological or **adopted** child (often by way of **child support** when a **divorce** has occurred) until she reaches the **age of majority**, become **emancipated**, or is adopted. In some states, the support duty continues after the child becomes an adult if the child is disabled, unable to care for herself, or in school.

Contraception: See *Birth Control.*

Convertible Divorce: A convertible divorce is one which is obtained by converting a **legal separation** to a **divorce**.

> **EXAMPLE**
>
> Kate and Robert have been married for 15 years. Kate has severe back problems and is unable to work. She has received extensive medical care, which has been paid for through Robert's medical insurance; she is unable to obtain her own insurance. Kate and Robert agree that their **marriage** is not working. But because if they divorce, Kate will have no health insurance, they legally separate so that Kate is able to remain on Robert's health plan. After a few years, Kate undergoes extensive surgery and her back problems are gone. She also obtains a job in which her employer is willing to provide her with health insurance. Because Kate no longer needs Robert's insurance, Kate and Robert now convert their legal separation into a divorce.

The significance of a convertible divorce is that a couple who has been legally separated need not file preliminary divorce papers when they file a paper requesting the court to change their separation to a divorce. The terms of their divorce (**alimony, child support, custody, visitation** and **division of property**) have already been disposed of in the **separation agreement** or **separation decree**.

Cooling-Off Period: The "cooling-off period" is slang for the time a couple must wait from the date the court has issued a **judgment** in their **divorce** to the date the judgment becomes final. The wait can be three months to a year, depending on state law, and is meant to give the couple an opportunity to **reconcile**. Some states have no waiting period.

See *Interlocutory and Final Judgment.*

Co-Parent: An adult who is not legally responsible for the care, support and **custody** of a child, but who has assumed the care, support and custody of a child together with the child's legally responsible parent, is sometimes called a co-parent.

Stepparents who have not **adopted** their stepchildren are co-parents, however, the term is rarely used for stepparents. It is more commonly used by unmarried couples jointly raising a child for whom only one of them is legally responsible. Because **same-sex couples** cannot biologically parent one child, cannot **marry** (and become stepparents) and virtually all have been denied the right to jointly adopt (usually one person adopts and together they raise the child), co-parenting has become an important concept in the lesbian and gay community.

Co-Respondent: The "other man" or "other woman" named in the **court papers** for a **fault divorce** alleging **adultery** is called the co-respondent.

Corroboration: Corroboration is additional **evidence** that supports an accusation or item of **circumstantial evidence**. For instance, in the **case** of alleged **adultery**, corroboration might consist of a love letter or a hotel clerk's testimony that the spouse and the **co-respondent** rented a room together.

Cost of Living Adjustment (COLA) Clause: A COLA clause in an **alimony** or **child support** order means that payments are to increase annually at a rate equal to the annual **cost of living increase**, as determined by an economic indicator (such as the Consumer Price Index) identified in the **order**. Some judges include COLAs in their orders when setting alimony and child support. This eliminates the need for any **requests for modifications** from the recipient claiming the cost of living increase as a **changed circumstance**.

Cost of Living Increase: When inflation reduces the value of **alimony** or **child support** payments, the recipient may cite her increased cost of living as a **changed circumstance** and request an increase in alimony or child support.

County Adoption: See *Agency Adoption.*

Court Calendar: See *Calendar.*

Court Clerk: See *Clerk.*

Court Commissioner: A court commissioner is a person appointed by a judge to assist her in finding facts, hearing testimony from witnesses and resolving issues. Court commissioners are frequently lawyers or retired judges. In many states, court commissioners commonly hear testimony concerning the validity of **wills**, preside over **default divorces** and other default hearings, decide **alimony** and **child support** modifications, and decide **discovery motions**.

Court Costs: Courts usually charge a fee for filing a document. The fee can be as high as $250 for the first paper filed by each side (called the pleading) in a lawsuit, depending on the state and type of pleading. The filing fee for subsequent papers which request some action by the court (**motions**) is usually substantially less. These fees help pay the costs of running the courts, sometimes paying the salaries of the judges and their staffs, maintaining the courthouse law library, and paying the costs of any **conciliation service** or **mediation**.

Court Forms: A number of states have developed pre-printed legal forms for use in court proceedings involving such matters as **divorces, guardianships** and **temporary restraining orders**. These forms are especially helpful to people handling their own **cases** without lawyers; filling in blanks is usually much easier than figuring out what needs to go into a document that must be typed from scratch. On the other hand, some forms are so confusing that they intimidate all but the most knowledgeable lawyers or paralegals.

Court Mediator: See *Mediation* and *Mediator*.

Court Opinion: When an **appellate court** decides an **appeal**, it usually issues a written opinion (called the **case**) explaining its decision (see **majority opinion**, and **concurring and dissenting opinion**). Important cases are collected and published in hardbound books as they come out. They serve as guidance for **courts** and **litigants** who must later come to grips with the same or similar issues.

See also *Precedent*.

Court Papers: All papers filed with a court regarding a lawsuit are called court papers. They typically consist of pleadings (**complaint** or petition and **answer**), **motions** (written requests to the court to take some specific action), and court **orders** (written orders resulting from a **trial** or hearing).

Court Reporter: A court reporter is a person trained to take down a verbatim account of all proceedings in the courtroom (but usually not in the judge's **chambers**). Most court reporters today use special machines that enable them to get down every word. Later, they prepare typed transcripts for use by the **parties** and the judge on **appeal**. Court reporters also record and transcribe **depositions**.

Until recently, court reporters had to manually type out the transcript from their shorthand notes. Now, however, many reporters have machines that read the recording machine tape and create a text file that can be printed out on a standard computer printer.

Court Rule: Every court has rules governing the procedures specific to that court.

Details such as the size and length of the **court papers**, time limits for filing certain documents, the cost of filing, when a **case** may be placed on a **calendar**, etc. are dictated by these rules. In some states, court rules govern the amount of **alimony** and **child support** to be paid based on the incomes of the spouses and the number of children. Court rules are usually formulated by legislative and administrative judicial bodies, or by the courts themselves.

Court Trial: See *Bench Trial*.

Creditors and Marital Debts: See *Debts Accumulated Between Separation and Divorce* and *Debts Incurred During Marriage*

Criminal Contempt: See *Contempt of Court*.

Criminal Conversation: Criminal conversation is a ground for a lawsuit brought by a husband for damages against a man who has seduced the husband's wife. This action is no longer available in most states. See also *Heart-Balm Lawsuits*.

Cross Examination: See *Direct and Cross Examination*.

Cruelty: Cruelty is often defined as any act of inflicting unnecessary emotional or physical pain. In the states which still allow **fault divorces**, cruelty or mental cruelty is often used as a **ground for divorce** because as a practical matter, courts will accept minor wrongs or disagreements as sufficient evidence of cruelty to justify the **divorce**.

Curtesy: Under the traditional **common law**, a spouse was automatically entitled to inherit a portion of the other spouse's **property**. Curtesy was the portion of a wife's property that the husband was entitled to when the wife died, while **dower** was the portion of the husband's property that the wife was entitled to receive when he died. Commonly, a husband received 100% of his wife's property if she died leaving children, who could later inherit the property from their father. If the woman died without children, her property returned to her parents, **siblings** or other relatives. Some states, however, did not require the women to leave children in order for her husband to receive her property. Curtesy and dower laws don't exist in **community property states**, and many other states abolished or modified the laws when they adopted **equitable distribution** rules.

Custodial Parent: The parent who has **physical custody** of a child is called the custodial parent. The other parent is termed the **non-custodial parent**. This is true even if the parents share **legal custody**. Some states now grant **joint** (physical) **custody**, where the parents share the physical custody of their child (e.g., alternate months or years, three days a week in one home and four in the other, or **bird's nest custody**). In joint custody arrangements, a parent is considered the custodial parent when she actually has the child.

has the child.

Custody: Custody includes both the legal authority to make decisions about the medical, educational, health and welfare needs of a child (**legal custody**) and physical control over a child (**physical custody**). Traditionally, legal and physical custody were granted to the mother and **visitation** rights to the father. This arrangement is still the norm in many states. Some states, however, have **joint custody** laws which allow **divorced** parents to share physical custody, legal custody, or both. When only legal custody is shared, one parent is given physical custody and the other is given visitation rights. When physical custody is shared, usually so is legal custody. The primary standard used by courts when awarding custody is the **best interests of the child**.

Custody should not be confused with **child support**. Every parent has an obligation to support his children. When one parent has physical custody and the other visitation rights, the parent with visitation rights (called the **non-custodial parent**) is usually ordered to pay some child support to the other parent, while the **custodial parent** is deemed to meet her obligation through the custody itself.

RELATED TERMS

Agreement to Modify Alimony, Child Support, Custody or Visitation
Changed Circumstance
Changing Child's Name
Child's Preference for Custody Arrangement
Childnapping
Cohabitation
Day Care
Established Living Pattern
Family Home
Gay or Lesbian Lifestyle: Effect on Custody and Visitation
Geographic Move: Effect on Custody and Visitation
Grandparents' Rights
Guardianship
In Loco Parentis
Lifestyle and Social Factors: Effect on Custody and Visitation
Modification Agreement
Parental Kidnapping Prevention Act
Permanent Alimony, Child Support, Custody or Visitation
Request for Modification of Alimony, Child Support, Custody or Visitation
Standards for Custody
Temporary Modification of Custody or Visitation
Temporary Provision for Alimony, Child Support, Custody or Visitation
Tender Years Doctrine
Termination of Parental Rights
Transportation of Children
Unfitness of Parent
Uniform Child Custody Jurisdiction Act

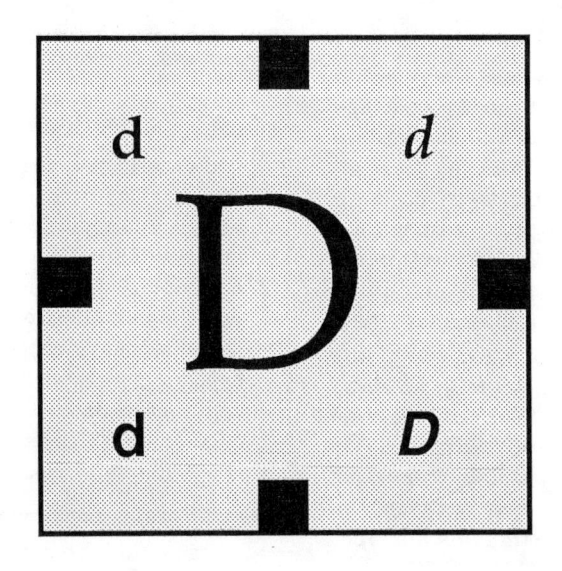

Day Care: Day care centers take care of pre-school-aged children while their parents work. They may be publicly or privately funded. Quality day care, while increasingly in demand in our society because most parents now work outside the home, is in dramatic short supply.

Working married couples with children or working single parents are entitled to claim on their federal income tax return an "employment-related expense" credit of up to $800 for one child or $1600 for two or more children for day care costs incurred to allow the parents to be gainfully employed.

Debt: A debt is money owed. Common debts are home mortgages, **alimony** and **child support** obligations, credit card bills, phone bills, gas bills, car payments and student loans.

For a married couple, responsibility for paying a debt depends on when the debt was incurred (before **marriage**, during marriage, or after **separation** but before **divorce**), the state in which the couple lives, who incurred the debt (one spouse or both), and for what the debt was incurred. As a general rule, both spouses are responsible for debts incurred by either or both during marriage if the debt is for property or a service which benefits both spouses.

See also *Community Debts; Debts: Effect on on Alimony and Child Support; Debts Incurred Before Marriage; Debts Incurred BetweenSeparation and Divorce;* and *Debts Incurred During Marriage.*

Debts: Effect on Alimony and Child Support: Upon divorce, the court allocates **debts incurred during marriage** between the spouses based on who can pay and who benefits most from the **asset** attached to the **debt**. If the court orders a spouse to pay a large portion of marital debts, it often reduces the amount of **alimony**, and on rare occasions the amount of **child support**, that spouse is ordered to pay.

See also *Community Debts; Debts Incurred Before Marriage; Debts Incurred Between Separation and Divorce;* and *Debts Incurred During Marriage.*

EXAMPLE

When Marie and Pierre married, Marie had student loan debts of $10,000. She had defaulted on four payments of $150 each, and continued not to pay during the marriage. Pierre kept his earnings in a separate bank account. When the bank which loaned Marie the money sued her for repayment, it could go after Marie's separate property, and Marie and Pierre's community property (except for his earnings). None of Pierre's separate property, however, can be used.

See also *Community Debts; Debts: Effect on Alimony and Child Support; Debts Incurred Between Separation and Divorce* and *Debts Incurred During Marriage.*

Debts Incurred Before Marriage: In **community property states** and many **equitable distribution states**, **debts** incurred by a spouse before **marriage** are the responsibility of the spouse incurring them. During the marriage, the debtor-spouse's **separate property** must first be looked to by creditors to pay the pre-marital debt. After that, **marital property** may be used. In no case, however, is the separate property of one spouse liable for **debts** incurred by the other spouse before marriage. In some community property states, community property **earnings** of the non-debtor spouse are not liable for the other's pre-marital debts if the earnings are kept in a separate bank account and not mixed with other marital property.

Debts Incurred Between Separation and Divorce: State law varies on who is responsible for **debts** incurred after a **married** couple permanently **separates** but before the **divorce** is final. In some states, each spouse is responsible for his own debts. In many states, however, creditors may sue both the husband and the wife for a debt incurred by either one of them before the official divorce. If a creditor obtains payment from the wife, but the husband incurred the debt, the wife must request the court to order her husband to **reimburse** her.

In a few states, debts incurred between separation and divorce for **necessaries** (food, housing, clothing and health care) for

-50-

the spouse or children (unless there is a **child support order** stating who must pay) are considered joint debts. A creditor may obtain payment from either spouse. If the wife pays, but the husband incurred the debt, the wife will not be entitled to reimbursement.

> **EXAMPLE**
>
> George and Fran separated in October and planned to divorce. In December, George was in a car accident, and was billed $250 for fixing the car and $100 toward his medical costs. In March, when George and Fran drafted their **divorce agreement**, George requested that Fran contribute toward the bills. Fran refused, and so they brought the question before a judge. The judge ordered George to pay the full car bill, but ordered Fran to help with the medical costs (a necessary of life).

See also *Community Debts; Debts:Effect on Alimony and Child Support; Debts Incurred Before Marriage;* and *Debts Incurred During Marriage.*

Debts Incurred During Marriage: Debts incurred during a marriage are usually considered joint debts—that is, during the marriage, both spouses are legally responsible for them. Creditors first look to jointly owned **property** to satisfy debts; if there is no jointly owned property, they look to each spouse's **separate property**.

If a couple **divorces**, responsibility for marital debts is allocated in accordance with the **property** division laws of the state. This usually means that the debts are divided equally or equitably, especially when they were incurred for food, shelter, clothing and medical care (called **necessaries**). The court also considers who is better able to pay the debts (the spouse with the higher income and/or lower living expenses). If a couple has many debts but also has much property, a common result is for the spouse better able to pay the debts to assume their payment and also to receive a larger share of the property to even up the division.

> **EXAMPLE**
>
> Aaron and Alice purchased a table for cash, bought a car on credit and charged a vacation to Hawaii on their credit card while they were married. After they divorced, Alice agreed to pay off the vacation (in exchange for keeping the table), and Aaron took the car and assumed the car payments. If Alice doesn't pay off the vacation, or if Aaron doesn't make the car payments, the creditor can seek payment from the other and leave the two of them to fight out who must pay and who is entitled to reimbursement.

Regardless of the court's assignment of responsibility, in **community property states** and many **equitable distribution states**, a creditor may sue either or both spouses and will do so on the basis of who is

-51-

more likely to pay. Any agreement which the husband and wife may make regarding these debts is not binding on creditors, but entitles a spouse to **reimbursement** if the agreement is not honored by the other.

One member of a couple may also incur a separate debt during the marriage, but only that partner is responsible for repayment. In most states, a separate debt is when the creditor requested credit information about only one spouse when making the debt and intends for only that spouse to repay the debt.

EXAMPLE

Ellen bought a plot of land before her marriage to Bob, and during her marriage decided to landscape the property; the bank which loaned Ellen the money relied solely on Ellen's credit in making the loan. Ellen has incurred a separate debt. Regardless of when the debt is repaid, only Ellen's separate property is legally responsible. If jointly owned property is used, Bob is entitled to request from Ellen that he be reimbursed for his portion of that property paid to the bank. In community property states, this would be one-half.

See also *Community Debts; Debts: Effect on Alimony and Child Support; Debts Incurred Before Marriage;* and *Debts Incurred Between Separation and Divorce.*

Declaration: A declaration is a written statement submitted to a court in which the writer swears "under penalty of perjury" that the contents are true. That is, the writer acknowledges that if he is lying, he may be prosecuted for perjury. (See *Oaths and Affirmations*). Declarations are normally used in place of live testimony when the court is asked to **order temporary provisions for alimony, child support, custody, visitation and property division.**

A typical declaration sets forth the factual assertions of the person signing it (called the declarant) and ends with the statement worded like this one: "I declare under penalty of perjury that the foregoing is true and correct, and would be my testimony if I were in a court of law." The date and place of signing are usually included.

Declarations are different from **affidavits**, which are signed in the presence of a **notary public.** Some states allow declarations to be used in the place of affidavits, thus avoiding a trip to the notary public.

Decrease in Income: When a parent or ex-spouse paying **alimony** or **child support** suffers a temporary decrease in **earnings,** she may be able to obtain from the court a downward **temporary modification of alimony or child support.** If the payor suffers a permanent decrease in income, she should file a **request for modification** with the court, citing the decrease as the **changed circumstance** that justifies the request for a reduction.

Decreased Ability to Pay: See *Decrease in Income.*

Decreased Need for Alimony: When a former spouse's need for **alimony** decreases or ceases, the court may reduce or terminate the alimony if the paying spouse files a **request for modification.** Such a request can be made if the alimony recipient gets a job, an increase in pay, or sometimes if he begins intimately living with someone of the opposite sex (**cohabitating**).

Decree: In most states, the court **order** granting a **divorce** and ruling on the issues associated with the divorce (**alimony, child support, custody, visitation,** and **division of property**) is called a decree. Decrees are **temporary, interlocutory** (semi-permanent), or **permanent.** For all practical purposes, a decree is the same thing as a **judgment.**

Decree, Final or Interlocutory: See *Interlocutory and Final Judgments.*

Deed: A deed is a written document, signed by the owner of **real property,** that transfers **title to the property** to another person. There are several types of deeds:

• bargain and sale deed—document includes getting something of value in exchange for the transference of the property.

• grant deed—document guarantees that the title hasn't already been passed to someone else or isn't encumbered (burdened with a mortgage, lien or past due tax bill) except to the extent disclosed by public records or the person signing the deed.

• quitclaim deed—one person transfers what ownership interest in the property he has, but makes no promises about the title. When **divorcing** spouses jointly own **real property,** often one spouse is required to sign a quitclaim deed in favor of the other spouse as part of the overall **property** division.

• sheriff's deed—document is given to purchaser and signed by the sheriff after property is sold at a sheriff's sale (i.e., sold to pay a court **judgment** on a foreclosure).

• tax deed—document is given to the purchaser and signed by the government after property taken by the government from a previous owner is sold to pay due taxes.

• warranty deed—the person signing the deed guarantees that he has good title to the property. These deeds are rarely used today, as their function has been replaced by title insurance.

Default Divorce: If a spouse who is **served** with a **summons** and **complaint** (or petition) for **divorce** fails to file a formal response with the court, a divorce is automatically granted and is termed a default or uncontested divorce. Many divorces proceed this way because the spouses have worked everything out and there's no reason for both to go to court (and pay the **court costs**). Without such cooperation, however, a summons and complaint should never be ignored unless a person truly does not wish to contest the matter.

Defendant: The person against whom a lawsuit is filed is usually called the defendant. In some states, or in certain types of

-53-

actions, the defendant is called the respondent. The term respondent is also used to designate the person responding to an appeal.

See also *Appellant; Appellee* and *Plaintiff*.

Defense to Annulment: When one spouse sues for an **annulment** and the other does not want the **marriage** to end, the **defendant** may raise a defense. Annulments, however, are not usually contested. When a **defendant** does contest, she usually claims that the **plaintiff** (the spouse who filed for annulment) knew at the time of the marriage whatever facts are being relied on for the annulment.

EXAMPLE

When Jan and Dean married, Jan knew that Dean had a criminal record of theft and assault. She agreed to marry him nonetheless. After the marriage, Jan decided that Dean wasn't right for her and sued for an annulment, claiming that Dean didn't tell her of his past. If Dean raises the defense that Jan knew about his past and agreed to marry him regardless, the annulment is unlikely to be granted. (Jan and Dean will have to go the route of a **divorce**.)

Defense to Divorce: Under the traditional **fault divorce** scheme, a spouse who did not want to get **divorced** usually defended against the divorce **action** by simply denying whatever the other spouse alleged. Sometimes, however, the evidence of the **defendant's** fault (also called **marital misconduct**) was overwhelming, and the defendant needed something other than just a denial. Under the laws of many states, the defendant was permitted to defeat a divorce **action** by proving that the **plaintiff** was also at fault and therefore shouldn't be granted the divorce. If both **parties** were deemed at fault, neither could be granted the divorce, and they were forced to remain married. (Courts sometimes got around this, however. See, *comparative rectitude.*)

Under this system, women who were financially dependent on their husbands could threaten to block a divorce by proving that a husband was at fault, unless he agreed to provide a greater share of **marital property** or **alimony** than he might otherwise be required to pay. Although it is still possible to obtain a fault divorce in most states, the fact that **no-fault divorce** is now also available in every state has made this type of bargaining much less common.

Other defenses to a divorce based on marital misconduct include **provocation** (the plaintiff provoked the defendant into committing the misconduct), **condonation** (the plaintiff condoned the defendant's action), **connivance** (the plaintiff set up the defendant's activity in order to obtain a ground for divorce) and **collusion** (the plaintiff and defendant secretly cooperated by claiming one was at fault in order to obtain the ground for the divorce).

See also *Statute of Limitation.*

Delinquent Alimony: See *Enforcement of Alimony.*

Delinquent Children: When a person under the **age of majority** engages in an act which would be a crime if committed by an adult, she is said to have committed a delinquent act and is referred to as a juvenile delinquent, delinquent or delinquent child.

See also *Incorrigible Children* and *Juvenile Court*.

Delinquent Child Support: See *Enforcement of Child Support*.

Denial of Allegations in Complaint: See *Allegation* and *Answer*

Dependent Child: When a child under the **age of majority** is found by a court to have been neglected or abused by his parents or **guardians**, he is placed under the protection of the court or appropriate social welfare agency and is called a dependent child. The court procedure used to determine a child's neglect or abuse is called a dependency proceeding.

The term dependent child is also used to mean a child who still depends on his parents for financial support, a child who can be claimed by an adult on an income tax return because he receives at least one-half of his support from that adult, or a child who is eligible to receive **Aid to Families with Dependent Children (AFDC)**.

See also *Tax Consequences of Alimony and Child Support*.

Deposition: A deposition is a proceeding in which a witness or **party** is asked to answer questions orally under **oath** before a **court reporter**. If at the time of trial the witness is unavailable, or testifies differently from his deposition, the deposition (or parts of it) can usually be introduced into **evidence**—that is, read out loud in court by an attorney. All parties can attend a deposition and ask questions of the witness. Some courts are beginning to allow depositions to be recorded on videotape, especially when the witness is very ill or may not live until the trial.

See also *Discovery*

Desertion of Child: See *Abandonment of Child*.

Desertion of Spouse: Desertion is the voluntary abandonment of someone by his spouse without the abandoned spouse's consent. It is a frequent **ground for divorce** in states with **fault divorces**. Commonly, desertion occurs when a spouse leaves the marital home for a specified length of time (which varies among the states).

Destabilized Household: A home in which a devastating event has occurred may be referred to as a destabilized household. Examples of such events include the arrest of a parent for a violent crime, the death or desertion of a parent, or an allegation that a parent has sexually abused his child. If a **non-custodial parent** can prove to a judge that the **custodial parent's** home has become destabilized and that the event is devastating to the child, a **request for modification of custody** may be granted.

Direct Examination and Cross Examination: Witnesses who testify at a **trial** or **hearing** are questioned by two basic techniques: direct examination and cross examination. Lawyers, or the **parties** themselves if they aren't represented by lawyers, do the examining (questioning).

Direct examination consists of questions asked in a direct form, that is, a form which does not suggest the answer, such as "where were you on July 18th?" Direct examination is conducted of witnesses who are friendly to the questioner.

A question that suggests the answer, e.g., "you were at the shop on July 18th, weren't you?" is called a leading question and can be used only on cross examination. Cross examination questions are asked by the party whose position is opposed by the witness.

Sometimes when parties aren't represented by lawyers, these formal rules of questioning are not used. Instead, witnesses use narrative formats and simply tell their stories.

Disability: Disability in **family law** generally means the inability to earn enough income to support oneself through work because of a physical or mental condition. A temporary disability suffered by a person paying **alimony** or **child support** may warrant a downward **temporary modification of alimony or child support**. For example, if a construction worker with a child support obligation breaks her leg, a court may suspend her child support until she recovers and goes back to work. A permanent disability may warrant a **request for modification** of alimony or child support based on **changed circumstances**. Similarly, if a recipient of alimony or child support becomes disabled, a court may order an increase if her **earnings** decreased or her expenses increased (e.g., health care or child care) as a result.

The word disability means something else under government programs such as Social Security Disability Insurance and Supplemental Security Income (SSI). Being disabled and therefore entitled to benefits under Social Security and SSI means:

• having a medically proven physical or mental impairment

• which prevents the person from doing any "substantially gainful work"

• which is expected to last at least twelve months or result in death.

Discovery: The formal procedures used by **parties** to a lawsuit to obtain information before a **trial** is called discovery. Discovery helps a party find out the other side's version of the facts, what witnesses know, and other **evidence**. Rules dictating the allowable methods of discovery have been set up by Congress (for federal courts) and by state legislatures (for state courts). Common discovery devices include:

• **Deposition**—a proceeding in which a witness or party is asked to answer questions orally under **oath** before a **court reporter**.

• Interrogatories — written questions sent by one party to the other party for the latter to answer in writing under oath.

• Request for physical examination—a

request to a party that he be examined by a doctor if his health is at issue.

• Request for production of documents—a request to a party to hand over certain defined documents. In **family law** cases, parties often request from each other bank statements, pay stubs, and other documents showing **earnings, assets** and **debts**.

• Request for inspection—a request by a party to look at tangible items (other than writings) in the possession or control of the other party. Items to be inspected include houses, cars, appliances, and virtually any other physical item.

• Subpoena—an **order** telling a witness to appear in court or at a deposition. A subpoena is issued by the court, and if the witness fails to comply, he can be held in **contempt of court**.

• Subpoena duces tecum—an order telling a witness to turn over certain documents to a specific party. A subpoena duces tecum is issued by the court, and if the witness fails to comply, he can be held in contempt.

The scope of information obtainable through discovery is quite broad and not limited to what can be used in a trial. Federal courts and most state courts allow a party to discover any information "reasonably calculated to lead to the discovery of **admissible evidence**." Because of this broad standard, parties often disagree about what information must be exchanged and what may be kept confidential. These disputes are resolved through court rulings on **discovery motions**.

EXAMPLE—DEPOSITION

Ellen and Amy have been living together for seven years and have purchased a car, some furniture and much household goods. They're going separate ways, but cannot agree on how to divide their **property**. Their dispute becomes nastier as the days progress, and Ellen sues Amy, claiming Amy has breached an oral agreement. Amy's lawyer wants to know Ellen's understanding of how they owned their property, so he schedules Ellen's deposition. He will ask Ellen what she understood to be the arrangement and further will ask her to identify any documents supporting her position, such as agreements, receipts, or bank statements.

EXAMPLE— REQUEST FOR INSPECTION

Bill and Bernice are **divorcing**. The court ordered Bill out of the **family home** to allow Bernice to stay there with the children. Bill and Bernice have decided to sell the house, but don't agree on the value, and therefore each plans to have an appraiser submit an **appraisal**. If Bernice refuses to allow Bill's appraiser access to the house, Bill will have to request an inspection.

Discovery Motions: When **parties** disagree over whether certain information is obtainable through the **discovery** process, they can request that the court resolve their dispute. They submit their requests in the form of written **motions**. Normally, a discovery motion asks either for an **order** compelling the other side to respond to discovery requests or for a **protective order** limiting the discovery efforts of the other side.

Discretion of Judge: When judges make decisions on questions of **child custody, alimony** and **property** division, they must, of course, follow the standards set out by state law. These standards, though, often allow judges a lot of leeway (which is called discretion). Judges are given this discretion so they can make decisions that are fair in a particular **case**, instead of being locked into a formula that may not suit every situation.

The exercise of judicial discretion is difficult to attack on **appeal**, because the decision, by law, was left to the judge in the first place. Nevertheless, judicial discretion must be exercised fairly and impartially, and a showing to the contrary may result in the ruling being reversed as an "abuse of discretion."

Dispute Resolution: Any process which helps people put an end to their disputes is called dispute resolution. Among the more common methods of dispute resolution used in **family law cases** are:

• the judicial system (courts and the court process)
• **arbitration** (the **parties** select a third person, present their case to him, and agree to be bound by that decision)
• **mediation** (the parties meet—antagonistically or unantagonistically—with a third party who helps them reach an agreement)
• **conciliation** (the parties meet unantagonistically with a third party who helps them reach an agreement).

Dissolution of Marriage: Some states now formally refer to **divorce** as dissolution of marriage.

Divisible Divorce: A divisible divorce (also called a **bifurcated** divorce) is one where the **divorce** itself is granted, terminating the **marriage,** but issues incident to the divorce, such as **alimony, child support, custody, visitation** and **division of property** are decided at a later **hearing** or **trial.** Divisible divorces usually occur when a couple cannot agree on the custody, support or property, but one spouse wishes to **remarry** or be divorced for income tax reasons. Divisible divorces may also occur when a court has **subject-matter jurisdiction** over the divorce (because the **plaintiff** lives in the state), but doesn't have **personal jurisdiction** over the **defendant.** In this situation, the court is authorized to grant the divorce itself, but can't on the other issues without personal jurisdiction over the defendant.

Division of Bills or Debts: See *Community Debts; Debts: Effect on Alimony and*

Child Support; Debts Incurred Before Marriage; Debts Incurred Between Separation and Divorce and *Debts Incurred During Marriage.*

Division of Property: In the course of a **divorce**, a couple must divide the **property** and **debts** accumulated during their **marriage**. It is common for the couple to do their own dividing rather than leave it to the judge. There is no requirement that the couple follow their state's laws in making the division. But if a couple cannot agree on a division, they may submit their property dispute to the court, which will use state laws to **characterize** and divide their marital property (usually, more or less equally).

Division of property does not mean a physical division. Rather, each **party** is awarded by a court a percentage of the property. Each item of property is then assigned a monetary value and the values are totalled. The items are distributed, with each party getting items totalling his or her percentage.

In some states, regardless of whether **fault divorces** are still available, fault is a factor in dividing property and a guilty spouse might not receive her full share of the marital property.

See also *Agreement Before Marriage; Agreement During Marriage; Common Law Property; Community Property; Equitable Distribution;* and *Separate Property.*

See chart, **FAULT CONSIDERATIONS IN DISTRIBUTING MARITAL PROPERTY.**

Divorce: Divorce is the legal termination of a **marriage**. In some states, divorce is now called "dissolution" or "dissolution of marriage."

RELATED TERMS

Active Military Duty
Alimony
Annulment
Debts Accumulated Between Separation and Divorce
Decree
Default Divorce
Defenses to Divorce
Divisible Divorce
Division of Property
Divorce Agreement
Entry of Judgment
Family Home
Fault Divorce
Foreign Divorce
Grounds for Divorce
Interlocutory and Final Judgments
Legal Separation
Living Apart
No-Fault Divorce
Nunc Pro Tunc
Residency: Effect on Marriage and Divorce
Separation
Temporary Provisions for Alimony, Child Support, Custody, Visitation and Property Division
Travel: Effect on Residency
Uniform Marriage and Divorce Act

FAULT CONSIDERATIONS IN DISTRIBUTING MARITAL PROPERTY

Although no-fault divorce is available in every state, some states reduce a spouse's share of marital property for marital fault (e.g., adultery, mental cruelty, desertion). In addition, some states reduce a spouse's share of the marital property for economic misconduct (e.g., fraud, concealing assets).

Marital Fault Irrelevant	Marital Fault May Reduce Share	Economic Misconduct May Reduce Share
Alaska	Alabama	Arizona
Arizona	Arkansas	California
California	Connecticut	Colorado
Colorado	Florida	Connecticut
Delaware	Georgia	Delaware
Idaho	Hawaii	Florida
Illinois	Maryland	Georgia
Indiana	Michigan	Illinois
Iowa	Mississippi	Indiana
Kansas	Missouri	Kansas
Kentucky	New Hampshire	Maine
Louisiana	North Carolina	Minnesota
Maine	North Dakota	Montana
Massachusetts	Rhode Island	Ohio
Minnesota	Texas	New York
Montana	Utah	North Carolina
Nebraska	Vermont	Pennsylvania
Nevada	Virginia	South Dakota
New Jersey	Wyoming	Vermont
New Mexico		West Virginia
New York		Washington, DC
Ohio		
Oklahoma		
Oregon		
Pennsylvania		
South Carolina		
South Dakota		
Tennessee		
Washington		
West Virginia		
Wisconsin		
Washington, DC		

Divorce Agreement: When a couple divorces, they may agree on some or all of the issues relating to the **division of property**, **custody** and **visitation** of the children, **alimony** and **child support**. If the agreement is put in writing, signed by the parties, and accepted by the court, it is called a divorce agreement or marital settlement agreement. The agreement becomes part of the divorce **decree** and does away with the necessity of having a **trial** on the issues covered by the agreement.

Divorce by Consent: See *No-Fault Divorce*.

Divorce Conciliation or Mediation Service: See *Conciliation Service* and *Mediation*.

Docket: A list of **cases** scheduled to be heard by a judge is called that judge's docket. These lists (containing the names of the **parties**, the **case numbers**, the date and place of the **hearing**, and in some cases, the judge's tentative decision based on the papers submitted by the parties in advance of the hearing) are usually prepared daily and posted at the courthouse. In many large cities, they are published in legal newspapers.

EXAMPLE

	Case No.	Time	Dept.
Black v. Black	65-2983	9:00 am	13
Marriage of Alvarez	76-8331	9:45 am	13
Marriage of Shapiro	23-3331	10:30 am	13
Slate v. Slate	66-2999	2:15 pm	16
Li v. Chin	87-1415	3:00 pm	16

Docket Sheet: A docket sheet is a document kept in a **case** file at the courthouse. It lists all papers filed and actions taken in a case. The judge may also note on it any action taken during a **hearing** or **trial**. Except for **juvenile court** and certain other types of confidential matters (such as **adoptions**), case files and docket sheets are public records and can be inspected by anyone.

EXAMPLE

Estelle and Ira Green's **alimony** hearing was held on Tuesday morning before Judge Garcia. At the hearing, the judge ordered Estelle to pay Ira $250 per month for six months, and further ordered that the **parties** return to court in six months in order for her to decide whether Ira will need alimony any longer. In the courthouse case file for the *Marriage of Green* (the title of the case), Judge Garcia will place a sheet of paper (often a form) on which she has written "Wife to pay husband $250 per month for six months. Parties to return to court in six months for further order."

Domestic Violence: When a spouse or lover physically assaults his partner or a child, it is called domestic violence or abuse. When a child is the victim, it is called **child abuse**. Many states offer simplified civil court procedures through which the victim of domestic violence (or a parent, in the case of a child victim) may get a **temporary restraining order** (TRO) from the court barring the abuser from entering the **family home** and prohibiting further acts of violence. In many localities, a TRO is registered with the local police so that immediate action may be taken if the abuser violates it and the victim phones the police for assistance. Violation of a TRO can result in criminal prosecution in most states. Many police officers, however, are reluctant to get involved in domestic violence situations; prosecutions are therefore often difficult to bring.

Domestic violence is also a crime. Victims may make formal complaints to their police departments, regardless of whether they have obtained or registered TROs. Unfortunately, however, because of police reluctance and victim fear of retaliation by the abuser, arrests and prosecutions are often difficult to obtain.

Domicile: Domicile is the act of living in a state with the intent to remain there.

See also *Residency: Effect on Marriage and Divorce.*

Dominican Republic Divorce: Divorces granted by the Dominican Republic are called Dominican divorces. **Married** couples can obtain Dominican divorces without actually going to the Dominican Republic. Most states, however, do not recognize this divorce as valid unless at least one spouse was present in the Dominican Republic at the time the Dominican divorce was obtained.

The Dominican Republic is the current nation offering fast, mail-order divorces, but is by no means the only nation to do so. In past years, Mexico and Haiti were popular "quickie" divorce spots.

See also *Foreign Divorce; Jurisdiction;* and *Uniform Divorce Recognition Act.*

Dower: Under traditional **common law**, a dower was the portion of a husband's **property** which he brought into the **marriage** or acquired during the marriage to which his wife was automatically entitled if he died leaving children. Dower laws barred a husband from selling, giving away or disposing of in his **will**, the portion his wife was entitled to, unless she consented. Some dower laws provided the wife and children use of the husband's property until the wife died, and then passed the property as laid out in the husband's will or under the state's **intestate succession** laws if he died without a will. Other dower laws provided the wife with one-third of the husband's property on his death, even if his will left her less. Most states have abolished or modified their dower laws, although the term is sometimes used today when a married couple jointly purchases property. There, if the property is neither **community property** nor **joint tenancy**, a wife will often sign away her "dower rights" so that the husband may dispose of his portion of the property as he chooses when he dies.

See also *Curtesy.*

Duces Tecum: See *Discovery.*

Due and Payable: "Due and payable" means that each installment of court-ordered **alimony** or **child support** is owed and to be paid according to the date set out in the **order**. Failure to pay on time results in

-62-

an **arrearage**.

See also *Retroactive Modification*.

Due Process: Due process is best defined in one word—fairness. Throughout America's history, its constitutions, **statutes** and **case law** have provided standards for fair treatment of citizens by federal, state and local governments. These standards are known as due process. When a person is treated unfairly by the government, including the courts, he is said to have been deprived of or denied due process.

EXAMPLE

Ezra and Sharon married in New York and had a son, Darwin. They **divorced** and Sharon moved to California; Darwin stayed with Ezra. Darwin later moved to California to live with Sharon; Sharon sued Ezra for **child support** in California. Ezra claimed that because he didn't live in California and had never been to California it would be unfair (a denial of due process) for him to defend the child support lawsuit in California. The United States Supreme Court agreed, saying that Sharon should file her child support request in New York. (This example is based on a case called *Kulko v. Superior Court*, 436 U.S. 84 (1978).)

Durable Power of Attorney: A durable power of attorney is a document written and signed by an adult (called the "principal") which authorizes another adult (called the "attorney in fact") of the principal's choosing to make financial and/or medical decisions on the principal's behalf. This authorization can take place upon the signing of the document or at a later time specified in the document (e.g., when two doctors certify that the principal is incompetent). The term durable refers to the fact that the power of attorney survives the incapacity of the principal, whereas a regular power of attorney automatically expires upon the principal's incapacity. In that case, or if no durable power of attorney has been executed, a court must appoint a **conservator** or **guardian** to make these decisions.

EXAMPLE

Fred developed the first symptoms of Alzheimer's disease several years ago. Recently his mental acuity has deteriorated to the point where he is unable to handle his financial affairs or make medical decisions for himself. While still competent, however, Fred executed a durable power of attorney, placing authority over his finances and health care decisions in his brother Benjamin. This means that no court proceedings are necessary to decide who will be responsible for Fred's financial affairs or his medical decisions. Benjamin may sign checks, make bank deposits, sell securities, decide Fred's medical care, and do whatever else is necessary to manage Fred's affairs. If Fred had chosen, he could have delayed the effect of the durable power of attorney until he actually became incompetent.

Duration of Alimony: See *Length of Alimony*.

Durational Residency Requirement: See *Residency: Effect on Marriage and Divorce*.

> *In Japan, if a married couple wants to dissolve their marriage and agree about children and property, they can simply "de-register" with government authorities and avoid judicial involvement.*

Earning Power: See *Ability to Earn*.

Earnings: Earnings are the wages, salaries and benefits (such as health and **life insurance** policies, **pensions**, severance pay and stock options) received by an employee or paid to oneself if one is self-employed.

See also *Ability to Earn*; *Ability to Pay* and *Earnings During Marriage*.

Earnings During Marriage: In most states, wages and salaries of spouses during **marriage** are considered **marital property**. This means that in **community property states**, the earnings are jointly owned, and in **equitable distribution states**, **assets** acquired with those earnings are equitably divided at **divorce**. Employment benefits, such as pensions and stock options, however, are considered marital property in only some community property and equitable distribution states.

In Mississippi (the **common law property state**), a spouse's earnings are considered his **separate property**, and assets acquired with those earnings are not divided at divorce unless they have been **commingled** with jointly owned property or the property of the other spouse.

Educational Degree: See *Professional Degree or License*.

Emancipated Minor: A minor demonstrating freedom from parental control or support is considered emancipated, or may be declared emancipated by a court. An emancipated minor is considered an adult for purposes such as entering into contracts (for employment, buying a car, etc.) and signing a **will**.

A minor who goes on **active military duty** is considered emancipated without a court **order**. A minor who gets a job and moves out of the **family home** is usually considered emancipated, but some states require a court order of emancipation before a parent's **continuing duty to support** ends. In most states, minors who wish to get married before reaching the **age of majority** need to obtain a court order of emancipation or, in some states, their parent's consent.

Child support obligations to the parents of emancipated minors may be cancelled by the court. For obvious reasons, most states do not allow parents to unilaterally declare their children emancipated; rather, a special proceeding must be brought to have the child declared emancipated by a court.

End of Alimony or Child Support: See *Termination of Alimony* and *Termination of Child Support*.

Enforcement of Alimony: When an ex-spouse ordered by a court to pay **alimony** does not comply, the overdue payments are called **arrearages**. Because the majority of people ordered to pay alimony don't, and a growing number of women who are **awarded** (but not paid) alimony are poor, many (but unfortunately, not enough) courts are becoming more strict than they were a few years ago about enforcing alimony **orders** and collecting alimony arrearages.

No federal laws have been passed specifically to aid in the collection of alimony. The Child Support Enforcement Act of 1984 (see *enforcement of child support*), however, gives states the option of allowing their district attorneys to pursue alimony arrearages when seeking back owed **child support**. In addition, a number of states are using enforcement laws such as **wage attachments** and **contempt of court** proceedings to collect alimony arrearages.

Enforcement of Child Support: When a person ordered by a court to pay **child support** does not comply, the overdue payments are called **arrearages**. Courts have become very strict about enforcing child support **orders** and collecting arrearages, and to that end, many state and federal laws have been passed to aid in collection.

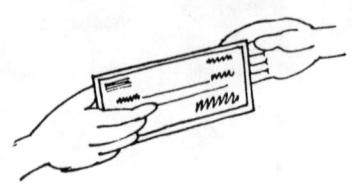

Under the federal Child Support Enforcement Act of 1984, the district attorneys of every state (sometimes called other titles, e.g., the State's Attorney in Illinois) must offer collection assistance to the recipient parent. Sometimes this means serving (see *service of court papers*) the other parent with papers requiring him to meet with the D.A. and arrange a payment schedule (and telling him that if he refuses to meet or pay, he could go to jail). If the non-paying parent has moved out of state, the D.A. or the recipient parent can use the Uniform Reciprocal Enforcement of Support Act (URESA) or **Revised Uniform Reciprocal Enforcement of Support Act (RURESA)** to locate him and seek payment. Federal and state **Parent Locator Services** can also assist in locating missing parents. In addition, federal laws permit the interception of tax refunds to enforce child support orders. Other methods of enforcement include **wage attachments** and **contempt of court** proceedings.

Enjoin: Enjoin is the effect of an **injunction**.

Entry of Judgment: When a court **judgment** (such as a judgment of **divorce**) is actually written into the official court records by the court **clerk**, the "judgment is entered." The court clerk sends a notice of the entry to each **party**. The date the judgment is entered can be important. For example, if one party wants to **appeal**, he usually has 10 to 30 days from the date of entry of judgment to file a paper indicating his intent to appeal. Also, some states require an individual to wait a period of time (20 days to 18 months) after the entry of judgment of divorce before **remarrying**.

Equitable Distribution: Equitable distribution is a principle under which **assets** and **earnings** accumulated during **marriage** are divided equitably (fairly) at **divorce**. In theory, equitable means equal, or nearly so. In practice, however, equitable is often 2/3 to the higher wage earner and 1/3 to the lower (or non) wage earner, unless the court believes it is fairer to **award** one or the other spouse more. In some **equitable distribution states**, if a spouse obtains a **fault divorce**, the "guilty" spouse may receive less than her share of the **marital property** upon divorce. Equitable distribution principles are now followed in 40 states.

Equitable Distribution States: The forty states (and Washington, D.C.) which require their **courts** to employ **equitable distribution** principles when dividing **property** at **divorce** are called the equitable distribution states. These are every state *except* Arizona, California, Idaho, Louisiana, Nevada, New Mexico, Texas, Washington (the **community property states**), Wisconsin (modified community property state) and Mississippi (**common law property state**).

EXAMPLE

Maureen and Frank, who live in New York (an equitable distribution state), are divorcing after 10 years of marriage. During their marriage, they bought a house, some furniture and a car with their earnings and investments. Maureen earns substantially more than Frank; they shared the work around the house. Upon divorce, a court is likely to divide the property in a way which takes into account the money and work put into the marriage and property as well as the economic realities of the parties. Maureen, because of her higher earnings, will probably keep the house (and its mortgage), the furniture will be divided, the party who needs the car more will get it, and Maureen will pay Frank a sum of money equal to his portion of the house (a little less than half).

Equitable Power: If strict application of the law would be unfair to a person, most courts have the authority, called equitable power, to bend the rules to prevent such an outcome. English Courts of Equity were established hundreds of years ago to temper the legalistic rigors of English Common law. Equity principles were adopted by American courts when the United States was formed. Today, when a court exercises equitable powers, it often does so to prevent one **party** from taking unfair advantage of another or from profiting by her own wrongdoing.

See also *Equitable Relief.*

Equitable Relief: In many situations, a court cannot achieve a fair result simply by **awarding** the winner a sum of money. A non-monetary award by a court is called equitable relief. For example, if a woman is the victim of **domestic violence**, a later award of money may compensate her for her medical costs, but will not prevent her from being further injured. In this situation a court may grant equitable relief in the form of **temporary restraining order** (TRO), ordering the abuser to stop the abuse and leave the **family home**. Violation of the TRO (called **contempt**) can be punished by a jail sentence.

Other examples of equitable relief include:

• Ordering **property** returned to its owner. This may arise if one spouse locks the other out of the family home and refuses to turn over his belongings.

• Rewriting a **divorce agreement** (or any other contract) to reflect the actual intentions of the parties if a mistake was made in drafting.

• Ordering an agreement, such as a contract for sale of a house, to be carried out.

Equity: Equity in property is the portion of the property's value that is claimed by the property owner. For example, a real property owner's equity in her property is the **fair market value** of the property less the mortgage and taxes due. In evaluating real property as part of a division of property during a **divorce**, other debts which must be subtracted from the fair market value are any real estate commission, closing costs or lawyer's fees necessary to sell the property.

See also *Appraisal* and *Valuation of Property.*

Equity also describes the principles under which a court may exercise **equitable powers** to grant **equitable relief**.

EXAMPLE

Terry owns a house with a fair market value of $125,000, and owes $50,000 on the mortgage and $2500 in taxes. The equity in her house is $72,500, that is, $125,000 - ($50,000 + $2500).

If Terry and her husband own the house and are dividing it as part of their divorce settlement, the equity must take into consideration the costs of selling the house; the closing costs, commissions and lawyer's fee would be approximately $5000. The equity in the house is now $67,500, that is, $125,000 - ($50,000 + $2500 + $5000).

Error in Trial Court: When a **trial court** makes a mistake about the law or finds certain facts to be true without adequate **evidence**, the court is in error. If the error affects the outcome of the **case**, it is called a prejudicial error, and the decision may be reversed on **appeal**. If this happens, the case is usually returned to the trial court for **new trial**. If, however, the error made in the course of a **trial** does not affect the outcome of the case (called a harmless error), an **appellate court** will not **reverse** the trial court decision.

Escalator Clause: An escalator clause sometimes is included in a **divorce agreement** or **decree** to provide an **alimony** recipient with an automatic specified share of any increase in the payor's **earnings**.

Note: Escalator clauses are not used with child support.

Established Living Pattern: When a parent seeks **custody** of, or more **visitation** with, a child, the court's decision will normally favor the parent who will best maintain stability in the child's surroundings. There is no set standard as to what constitutes "stability," but a judge looks for continuity in a child's life. It is important that the child, to the degree possible, keep the same school, community and religious ties. If maintaining the same contacts is not possible, the judge looks to which parent is best able to create a stable environment for the child.

See also *Best Interests of the Child*.

EXAMPLE

Byron is eight years old. He's in the third grade, Boy Scout troop 1376, and takes kiddie cooking classes once a week. Byron's parents have recently separated, and both want custody. Byron's family has moved every other year due to his father's business obligations. Byron's father argued to the judge that frequent moving is not harmful to Byron, and gives him an opportunity to experience different places and people while growing up. Byron's mother emphasized that she has no plans to move and that she feels Byron needs to settle in one place. The judge agreed with the mother, **ruling** that stability in Byron's life was more important than the opportunities to live in many places and meet many people.

Estoppel: In certain situations, the law refuses to allow a person to deny facts when another person has relied on and acted in accordance with the facts. This is called estoppel.

There are a number of kinds of estoppel. Collateral estoppel prevents a **party** to a lawsuit from raising a fact or issue which was already decided against him in another lawsuit. For example, if Donna obtained a **paternity judgment** against Leroy and then sued him for **child support**, Leroy would be collaterally estopped from claiming he isn't the father.

Equitable estoppel prevents one party from taking a different position at **trial** than she did at an earlier time if the other party would be harmed by the change. For example, if after obtaining the paternity judgment, Leroy sues Donna for **custody**, Donna is now equitably estopped from claiming in the custody suit that Leroy is not the father.

Promissory estoppel prevents one person from going back on a promise if the other person was reasonably induced to act because of the promise. Example: John promises to sell his car to Ed, and in preparation Ed obtains a bank loan and buys an alarm, new tires, a car stereo system and paint to repaint the car. If John changes his mind and decides he doesn't want to sell, a court would probably require John to keep to the agreement and sell the car.

Et Ux: Et ux is Latin for "and wife." It was used in referring to **married** men when married women had few legal rights. The phrase is rarely, if ever, used today.

Evaluation of Property: See *Appraisal* and *Valuation of Property*.

Evidence: Evidence is any item or information which a **party** wants to present to the jury (or judge if there is no jury) at a **trial** or **hearing** to prove her contention. Evidence may be oral testimony, **affidavits**, documents, items of clothing, automobiles, typewriters, maps, the results of medical tests, to name a few examples. Evidence which by law may be considered by the judge or jury is called **admissible evidence**, whereas evidence which does not meet specific legal standards for reliability and fairness is called inadmissible evidence. For example, **hearsay** is often deemed inadmissible evidence because it is unreliable.

> **RELATED TERMS**
> *Admission*
> *Authentication of Evidence*
> *Burden of Proof*
> *Character Evidence*
> *Circumstantial Evidence*
> *Discovery*
> *Expert Witness*
> *Immaterial Evidence*
> *Incompetent Evidence*
> *Irrelevant Evidence*
> *Privileged Communication*
> *Relevancy*
> *Rules of Evidence*

Ex Parte: Ex parte means "by one side." Although a judge is normally required to meet with all **parties** in a **case** and not with just one, there are circumstances where this rule does not apply and the judge is allowed to meet with just one side (ex parte). In addition, sometimes judges will issue temporary **orders** ex parte (i.e., based on one party's request without hearing from the other side) when time is limited or it would do no apparent good to hear the other side of the dispute. For example, if a wife claims **domestic violence**, a court may immediately issue an ex parte order telling her husband to stay away. Once he's out of the house, the court holds a **hearing**, where he can tell his side and the court can decide whether the ex parte order should be made permanent.

Expert Witness: An expert witness is a person who testifies at a trial because she has special knowledge in a particular field. This entitles her to testify about her opinion on the meaning of facts. Non-expert witnesses are only permitted to testify about facts they observed and not their opinions about these facts. In **family law** trials, common expert witnesses include:

• Actuaries, who testify about values of spouses' **pension** plans for the purpose of dividing them at **divorce**

• Child psychologists or development specialists, who testify about the **best interests of the child** when **custody** or **visitation** is in dispute

• Appraisers, who testify about **property** values when the **parties** cannot agree and

• Career counselors, who testify about a homemaker's ability to return to the work force for the purpose of determining the amount and duration of **alimony**.

Extended Family: An extended family is one which includes persons in addition to or other than parents and children. Some extended families include grandparents, stepparents and stepchildren, nieces and nephews, etc.

Extended family can also mean a circle of people in a close relationship. For example, for many lesbians, gay men, and other non-married people, the term extended family refers to a small, close group of friends who provide support for one another in much the same way a traditional **family** supports its members.

Extension of Alimony: Although alimony is usually set for a limited amount of time, the period is usually extended by the court if the recipient presents **evidence** of **changed circumstances**. The recipient must file a **request for a modification of alimony** before the existing alimony expires. This is because once there is a **termination of alimony**, the court cannot reinstate it.

EXAMPLE

As part of Jody and Tim's **divorce agreement**, Tim is to pay Jody $400 per month in alimony for three years or until she obtains a job, whichever comes first. Jody and Tim agree that the purpose of the alimony is to give Jody adequate time to learn a skill and find work. Six months ago, Jody completed a computer course in which she learned how to program. En route to a job interview, however, she was in a car accident and has been laid up ever since. The three year period ends in two months. Jody has filed a motion requesting an extension of the alimony until she is well enough to interview and work. Because she did her best to obtain a skill and find a job, the court is likely to grant her an extension until she gets a job.

In many states, **divorce agreements** or **decrees** may state that alimony amounts and periods are "non-modifiable," which means that they cannot be changed once they are established.

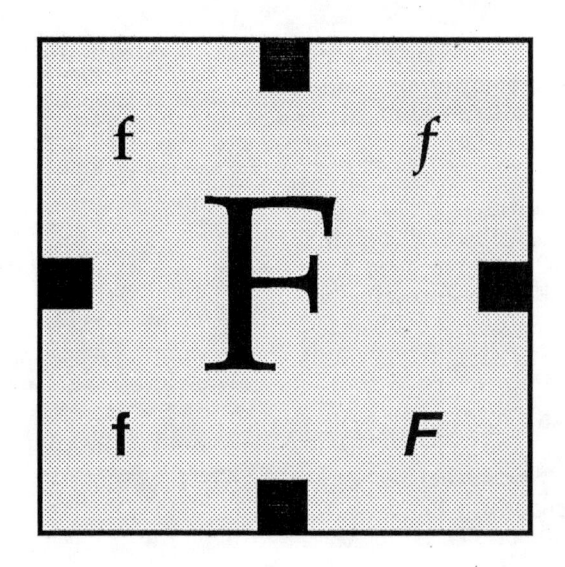

Failure to Appear at Court Hearing: If one **party** files with the court a **request for modification** or other **motion** and the other party files a written response but then fails to show up for **hearing**, the proceedings usually go forward without her. In these circumstances, usually the party who filed the motion will normally get what he requested unless it is beyond the court's authority to grant the request.

If a person is served (see *service of court papers*) with a **subpoena** ordering him to appear at a hearing but fails to show up, he may be guilty of **contempt of court** and subject to arrest, fine or imprisonment. Therefore, a person who is unable to attend a hearing when it is scheduled should call or write the **court clerk in advance** and request a **continuance**.

See also *Contested Hearing*.

Failure to Respond to Complaint: See *Default Divorce*.

Fair Amount of Child Support: In addition to providing for the needs of the child, the courts are supposed to strive for fairness to the parents in establishing the dollar amount of **child support** obligations. They are thus given **discretion** to apportion child support responsibility between parents according to their relative financial circumstances. Some states' laws specify factors which must be considered in determining who pays child support, and how much. These include the **needs of the child**, the needs of the **custodial parent**, the payor's **ability to pay** and the **standard of living** of the child before **divorce**. Under the Child Support Enforcement Act of 1984 (see *enforcement of child support*), federal law now requires each state to develop guidelines to calculate a range of child support to be paid, based on the parents' incomes and expenses.

Fair Market Value: The fair market value of an item of **property** is the amount a willing buyer would pay a willing seller. Fair market value can de be determined by comparing the price for which similar items recently have been sold. Factors that commonly influence an item's fair market value are:
 • Supply—if an item is relatively rare, its fair market value will tend to be higher than if the item is commonly available.
 • Demand—if demand for the item is high, the fair market value will be higher than if the item is not wanted.

Divorcing couples (or the court if the spouses cannot agree on the property division) need to know the fair market value of their **assets**. This is because **marital property** is usually divided by totalling up the value of the items to be divided, and then giving each spouse a more or less equal share.

See also *Appraisal; Community Estate* and *Valuation of Property*.

Family: The word family may be used to define immediate relatives (parents and children), people related by blood, **marriage** or **adoption**, or any extended group of people living together.

See also *Extended Family; Head of Family; Incest; Intact Family* and *Zoning*.

Family Abuse: See *Domestic Violence*.

Family Allowance: When a husband or wife dies leaving **property**, courts in many states are authorized to order some of the property used for support and care of the surviving family members until the court distributes the property to its new owners.

Family Car Doctrine: The family car doctrine holds the owner of a **family** car legally responsible for any damage caused by a family member when driving if the owner knew of and consented to the family member's use of the car. This doctrine is followed by the courts of approximately 20 states.

Family Conciliation Court: See *Conciliation Service* and *Mediation*.

Family Court: Many states have special courts that hear only **family law cases**; they are often called family courts.

Family Home: The family home is any home in which a family resides. In **divorces**, the term refers specifically to an owned (as opposed to rented) house in which the family lived before the divorce. In many states, if **minor** children are in the family, the family home won't be divided—that is, it's neither sold with the proceeds split, nor awarded to one **party** with the other **awarded property** of equivalent value—at the divorce. In fact, a few states, including Maryland, prohibit the sale of a family home when there are children. Instead, the home is given temporarily to the parent with **physical custody** of the children. When the children leave the home or the **custodial parent remarries** or moves, the house is then divided.

If one spouse has abused the other spouse or the children, he may be barred from the family home (whether it is rented or owned) if the victims obtain a **temporary restraining order** from the court.

When cohabitating couples break up in West Germany, a court will grant the right to use the rental residence to the party who needs it most.

Family Law: Family law is a general term used to refer to the body of law relating to **marriage, divorce, adoption, paternity,** and marital-type relationships.

Family Living Expenses: See *Debts Incurred During Marriage*.

Family Support: When **alimony** and **child support** are combined into one payment without regard to which portion is alimony and which is child support, some states call it family support. Because of the increased concern over enforcement of child support, however, the courts of many states require that child support and alimony be specified separately.

See also *Integrated Property Settlement Agreement* and *Tax Consequences of Alimony and Child Support*.

Fault Divorce: Traditionally, in order for a **married** couple to obtain a **divorce,** one spouse had to prove that the other spouse was legally at fault (see *grounds for divorce)*. The "innocent" spouse was then granted the divorce from the "guilty" spouse. If a husband was the guilty spouse, he would usually have to pay a substantial amount of **alimony;** if a wife was at fault, her alimony might be reduced or eliminated.

Today, although 32 states and the District of Columbia still allow a spouse to allege fault in obtaining a divorce, all states have some form of **no-fault divorce.** In addition, fault and alimony are linked less and less. For example, although a fault divorce is still available in Illinois, alimony is **awarded** and **property** divided regardless of fault. Conversely, although fault divorces have been eliminated in Florida, a spouse who is able to prove that the other is at fault may pay less or be awarded more alimony.

See also *Defense to Divorce*.

Federal Statutes: Laws passed by the United States Congress are called federal statutes. Although most **family law** comes from state statutes, a few federal statutes pertain to family law, such as the **Child Support** Enforcement Act of 1984, federal tax laws, the **Parental Kidnapping Prevention Act**, and **Aid to Families with Dependent Children (AFDC)**.

Fiduciary Relationship: See *Confidential Relationship*.

Filiation: A filiation proceeding is a **paternity** proceeding, usually brought by a mother, to establish that a certain man is the father of her child.

Final Decree or Judgment: See *Interlocutory and Final Judgments*.

Financial Emergency: A financial emergency occurs when a person is unexpectedly required to lay out money (e.g., to pay sudden medical bills). When a person who pays **alimony** or **child support** suffers a financial emergency, he may file a request with the court for a downward **temporary modification of alimony or child support**. When a person who receives alimony or child support suffers a financial emergency, she may ask the court for a upward temporary modification.

Financial Statement: A financial statement is a **court paper** which requires a **party** to specify her monthly income and expenses. The court often requires each **divorcing** spouse to fill out a financial statement so that the court has a complete picture of the parties' financial situations before making a decision on **alimony, child support**, payment of **attorneys' fees**, or other financial matters.

Findings of Fact and Conclusions of Law: After **trial** of a **family law case**, the judge often must issue findings of fact and conclusions of law. These set forth the facts the judge found to be true and the conclusions of law he reached regarding those facts. This allows a losing **party** to know how and why the judge reached his decision and whether an **appeal** is warranted. If the losing party appeals, the **appellate court** will determine whether the factual findings are supported by the **evidence** and whether the legal conclusions are correct. If the court answers either question negatively, the case will usually be reversed and sent back to the **trial court** for a **new trial**.

Foreign Divorce: A **divorce** obtained in a different state or country from where the person has her residency is called a foreign divorce. As a general rule, foreign divorces are recognized as valid in all states if at least one spouse has become a resident of the state or country granting the divorce and if both **parties** consented to the **jurisdiction** of the foreign court to grant the divorce. A foreign divorce obtained by one person without the consent of the other is normally not valid, unless the non-consenting spouse later acts as if the foreign divorce was valid, for example, by **remarrying**.

> **EXAMPLE**
>
> LuAnn and Jay have been married for seven years, and LuAnn wants a divorce. They live in New Mexico. LuAnn can file papers in New Mexico and proceed via the regular route, or she can try to obtain a divorce elsewhere (a foreign divorce). LuAnn can go to another state, such as Nevada, or another country, such as Mexico, both of which have a short divorce residency requirement; Jay must either personally appear or consent in writing for the foreign divorce to be valid. LuAnn cannot obtain a valid divorce by filling out papers in New Mexico and then having them sent to another country (such as the Dominican Republic) for a foreign divorce.

See also *Dominican Republic Divorce* and *Uniform Divorce Recognition Act*.

Forms: See *Court Forms*.

Fornication: Fornication means sexual intercourse between unmarried persons. (In some states, if one person is married it is still fornication; other states call sexual intercourse between an unmarried person and a married person **adultery**. Other states, when referring to sexual intercourse between an unmarried person and a married person, call the unmarried person a fornicator and the married person an adulterer.) Fornication is illegal in many states. If a state prohibits fornication, a court may refuse to uphold a **cohabitation agreement** on the ground that because the relationship covered by the agreement is illegal, the agreement is unenforceable.

Forum: The state, county or district in which a lawsuit is filed or a **hearing** or **trial** in that **action** is conducted is called the forum. Forum also refers generally to a court.

Forum Non Conveniens: Forum non conveniens means inconvenient **forum**. Although there are rules which govern where a lawsuit must be filed (the state, county or district), sometimes the location is inconvenient for the witnesses or **parties**. If a party makes an adequate showing of inconvenience, the principle of forum non conveniens allows a judge to decline to hear a **case** even though the court is an appropriate court for the case.

See also *Jurisdiction*.

> **EXAMPLE**
>
> Vince and Claire's **divorce** case was decided in Miami, Florida, but both have since moved to Orlando. Any **request for modification** must first be filed in Miami, but either party could request that the court decline to hear the case, and instead, transfer it to Orlando for the **hearing**.

Foster Home: When a child is temporarily placed by a court or welfare department in a home other than her parents', it is termed a foster home.

See also *Abandonment of Child* and *Foster Parent*.

Foster Parent: Adults who take children into their homes when those children have been removed from their biological parents' home by a court are called foster parents. Foster parents usually become the **guardians** of the children placed in their homes. If the biological parents are unable to make the necessary changes to have the children return to them, their parental rights may be terminated and the children made available for **adoption**. When this occurs, foster parents usually have priority in adopting. In fact, many states have Fost-Adopt programs, where the foster placement is intended to lead to the adoption of the children by the foster parents.

Foster parents are often entitled to receive payments from the state welfare department to assist them in supporting the children. Foster parents who parent disabled children may receive even higher payments. The payments usually terminate, however, if the foster parents adopt the children.

See also *Termination of Parental Rights*.

Fraud: Fraud is intentional perversion of the truth in order to gain an advantage (usually economic) over another person. Common types of fraud are deceit, misrepresentation and concealment. To prove deceit or misrepresentation, a person must show that another person made a material false statement with the intention of deceiving the first person, who justifiably relied on the statement and was hurt by it. To prove concealment, a person must show that the other person withheld something that she had a duty to disclose, and that the first person was were hurt by the withholding. A spouse who conceals jointly owned **property** may be **awarded** less than her full share on **divorce**.

EXAMPLE

Vronsky and Svetlana are married and live in a **community property state** (i.e., **earnings** during **marriage** are jointly owned). Vronsky earns $2,000 per week. He tells Svetlana that he'd like to put $400 of the $2,000 into an interest bearing account for a "vacation of a lifetime" for them. Unbeknownst to Svetlana, the money is really being used to pay off Natasha, a woman with whom Vronsky had an affair. When Svetlana learns, she sues for divorce. Svetlana should be entitled to recover one-half (her share) of the money paid to Natasha. Obviously, Svetlana cannot recover the money already paid to Natasha; however, Vronsky will receive less of his share of the **marital property** to make up the money owed to Svetlana.

Fraudulent Marriage: If a person marries relying on a false statement made by her spouse before the **marriage**, the marriage is considered fraudulent, and the defrauded spouse may obtain an **annulment**. The false statement must concern something of fundamental importance, such as the ability to have sex, the ability or desire to have children, or religious beliefs or practices. For example, if Ben represented himself to be Roman Catholic, but then confessed to being Shaker and having taken vows of celibacy, his wife could probably get an annulment.

See also *Sham Marriage*

Frivolous Appeal: An **appeal** without any arguable legal basis is called a frivolous appeal and can be dismissed (thrown out) by the **appellate court**. Because lawyers can create a plausible legal basis for almost any argument imaginable, however, few appeals are ever ruled frivolous. The most outrageous time-waster is usually only said to "border on the frivolous."

Full Faith and Credit: Full faith and credit is a legal principle requiring judges to recognize and enforce valid **decrees** and **judgments** issued by courts in other states. Thus, a Wisconsin judgment for back **alimony** can be enforced in Minnesota, if the recipient takes the steps necessary to convert it to a Minnesota judgment.

In the past, states often did not afford full faith and credit to **custody** decisions of courts in other states, preferring instead to decide the issues on the **evidence** before them. This often led to contradictory custody orders and sometime children were **childnapped** and thrown back and forth. Now, however, the **Parental Kidnapping Prevention Act** and the **Uniform Child Custody Jurisdiction Act** require states to give full faith and credit to custody decisions rendered in other states.

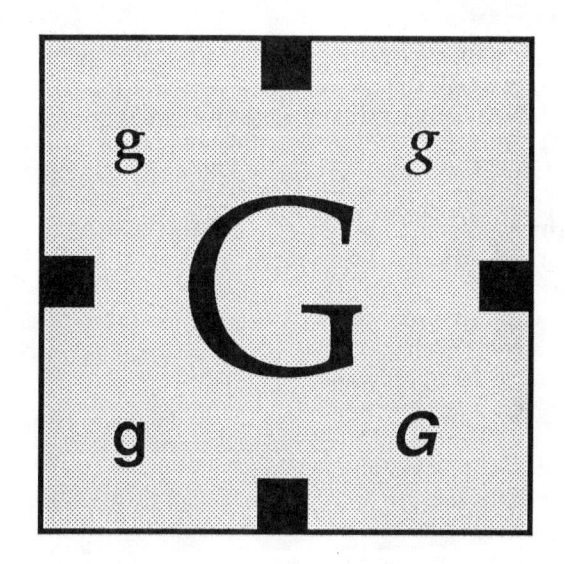

Garnishment of Wages: See *Wage Attachment*.

Gay or Lesbian Lifestyle: Effect on Custody: If a **divorced** or **separated** parent is gay or lesbian, many courts deny or strictly limit the parent's **custody** of or **visitation** with her children. In addition, some courts, when the parent's sexual orientation becomes known, modify existing custody and visitation **orders**. In a few states, however, a parent's sexual orientation cannot in and of itself prevent a parent from being given custody of her child. As a practical matter, however, lesbian and gay parents in those states may still be denied custody. This is because judges, when considering the **best interests of the child**, may be motivated by their own prejudices as well as by the prejudices of the community and may find reasons other than the parent's sexual orientation to deny the lesbian or gay parent custody.

General Denial and Specific Denial: See *Answer*.

Geographic Move: Effect on Custody and Visitation: If a **custodial parent** geographically relocates a substantial distance, the move may constitute a **changed circumstance** that justifies the court's modification of a **custody** or **visitation order** in order to accommodate the needs of the **noncustodial parent**. Some courts switch custody from one parent to the other. Other courts require that the relocating parent pay transportation costs for visits with the noncustodial parent. To discourage moves, some courts forbid parents to remove the children from the state of the **divorce** without first giving written notice to the other parent. This notice gives the non-custodial parent the opportunity to go to court and ask for a custody or visitation modification.

Good Will: See *Business Good Will*.

Grandparents' Rights: When parents **separate** or **divorce**, grandparents' relationships with their grandchildren are often at risk. To minimize the risk, all states but Nebraska have laws which allow grandparents to seek **visitation** rights with their grandchildren after divorce or separation.

When a child is **adopted**, the biological parents' and grandparents' rights are usually terminated. A growing number of states, however, allow the grandparent-grandchild tie to be preserved when the grandchild is adopted by a **stepparent**.

Gravamen of Case: The core legal issue in a **case** is sometimes referred to as the gravamen of the case.

Green-Card Marriage: See *Sham Marriage*.

Griswold v. Connecticut: *Griswold v. Connecticut*, 381 U.S. 479 (1965) is a United States Supreme Court decision which says that **married** couples have a constitutional right of **privacy**, which includes the right to use **birth control**. The **case** is significant because it was one of the first Supreme Court decisions recognizing a right to privacy under the U.S. Constitution.

Grounds for Divorce: All states require a spouse (or the couple, in the few states which allow **married** couples to jointly ask for **divorce**) to identify a legal reason for requesting a divorce when he initiates the proceedings by filing the **complaint** (or petition). (Some states also allow the other spouse to identify reasons in her **answer** in the event she, too, wants the divorce.) What constitutes a sufficient legal reason varies among the states; these reasons are laid out in state laws and referred to as the "grounds for divorce."

Grounds for divorce in Hindu law include renunciation of the world (entering a religious order), the husband's taking a second wife, and conversion to another religion. One ground for divorce in the border areas of China is opium-taking.

Until the 1970's, in every state a spouse had to allege the other spouse's **fault** as the ground for divorce. Common fault grounds included **adultery, constructive abandonment, cruelty, desertion,** and **physical incapacity**. Today, the grounds for divorce are as follows:

- Thirteen states are pure **no-fault divorce** states. This means that the only grounds for divorce are irreconcilable differences, incompatibility, or irretrievable or irremediable breakdown of the marriage.
- Four states have no-fault plus **separation**. This means that the only grounds for divorce are irreconcilable differences, incompatibility, irretrievable or irremediable breakdown, or separation (between six months and five years).
- Twelve states allow both traditional fault and no-fault divorces.
- Twelve states and the District of Columbia have retained fault divorces and added separation as a basis for divorce.
- Nine states allow traditional fault divorces, no-fault divorces, and separation divorces.

See chart, **GROUNDS FOR DIVORCE.**

Group Home: When **delinquent children** or **incorrigible children** are taken away from their parents by **juvenile courts**, they are supposed to be placed in the least restrictive environment. In most states, private individuals have obtained licenses to operate special group homes in which juvenile courts place children who don't need to be confined to state or county institutions or reform schools. These group homes function much like regular homes, except that the operators specialize in providing supervision to troubled children.

Guardian: A guardian is an adult given the legal right to control and care for a **minor** child or a disabled adult, called the **ward**. A guardian may be awarded **custody** of a minor. Courts order guardianships over children when their parents are unavailable to care for them and another adult has assumed that responsibility. For example, when a child is put into a **foster home**, the **foster parent** becomes the guardian of the child. Guardianships are necessary so that schools, hospitals, and other authority figures have an adult to turn to in the event a decision needs to be made about the child. Guardians are accountable to courts for the well being and financial best interests of their wards.

Guardianships are also established when adults cannot care for themselves. Increasingly, these guardianships are called **conservatorships**.

Guardian Ad Litem: If a **party** in a lawsuit is a **minor** or an adult unable to legally care for herself, the court must appoint a person to protect and manage the person's interests in any legal proceedings that directly affect her. That person is called a guardian ad litem and is often, although not always, a parent or close relative, or an attorney. Twenty-five states also authorize the appointment of a guardian ad litem to represent the child's interest, without the child actually becoming a party to the **case**, when **custody** is an issue.

If a guardian ad litem is not an attorney, the minor or disabled adult is frequently represented by an attorney as well. Both the guardian ad litem and the attorney are to act in and articulate the best interests of the

GROUNDS FOR DIVORCE

The grounds for divorce are the legal reasons a spouse (or the couple) must include in requesting a divorce. In 14 states, the only grounds are irreconcilable differences, incompatibility, or irretrievable or irremediable breakdown (called the pure no-fault grounds). Four states have irreconcilable differences, incompatibility, irretrievable or irremediable breakdown and separation. Twelve states have retained the traditional fault grounds (such as adultery, abandonment, cruelty and desertion) and added irreconcilable differences, incompatibility, or irretrievable or irremediable breakdown. Eleven states and the District of Columbia have retained the traditional fault grounds and added separation. Nine states have retained the traditional fault grounds and added irreconcilable differences, incompatibility, irretrievable or irremediable breakdown and added separation.

State	Fault Grounds	No-Fault Grounds	Separation	Length of Separation
Alabama	•	•	•	2 years
Alaska	•	•		
Arizona		•		
Arkansas	•		•	3 years
California		•		
Colorado		•		
Connecticut	•	•	• (1)	18 months
Delaware	•	•	•	6 months
Florida		•		
Georgia	•	•		
Hawaii		•	•	2 years
Idaho	•	•	•	5 years
Illinois	•	• (2)	• (2)	2 years
Indiana		•		
Iowa		•		
Kansas	•	•		
Kentucky		•		
Louisiana	•		•	6 months
Maine	•	•		
Maryland	•		•	1 year
Massachusetts	•	•		
Michigan		•		
Minnesota		•		
Mississippi	•	•		

(1) Separation divorce must also allege incompatibility.
(2) Must allege irretrievable breakdown and separation for no-fault; if both parties consent, 2 years reduced to 6 months.

GROUNDS FOR DIVORCE

State	Fault Grounds	No-Fault Grounds	Separation	Length of Separation
Missouri	•	• (3)		
Montana		•	•	180 days
Nebraska		•		
Nevada		•	•	1 year
New Hampshire	•	•		
New Jersey	•		•	18 months
New Mexico	•	•		
New York	•		•	1 year
North Carolina	•		•	1 year
North Dakota	•	•		
Ohio	•		•	1 year
Oklahoma	•	•		
Oregon		•		
Pennsylvania	•	•	•	3 years
Rhode Island	•	•	•	3 years
South Carolina	•		•	1 year
South Dakota	•	•		
Tennessee	•	•	• (4)	3 years
Texas	•		•	3 years
Utah	•		•	3 years
Vermont	•		•	6 months
Virginia	•		• (5)	1 year
Washington		•		
West Virginia	•	•	•	1 year
Wisconsin		•	•	1 year
Wyoming		•		
Washington, DC	•		•	6 months

(3) If contested, plaintiff must show adultery, abandonment, incompatibility or separation.
(4) Separation divorce allowed only if there are no children.
(5) May be reduced to 6 months if there are no children.

-85-

minor or disabled adult. When the attorney and the guardian ad litem differ, the attorney often disregards the guardian ad litem's advice.

Guardianship: See *Guardian*.

Guidelines for Temporary Alimony and Child Support: In some states, legislatures publish tables that calculate a range of **child support** to be paid. Courts use these tables as guidelines to determine the amount of temporary **alimony** and child support to be paid while the **divorce** works its way through the courts. If the **parties** cannot agree on an amount, these temporary amounts are imposed at a **preliminary hearing** and may be altered when the court has a better understanding of what will be best in the long run.

In Iran, the Ayatollah Khomeini has written, "A woman who has entered into a ... marriage is not allowed to leave the house without her husband's permission. She must submit herself to any pleasure he desires. She may not refuse herself on any ground other than religiously accepted ones."

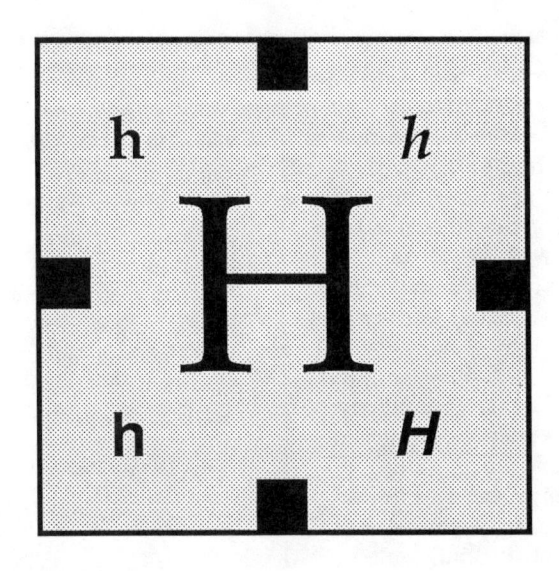

Habeas Corpus: Habeas corpus is Latin for "you should have the body." In legal terms, it is a petition filed with a court by a person who objects to his own or another's detention or imprisonment. The petition must show that the court ordering the detention or imprisonment made a legal or factual error. Habeas corpus petitions are usually filed by persons serving prison sentences. In **family law**, a parent who has been denied **custody** of his child by a **trial court** may file a habeas corpus petition. Also, a **party** may file a habeas corpus petition if a judge declares her in **contempt of court** and jails or threatens to jail her.

Half-Brother or Half-Sister: See *Siblings*.

Hardship: Hardship means suffering or adversity. If compliance with a legal obligation would cause a hardship on a person or his family, he may be excused from the obligation. For example, a payor's inability to meet an **alimony** or **child support** obligation without great economic suffering himself is a hardship. If a court finds this hardship substantial, the payor may be relieved of all or a part of his support obligation for a temporary or indefinite period.

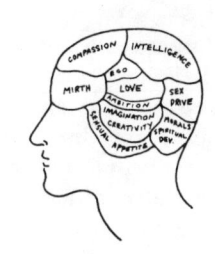

Head of Family: The head of the family is the person who supports and maintains one or more people who are related by blood, **marriage** or **adoption**. In some states, the head of the family has the legal right to choose and establish where the **family** resides.

-87-

Head of Household: Head of household is the federal income tax status of a single person who contributes more than one half toward the support of a non-spouse relative. The relative must be a parent (including step, grand, great-grand, etc.), child (including step, grand, great-grand, etc.) or **sibling** (including half-sibling). The head of household tax rate is higher than that for **married** persons filing jointly, but lower than that for single persons.

Head of household tax status is important for single parents, and **divorcing** parents often argue over which one is entitled to the head of household filing status. Because the one who claims head of household must contribute more than one-half of the support, both parents cannot claim it.

See also *Tax Consequences of Alimony and Child Support*.

Health and Welfare of Child: See *Best Interests of the Child*.

Hearing: In a lawsuit, a hearing is any legal proceeding (other than a **trial**) which is held before a judge or **court commissioner**. At a trial, disputed questions of fact and law are resolved and the **case** is concluded (although the parties may **appeal**). At a hearing, on the other hand, preliminary issues, procedural issues (including granting an uncontested or **default divorce**), and post-trial modifications and enforcements are heard.

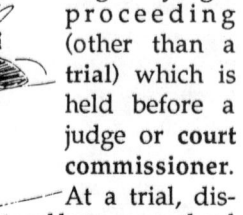

EXAMPLE

Paul has sued Taya for **divorce**. Their trial is to be held in nine months. Taya needs **alimony** now, however, so she files a request for **temporary** alimony. The court schedules a hearing at which Paul and Taya can appear before a judge and orally present their separate sides. After listening to Paul and Taya, the judge will decide if Taya is entitled to the alimony, and if so, how much and for how long.

EXAMPLE

Paul receives sporadic royalty payments from a book he wrote seven years ago. He claims that the income is speculative and hopes to keep it from being considered in the upcoming divorce trial where the amount of **permanent alimony** will be determined. A week before the trial, Paul requests a hearing to determine whether the law requires that the judge consider his royalty income in setting Taya's alimony.

See also *Administrative Hearing*.

Hearsay: Hearsay is any statement made outside a **hearing** or **trial** which is presented at the hearing or trial to prove the truth of the contents of the statement. All **evidence** rules begin with the premise that hearsay cannot be used in court because second-hand testimony is considered unreliable and because the person who made the original statement is often unavailable for cross-examination (see *direct and cross examination*). Statements in the forms of letters, **affidavits**, **declarations**, diaries, memos, oral statements, notes, computer files, legal documents, purchase receipts and contracts all constitute hearsay when they are offered to prove that their contents are true.

Testimony during a hearing or trial is not hearsay unless the witness tries to repeat something someone else said or wrote. In addition, a statement introduced to prove something other than its truth is not hearsay. For example, testimony may be offered to show the speaker's state of mind (e.g., anger or fear).

EXAMPLE

Dana and Bruce were fighting, and Dana shouted "Bruce, you are a lousy bastard." Marla heard the argument and was asked to testify at Dana and Bruce's **divorce** trial. Marla was permitted to repeat the statement "Bruce, you are a lousy bastard," because it is not hearsay. It was not introduced at the trial to prove that Bruce has lice or is an illegitimate child, but rather to show that Dana was angry.

A witness's earlier out-of-court statement may be presented at a trial or hearing if it contradicts his in-court testimony, because the statement is being used to cast doubt on the witness's credibility, rather than prove the statement's truth or falsity.

A great many exceptions to the hearsay rule exist and much hearsay tends to be admitted. Evidence which qualifies as exceptions are usually statements which are reliable and believed to be unfabricated. Some common exceptions are:

• Utterances made at the time of a startling event which provoked the observer into speaking (e.g., seeing one's spouse in bed with someone else)
• Statements describing a current condition (e.g., "I feel sick")
• Prior testimony from a hearing, trial or **deposition**
• **Admissions** by a party—statements which tend to support the other side's position or diminish the party's own position
• Religious records, family records, and **marriage** certificates
• **Property** documents (e.g., **deeds**)
• Statements made against one's own monetary or penal interest (i.e., an admission of a crime)
• Declarations made by someone who believes his death is imminent
• Business records made in the regular course of business
• Ancient documents
• Court **judgments**.

Heart-Balm Lawsuits: Heart-balm lawsuits are those brought to soothe broken hearts and include lawsuits for **alienation of affection**, **breach of promise to marry**, **criminal conversation** and **seduction**.

Heterologous Artificial Insemination: See *Artificial Insemination.*

Holding: An appellate court's resolution of an appeal is called the holding of the case. For example, if an appellate court reverses a trial court's decision declaring a father who hasn't paid child support in contempt of court, the reversal is called a holding.

Homologous Artificial Insemination: See *Artificial Insemination.*

Homosexual Lifestyle: Effect on Custody and Visitation: See *Gay or Lesbian Lifestyle: Effect on Custody.*

Homosexual Marriage: See *Same-Sex Marriage.*

In 1984, a Swedish government commission recommended that lesbian and gay couples be granted legal status similar to that granted married couples.

Illegitimate Children: Children born to parents not legally **married** to each other are sometimes termed illegitimate unless and until the parents later marry. This term is used infrequently today, and has little legal effect except where the law expressly gives rights only to legitimate children. For instance, illegitimate children are denied the right to inherit from their fathers in some states. Also, some states do not allow **unwed fathers** to sue for the **wrongful deaths** of their children, although married fathers and all mothers—married and unmarried—can.

In most states, once **paternity** of the child is established by acknowledgment of the father or by court **order**, there is no difference in the legal treatment between children born in and children born out of wedlock.

Immaterial Evidence: Evidence deemed too unconnected with the main issues of a **case** is considered immaterial and will be excluded from a **trial**.

Improvements to Property: In community property states, improvements to separate property (such as additions, renovations and substantial upkeep) are usually considered **community property** upon **divorce** if they were paid for out of community funds, unless there is a written agreement to the contrary. Also in community property states, improvements to community property paid for by separate funds usually remain separate property unless a written agreement states otherwise. The spouse making the separate contribution is entitled to **reimbursement** upon divorce. Community property improvements to community property remain community property, and separate property improvements to (one's own or one's spouse's) separate property remain the separate property of the contributor.

In **equitable distribution states**, separate property improvements by one spouse to the other's separate property or to jointly owned property may result in the first spouse acquiring a monetary interest (equal to the value contributed, or equal to any increase in the value of the property) in the improved property. In the **common law state** (Mississippi), the contributing party will obtain a monetary interest in the other's property generally only if **title to the property** was changed to reflect the contribution.

EXAMPLE

Bill owned a house before he married Tricia. During the marriage, Tricia used her inheritance from her Uncle Roy (Tricia's separate property) to build a $3,000 deck on to the house. Bill and Tricia are now divorcing.

If Bill and Tricia live in Idaho (a community property state), Tricia is entitled to either a $3000 reimbursement from Bill's separate property or $3000 more than Bill from the community property.

If Bill and Tricia live in New Hampshire (an equitable distribution state), Tricia may argue that she has a monetary interest in Bill's house for $3000 or an amount equal to the house's increase in value caused by the addition of the deck. More than likely, Tricia will receive $3,000 (plus any increased value) more than Bill in their marital property when they divide their assets. Or Tricia may file a **lien** against the house, giving her a right to be paid when the house is sold.

If Tricia and Bill live in Mississippi (the common law property state), Tricia will be entitled to reimbursement only if her name was added to the **title** to the house.

Inability to Live Together: See *No-Fault Divorce*.

Inadmissible Evidence: See *Admissible Evidence*.

In Camera: See *Chambers*.

In Camera Hearing: "In camera" means taking place in a judge's **chambers**. An in camera **hearing** is a hearing held in the judge's chambers and is not open to the public. In camera hearings usually take place to protect the privacy of the people involved and are common in cases of **guardianships**, **adoptions**, and **custody** disputes alleging **child abuse**.

Incest: Sexual relations (or **marriage**) between close relatives is called incest and is a crime. Relations between parent (including grand-, great-grand-, etc.) and child (including grand-, great-grand-, etc.), **stepparent** and stepchild, **siblings**, or aunt or uncle with niece or nephew are considered incest. In some states, relations or marriage between first cousins and other close relatives are also forbidden. Incest between an older relative and a **minor** is also punishable as **child abuse** under the laws of all states.
See chart, **INCEST AND MARITAL PROHIBITIONS**.

Inclination: Inclination is one element of **adultery** that a spouse must prove when suing for **divorce** based on adultery if there is no eyewitness to the adulterous act. Inclination means demonstrated signs of affection between the **defendant** and the person she is **alleged** to be having an affair with (the **co-respondent**).

Income and Expense Declaration: See *Financial Statement*.

Income Earned During Marriage: See *Earnings During Marriage*.

Incompatibility: Incompatibility refers to a conflict in personalities that makes **married** life together impossible, and is a **ground for divorce** in many states.
See also *No-Fault Divorce*.

Incompetent Evidence: Evidence considered inherently unreliable is called incompetent and is not **admissible** in a trial. Examples of incompetent evidence include **hearsay** and other types of second hand information, observations made while the witness was drunk or under the influence of drugs, and self-serving statements.

Incorporate by Reference: The method of including the contents of a document (such as a letter) in **court papers** or a contract without actually retyping it is called "incorporating by reference." This is usually done by attaching the document to the back of the court papers or contract and referring to it with convoluted language such as, "the letter is attached to this document as exhibit A and incorporated by reference as if fully set out within this document."

Incorrigible Children: Children who refuse to obey their parents are classified by the juvenile laws of many states as incorrigible. The same label applies to children who engage in behavior which is noncriminal, but prohibited for persons of their age (e.g., running away from home, chronic truancy, or endangering their own or another's health or morals).

INCEST AND MARITAL PROHIBITIONS

All states prohibit a person from marrying her/his sibling, half-sibling, parent, grandparent, great-grandparent, child, grandchild, great-grandchild, aunt, uncle, niece, and nephew. Additional prohibitions are listed below.

State	None	First Cousin	Step-child/ Step-parent	Parent-in-law/ Child-in-law	Spouse's Grandchild or Grandparent/ Grandparent's or Grandchild's Spouse
Alabama			•	•	
Alaska	•				
Arizona		•			
Arkansas		•			
California	•				
Colorado	•				
Connecticut			•		
Delaware		•			
Florida	•				
Georgia			•	•	
Hawaii	•				
Idaho		•			
Illinois		•			
Indiana		• (1)			
Iowa		•	•	•	•
Kansas		•			
Kentucky		• (2)			
Louisiana		•			
Maine	•				
Maryland			•	•	•
Massachusetts			• (3)	•	
Michigan		•			
Minnesota		•			
Mississippi		•	•	•	
Missouri		•			
Montana		•			
Nebraska		•			

(1) First cousins may marry if both over 65.
(2) Includes first cousin once removed.
(3) Includes step-grandparent and step-grandchild.

INCEST AND MARITAL PROHIBITIONS

State	None	First Cousin	Step-child/ Step-parent	Parent-in-law/ Child-in-law	Spouse's Grandchild or Grandparent/ Grandparent's or Grandchild's Spouse
Nevada		•			
New Hampshire		•	•	•	
New Jersey	•				
New Mexico	•				
New York	•				
North Carolina		• (4)			
North Dakota		•			
Ohio		•			
Oklahoma		•	•		
Oregon		•			
Pennsylvania		•			
Rhode Island			•	•	•
South Carolina			•	•	•
South Dakota		•	•		
Tennessee (5)	•				
Texas			•		
Utah		•			
Vermont	•				
Virginia	•				
Washington		•			
West Virginia		• (6)			
Wisconsin		• (7)			
Wyoming		•			
Washington, DC			• (3)	•	•

(4) Double first cousin.
(5) Additional prohibitions include great-aunt, great-uncle, grand-niece and grand-nephew.
(6) Includes double first cousin.
(7) First cousins may marry if the woman is 55 or older.

Incorrigible children are often referred to as "status offenders" because they would not be in court but for their status as **minors**. Incorrigible children may be brought into the court system by police, welfare or school officials, or by parents seeking help.

A child who is found to be incorrigible by a court (usually a **juvenile court**) is made a **ward** of the court, and either placed under the supervision of a probation officer while living at home or removed from the home and placed in a **foster home** or institution.

Increase in Income: When an **alimony** recipient's income increases, her ex-spouse may file with the court a **request for modification** of the alimony, claiming that the **changed circumstance** means his ex-spouse needs less alimony. Whether the court will agree depends on the particular facts of the situation.

When the paying spouse's income increases, alimony generally stays the same because alimony is based (theoretically) on the recipient's needs, not on her ex's income. **Child support**, however, is based on both parents' financial situations. Thus, when either a paying or recipient parent's income increases, child support may be modified accordingly.

Increased Needs of Child: See *Needs of Child*.

Incurable Insanity: Incurable insanity of a spouse often is a ground for either a **fault** or a **no-fault divorce**. It is rarely used because of the difficulty of proving that the insanity is incurable.

Independent Adoption: See *Private Adoption*.

Inflation: See *Cost of Living Increase*.

In Forma Pauperis: This is a Latin term meaning "in the character of a pauper." It refers to a petition filed by a poor person in order to proceed in court without having to pay **court costs** such as filing fees.

In forma pauperis proceedings are available in every state. A person with a low income (usually eligible for or receiving public assistance) fills out in forma pauperis papers (indicating income and expenses) before filing his first **court paper** (**complaint** or **answer**). The papers request that a judge decide whether or not the costs be paid. Although a **hearing** before the judge is sometimes needed, the more usual practice is for the judge to grant or deny the request without a hearing.

Inheritance: An inheritance is **property** inherited from someone who has died. It may be received through someone's **will**, or if the person died without a will, automatically under state laws (called **intestate succession**). An inheritance received by one spouse during **marriage** is considered the **separate property** of that spouse.

See also *Curtesy* and *Dower*.

Injunction: A court **order** requiring a person to do (or preventing a person from doing) a certain action is called an injunction. For example, if a **party** has threatened to remove **marital property**, or has threatened to **childnap**, a court might prohibit the party from touching any marital property or removing the child from the county.

Emergency injunctions that are in effect only a short time are called **temporary restraining orders**. Courts also issue "permanent injunctions" which stay in effect indefinitely.

See also *Equitable Power* and *Equitable Relief*.

In Loco Parentis: In loco parentis is a Latin phrase which means "in lieu of a parent." Teachers, camp counselors and others who take responsibility for children have a duty to act in loco parentis, which means they have the same power and authority over the children as do the parents, at least during the time that the children are under their control.

In Pro Per: See *Pro Per*.

In Pro Se: See *Pro Per*.

In Rem Jurisdiction: Rem is Latin for thing. When a court exercises in rem jurisdiction, it exercises authority over a thing, rather than a person. For example, if a **divorcing** couple asks a court to supervise the sale of their **family home**, the court exercises in rem jurisdiction over the house. Usually, the **property** must be located in the same county as the court for it to have in rem jurisdiction.

A court which grants a divorce exercises in rem jurisdiction over the **marriage**. One spouse must live in the same county as the court (therefore the marriage is in the county) for the court to exercise in rem jurisdiction over the marriage.

See also *Jurisdiction; Personal Jurisdiction;* and *Subject-Matter Jurisdiction*.

Instant Case: When a judge or attorney refers to "the instant case," she means the **case** which she is working on right then and there.

Insurance: Effect of Divorce: Divorce can affect a couple's life and health insurance. If a spouse is named as a beneficiary in a life insurance policy, some states laws change the beneficiary automatically if the couple divorces and the holder of the policy **remarries**. Thus, even if the policy holder forgets to change the beneficiary, the new spouse, not the ex-spouse, will get the proceeds. If there is no remarriage, the ex-spouse may still be automatically taken off the policy and the proceeds given to the insured's children. Some judges require an ex-spouse who pays **alimony** (or **child support**) to make the recipients of the support beneficiaries of a life insurance policy.

Divorce can also affect health insurance coverage. Some states have "automatic conversion" laws requiring the financially independent spouse to continue to cover the financially dependent spouse after divorce until the dependent spouse becomes financially independent. Also, federal law makes an ex-spouse eligible to receive for the three years following the divorce, any group rate health insurance provided by her ex-husband's employer.

Intact Family: A **family** which has not gone through a **divorce** or **separation** is sometimes called an intact family.

-97-

Integrated Property Settlement Agreement: Upon divorce, couples commonly enter into a **divorce agreement** which divides **marital property** and may set **alimony**. The agreement is called integrated if the **property** settlement and alimony payments are combined into either one **lump sum payment** or **periodic payments**. Integrated agreements are often used when the marital property consists of substantial intangible **assets** (e.g., future royalties, stock options, future **pension** plans) or when one **party** is buying the other's interest in a valuable tangible asset (for example, a home or business). In addition, if a spouse is entitled to little or no alimony, but is not financially independent, periodic payments may help that spouse gain financial independence.

Most integrated property settlement agreements cannot later be changed at the request of one of the parties unless he can show the agreement was entered into under **fraud** or duress. This is because the alimony and property division are so intertwined that a later modification would create a substantial risk of unfairness to one of the parties.

Child support is seldom included in integrated property settlement agreements, because courts want the power to modify child support orders in accordance with the **needs of the child** and the economic capability of the paying parent.

> **EXAMPLE**
>
> Sandy and Marc are divorcing. They have two minor children, of whom Marc will have **custody**. Sandy agrees to pay Marc a lump sum of $4,800 in alimony. He is also entitled to a portion of Sandy's stock option. (An accountant told them that Marc's share is $1,200.) Sandy is also buying Marc's half of their recently purchased, jointly owned house, in which they have **equity** of $24,000. Thus, the total amount Sandy must pay Marc is $18,000 ($4,800 + $1,200 + $12,000).
>
> Marc and Sandy execute an integrated property settlement agreement which combines the property and alimony payments into one. Sandy agrees to pay Marc $1,500 per month for a year. In a separate child support agreement the court approves of $500 monthly payments.

Interlocutory and Final Judgment: Interlocutory means interim, provisional or not final. In some states, a **divorce** occurs in two phases. The first is often called the interlocutory stage, where all the issues (e.g., **division of property, alimony, child support, custody** and **visitation**) get decided either by agreement of the spouses or by a judge after a **hearing** or trial.

The second phase, when the judgment of divorce becomes final, doesn't occur until after a waiting period—usually two to six months. The waiting period (sometimes referred to as the "cooling-off" period) is designed to give the divorcing couple every opportunity for **reconciliation**. It begins on the date the interlocutory judgment is entered. When the time period passes, if no **appeal** is pending and if the appropriate papers have been filed with the court, the final judgment is entered.

In some states, **a party** who is eager to **remarry** as soon as possible can get the waiting period shortened or set aside entirely, if the judge is convinced that the reasons are good. On the other hand, many people forget about the waiting period and remarry before the divorce is final. While such remarriage is technically invalid, the court, if requested, will validate the second **marriage** by finalizing the divorce to a date prior to the second marriage by issuing an order **nunc pro tunc**, which literally means "then for now."

Intermediary Adoption: See *Private Adoption*.

Intermediate Decree or Judgment: See *Interlocutory and Final Judgment*.

Interrogatories: See *Discovery*.

Interspousal Tort Suit: See *Intrafamilial Tort Suit*.

Intestate Succession: Intestate succession is the method prescribed by a state to distribute a person's **property** when he has not provided for its distribution in a will. Although the details of these laws vary from state to state, the normal scheme is to distribute the deceased person's property to his spouse and children. If there are no surviving children or spouse, the property is divided among other relatives, usually starting with parents and **siblings**.

Intrafamilial Tort Suit: Under traditional law, **family** members were prohibited from suing each other for **torts** (e.g., assault, false imprisonment, emotional distress). The justification was that allowing family members to sue each other would lead to a breakdown of the family. Today, however, more and more states recognize that if family members have committed torts against each other, there often already is a breakdown in family relationships. Thus, they no longer bar members from suing each other. In these states, spouses may sue each other either during the **marriage** or after they have **separated**.

Normally, these lawsuits are brought separate and apart from any **divorce**, **annulment** or other **family law case**. In a December 1987 divorce case in Texas, however, an attorney successfully argued that his client should be awarded **actual damages** because of her husband's tortious conduct during the marriage. The jury agreed, granting her a divorce, dividing the **property**, and awarding her $500,000 in damages for emotional distress. Although it is likely that divorce lawyers in other states will try to bring similar cases in the future, cases outside Texas are unlikely to succeed because Texas is the only state which does not have alimony.

In Vitro Fertilization: In vitro fertilization is fertilization that takes place outside a woman's body. An egg is removed from a woman, fertilized with a man's semen, and then placed back in the woman's womb where the embryo develops. Children conceived this way are often referred to as "test-tube babies."

Irreconcilable Differences: Irreconcilable differences are those differences between spouses that are considered sufficiently severe to make **married** life together more or less impossible. It is a **ground for divorce** in many **no-fault divorce** laws. As a practical matter, courts seldom, if ever, inquire into what the differences actually are, and routinely grant a **divorce** as long as the **party** seeking the divorce says the couple has irreconcilable differences.

Irrelevant Evidence: Any evidence which does not logically help a judge or jury decide a dispute is irrelevant, and a judge will not allow it to be considered.

EXAMPLE

Grace and Ian are **divorcing** in Michigan, an **equitable distribution state**. Grace and Ian have sold their marital home, and the only issue in their case is the division of the proceeds. The house was purchased with a combination of Grace's pre-marital savings (her **separate property**), Ian's pre-marital savings (his separate property), and their **earnings during marriage**. At the **trial**, Ian asks his friend Walter to testify that Grace didn't like the house and never wanted to buy it. Because Walter's testimony is irrelevant to dividing the proceeds, the judge will not let Walter testify.

Irremediable Breakdown: An irremediable breakdown in a **marriage** occurs when one spouse refuses to live with the other and will not work toward **reconciliation**. It is a **ground for divorce** in many no-fault divorce laws. As a practical matter, courts seldom, if ever, inquire into whether the marriage has actually broken down, and routinely grant a **divorce** as long as the **party** seeking the divorce says it has.

Irretrievable Breakdown: An irretrievable breakdown in a **marriage** occurs when one spouse refuses to live with the other and will not work toward **reconciliation**. It is a **ground for divorce** in many **no-fault divorce** laws. As a practical matter, courts seldom, if ever, inquire into whether the marriage has actually broken down, and routinely grant a **divorce** as long as the **party** seeking the divorce says it has.

Issue: Issue is the legal term used to denote a person's children, grandchildren, great-grandchildren, etc. down the line, especially in laws governing **wills** and **intestate succession**.

In quite another context, issue means a central point of dispute in a **case**.

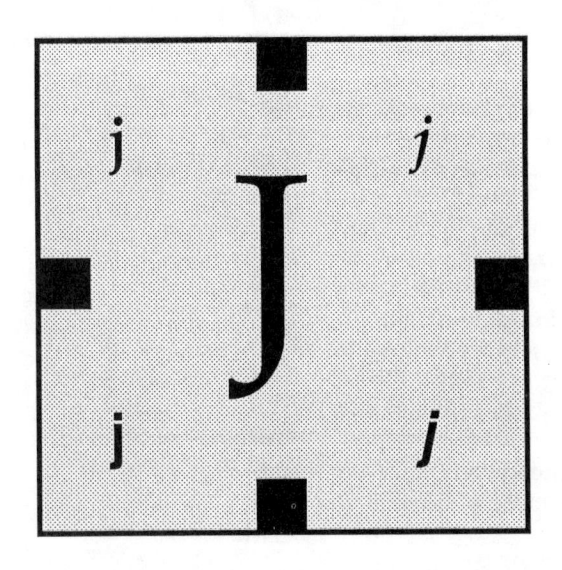

Joinder: Joinder is the process of bringing someone into an existing lawsuit as an additional **party** because his rights or obligations are involved in the **case**. For example, when a court divides a **pension** as **marital property** during a **divorce**, the pension plan administrator often must be joined as a party to the divorce, so that if the court **awards** a spouse payments under the other spouse's pension, the plan administrator can make the proper arrangements. (This is necessary because most pension plans prohibit the adminstrators from paying anyone other then the employee or other person named as beneficiary—i.e., someone entitled to benefits—of the pension.)

Joint Custody: Parents who don't live together have joint custody (also called shared custody) when they agree, or a court orders them, to share the decision-making responsibilities for, and/or physical control and **custody** of, their children. Joint custody can exist if the parents are **divorced**, **separated**, no longer **cohabitating**, or even if they never lived together. Joint custody may be joint **legal custody** (where the parents share in decision-making), joint **physical custody** (where the children spend approximately half the time with each parent) or both. It is common for couples who share physical custody to also share legal custody.

About 30 states have **statutes** which refer to joint custody. A few states, including California and Montana, have written a preference for joint custody into their laws, which means that judges are supposed to award joint custody of children unless there are circumstances that make it not in the **best interests of the child**. Some other states, including Nebraska and South Carolina, expressly disfavor joint custody awards, believing that parents who did not get along sufficiently to stay **married** will probably not cooperate in raising their children.

Usually, parents work out physical joint custody according to their schedules and housing arrangements. If the parents cannot agree, the court will impose an arrangement. A common pattern is for children to split weeks between each parent's house. Other joint physical custody arrangements include alternating years or six-month periods, or spending weekends and holidays with one parent while spending weekdays with the other.

Joint custody has the advantages of assuring the children continuing contact and involvement with both parents, and alleviating some of the burdens of parenting for each parent. There are, of course, disadvantages: children must be shuttled around, parents must cooperate, and maintaining two homes for the children can be expensive.

EXAMPLE

Ted and Dorothy had two children during their marriage. They are now divorced, but live in the same county and have joint physical and legal custody of the children. The children live with Ted Sunday through Wednesday morning, and live with Dorothy Wednesday after school through Saturday. Ted and Dorothy also share the decision making process.

EXAMPLE

LeMar and Shirley are divorced. LeMar lives in Kansas City, and Shirley lives in St. Louis. Joint physical custody is impossible because of the distance between them, but they speak at least once a week concerning the children's upbringing and share in the decision-making responsibility. This is joint legal custody.

Joint Debts: See *Debts Incurred During Marriage.*

Joint Income Tax Returns: A joint income tax return is a federal income tax return filed by a **married** couple. Only married couples, including ones who have **separated** but have not yet **divorced**, may file jointly. Married persons may file income tax returns separately; however, their tax will most likely be higher than if they filed jointly.

Joint Ownership: When any two or more people (including spouses) are the legal owners of a piece of **property**, they are generally said to be joint owners. Where the property is the type to which the owners have **title** (**real property**, cars, boats), the joint ownership is called "joint title." There are several different ways in which joint title may be held. States have different options. The most common are **community property; joint tenancy; marital property; tenancy by the entirety;** and **tenancy in common.**

Joint Tenancy: Joint tenancy is a method by which people jointly hold **title to property.** All joint tenants own equal interests in the jointly-owned **property**. When two or more persons expressly own property as joint tenants, and one owner dies, the remaining owner(s) automatically take over the share of the deceased person. This is termed the right of survivorship. For example, if two people own their house as joint tenants and one of them dies, the other person ends up owning the entire house, even if the deceased person attempted to give away her half of the house in her **will**.

In most states, one joint tenant may on her own end a joint tenancy by signing a new **deed** changing the way title is held; then she is free to leave her portion of the property through her will. Because joint tenancy property isn't passed through a will and thus doesn't go through probate, joint tenancy is a popular probate-avoidance technique.

In most **community property states**, property held in joint tenancy is presumed to be **community property** upon **divorce** unless there is proof to the contrary. This makes sense because a married couple's joint tenancy property is divided in half when they divorce, and a married couple's community property is divided equally at the end of their **marriage**.

In community property states, when purchasing real estate, or valuable personal property that comes with a written title (e.g., a recreational vehicle), a married couple must choose whether to take title to the property as community property or as joint tenants. If the property is taken as community property there will be significant federal income tax advantages if one spouse dies. On the other hand, if the property is held in joint tenancy and one spouse dies, that spouse's creditors (if she has any) will not be able reach the property.

Joint Title: See *Joint Ownership.*

Judge Pro Tem: A judge pro tem is not a regular judge, but someone (usually a lawyer) who is brought in to serve temporarily as a judge with the consent of the parties. Many courts use pro tem judges because there are too many cases for the regular judges to handle. Although every **party** has the right to have his case heard by a real judge, judges pro tem are often practitioners in the field in which they are asked to hear cases and have as much, if not more, knowledge than a real judge. Pro tem judges are used often in **family law** cases, especially in **default divorces.**

Judge's Chambers: See *Chambers.*

In Israel, if a husband dissolves a marriage against his wife's will without a court judgment, he may be imprisoned up to five years.

Judgment: A final decision made by a judge on a **material issue** during a **case** and written into the official case file at the courthouse is termed a judgment. A judgment can provide all or a portion of the relief sought in a case, including **property division**, **alimony**, **child support**, **custody** or an **injunction**.

See also *Appeal; Decree; Interlocutory and Final Judgments;* and *Order*.

Judgment Nisi: Nisi is Latin for "unless." A judgment nisi is an intermediate judgment which will become final unless a **party appeals** or formally requests the court to set it aside. An **interlocutory decree** is properly referred to as a judgment nisi.

Judicial Relief: Judicial relief is what the **parties** to a lawsuit are asking the judge for. Relief can be in such forms as a **judgment** for money, an **injunction**, an **award** of **custody**, an interim **order** such as a **temporary restraining order**, or an order compelling **discovery**. Different types of **cases** involve different kinds of judicial relief. For instance, an action by a wife against her former husband for assault and **battery** usually asks for money and an injunction, while the judicial relief commonly granted in a **divorce action** is an order settling issues of **property division**, **alimony**, **child support**, **custody** and **visitation**.

See also *Prayer*.

Jurisdiction: When a court has the authority to rule over a **case**, it is said to have jurisdiction over it. In all states, certain types of courts (often called, depending on the state, superior, circuit, county, district, or family courts) are given specific and exclusive jurisdiction to handle **family law** cases. This is called **subject-matter jurisdiction**.

In order for a court to have subject-matter jurisdiction over a **divorce** action, at least one spouse must have lived in the county where the court is located for a certain period of time. Some states also require the spouse to have lived within the state for a certain length of time, usually a few months longer than the time in the county. For example, to obtain a divorce in California, a person must have lived in California for at least six months, and in the particular county in which he wants to obtain the divorce for at least three months.

If the court is being asked to determine **alimony**, **child support**, **custody**, **visitation** or the **division of property**, the court must have the power to make orders concerning the individual **defendant** (called **personal jurisdiction**). For a court to have personal jurisdiction over the defendant, the defendant must have a minimum number of contacts with the state in which the court is located. No set number qualifies as the minimum; each situation must be analyzed case by case.

Jurisdiction is also used to refer to a political subdivision in which a particular set of laws apply. Individual states or countries are sometimes referred as jurisdictions.

Jury Trial: A jury trial is one in which factual disputes are resolved by a jury (not the judge). **Parties** are entitled to a jury trial by the federal constitution in those types of **cases** (such as breach of contract) which existed in 1789, the effective date of the constitution. Kinds of cases that have come into existence since then, however, such as **divorce** (which in 1789 still fell under the religious courts) and actions in **juvenile courts**, are not guaranteed jury trials. States are free to make jury trials available for such actions, but few have. In fact, only Texas and Georgia permit jury trials for divorces.

Justice of the Peace: A justice of the peace is a judge (often not a lawyer) who is empowered to perform certain limited judicial functions such as conducting **marriages** and hearing **cases** on violations of local **ordinances**.

Juvenile Court: Most states have established a special juvenile court to consider cases involving **minor** children who:
 • are neglected by their parents (see *child neglect*)
 • are considered **incorrigible** (also called status offenders)
 • or commit crimes

The original purpose of these courts was to provide a judicial procedure for troubled children that would be less harsh than the regular criminal court process. To this end, judges are given broad **discretion** in an effort to counsel and rehabilitate minors. In addition, many juvenile court systems have introduced new vocabulary: crimes are called delinquent acts; the court adjudges a minor to be a **ward** of the court rather than find him guilty; and the court "disposes of a case" rather than "pronounces sentence." Despite these new terms, many observers have noted that the system works more or less the same as the criminal **trial**, with similar results. In many cases, juveniles are sent to reform institutions for acts that would not constitute crimes if they were adults.

Juvenile Delinquent: See *Delinquent Children*.

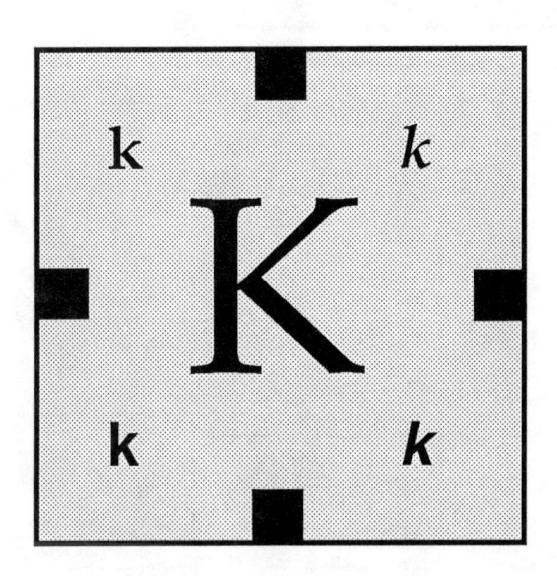

Kidnapping: See *Childnapping*.

Kin: Kin refers to persons related by blood. Kin can be close, as in brother and sister, or distant, as in third cousin twice removed. When used to determine the right of **inheritance** in the absence of a **will**, the term is commonly limited to specifically designated relationships.

See chart, **WHO IS YOUR KIN**.

WHO IS YOUR KIN?

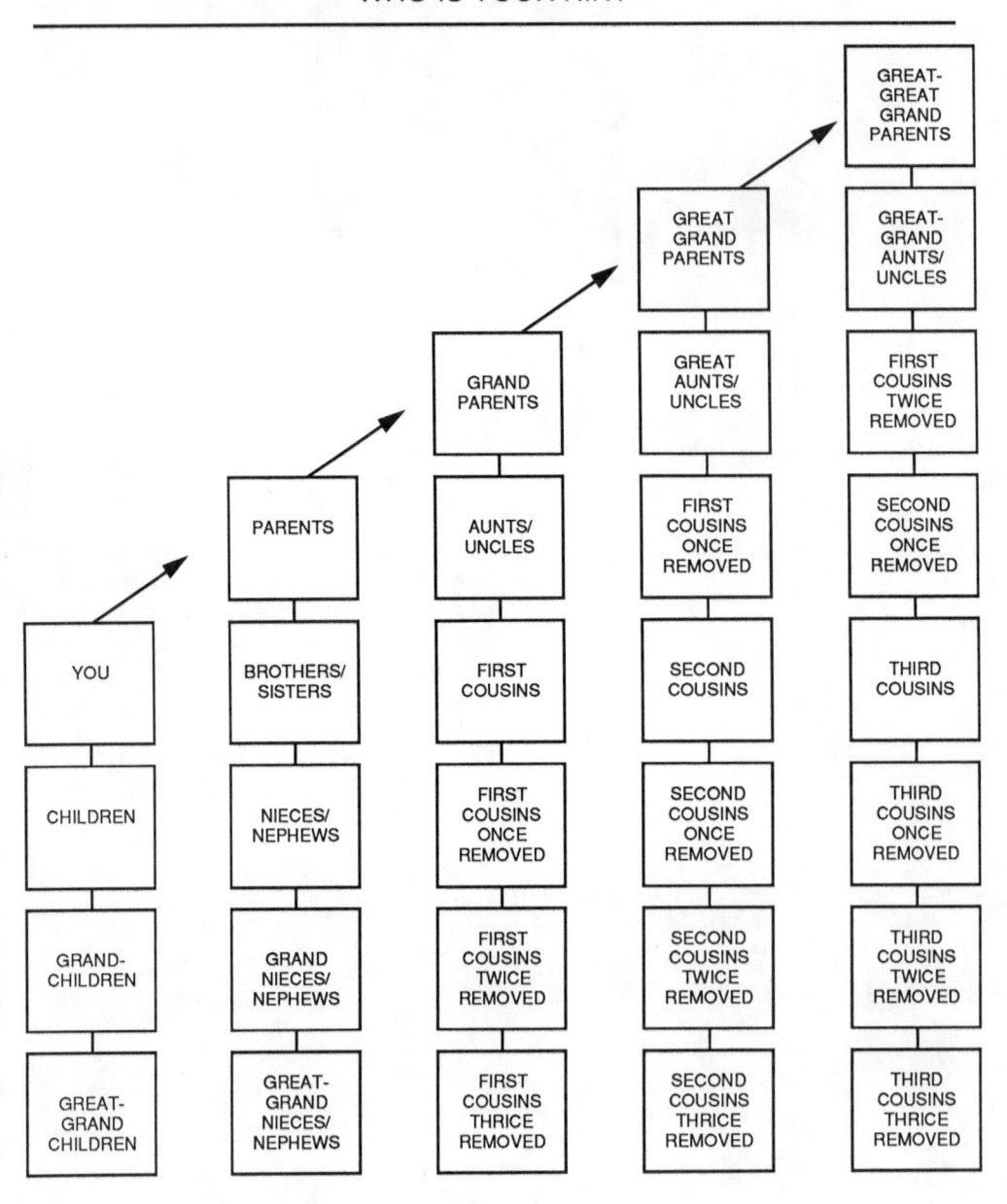

YOU	PARENTS	GRAND PARENTS	GREAT GRAND PARENTS	GREAT-GREAT GRAND PARENTS
				GREAT-GRAND AUNTS/ UNCLES
			GREAT AUNTS/ UNCLES	FIRST COUSINS TWICE REMOVED
		AUNTS/ UNCLES	FIRST COUSINS ONCE REMOVED	SECOND COUSINS ONCE REMOVED
YOU	BROTHERS/ SISTERS	FIRST COUSINS	SECOND COUSINS	THIRD COUSINS
CHILDREN	NIECES/ NEPHEWS	FIRST COUSINS ONCE REMOVED	SECOND COUSINS ONCE REMOVED	THIRD COUSINS ONCE REMOVED
GRAND-CHILDREN	GRAND NIECES/ NEPHEWS	FIRST COUSINS TWICE REMOVED	SECOND COUSINS TWICE REMOVED	THIRD COUSINS TWICE REMOVED
GREAT-GRAND CHILDREN	GREAT-GRAND NIECES/ NEPHEWS	FIRST COUSINS THRICE REMOVED	SECOND COUSINS THRICE REMOVED	THIRD COUSINS THRICE REMOVED

Law: See *Case Law; Common Law; Ordinance; Precedent;* and *Statute.*

Lawsuit: In Ambrose Bierce's words: A lawsuit is a machine you go into as a pig and come out as a sausage.
See *Litigation.*

Leading Case: The most important **appellate court** decision in a particular area of law is called the leading case. Such important **cases** are used as guidance by lawyers and judges who face similar issues later. For example, in the area of **abortion**, the leading case is *Roe v. Wade;* concerning **cohabitation**, the leading case is *Marvin v. Marvin.*

Legal Custody: Legal custody of a child is the right and obligation to make decisions about a child's upbringing. Decisions regarding schooling, and medical and dental care, for example, are made by a parent with legal custody. In many states, courts now award joint legal custody to the parents, which means that the decision making is shared.
See also *Custody; Joint Custody;* and *Physical Custody.*

Legal Duty to Support: See *Continuing Duty to Support.*

Legal Father: A legal father is the man recognized under law as the male parent of a child. Legal recognition is automatic if he was married to the child's mother when the child was born or has been declared the father in a **paternity** action. A male **stepparent** is not the legal father of his stepchildren unless he **adopts** them.

Legal Guardian: See *Guardian* and *Conservator*.

Legal Separation: A legal separation results when the **parties** separate and a court rules on the **division of property, alimony, child support, custody** and **visitation**, but does not grant a **divorce**. This separation is also called a separation from bed and board. The money **awarded** for support of the spouse and children under these circumstances is often called separate maintenance (as opposed to alimony and child support).

Legal separation is usually a substitute for, and not a step toward, divorce. It often occurs when there is a religious objection to divorce, or if a dependent spouse needs medical care and cannot afford it on her own. Most couples who intend to divorce begin **living apart** without going through formal separation procedures. Prior to **no-fault divorces**, however, legal separations were often obtained by couples wishing to live apart (they needed to get legal permission from the court to do so.)

See also *Convertible Divorce* and *Separation*.

Legally Divorced: See *Entry of Judgment*.

Legislative Intent: Legislative intent is what a legislature as a whole had in mind when it passed a particular **statute**. Normally, any given statute is interpreted by looking just at the statute's language. But when the language is ambiguous or unclear, courts try to glean the legislative intent behind words by looking at legislative interpretations (for instance, reports issued by legislative committees) which were relied upon by legislators when voting on the statute.

As a practical matter, statutes are often ambiguous enough to support more than one interpretation, and the material reflecting legislative intent is frequently sparse. This leaves courts free to interpret statutes according to their own predilections. Once a court interprets the legislative intent, however, other courts will usually not go through the exercise again, but rather will enforce the statute as interpreted by the other court.

Legitimate Children: See *Illegitimate Children*.

Length of Alimony: Although most **alimony** obligations are set up to continue indefinitely, many are limited to a specific period of time, depending on the **length of the marriage**, the spouses' **ability to earn**, the health and age of the spouses, and the supported spouse's **ability to be self-supporting**. In shorter **marriages**, alimony is usually **awarded** for a finite period of time to give the dependent spouse an opportunity to get training or skills and return to work, and is called **rehabilitative alimony**. In long-term marriages, however, especially where a spouse did not work outside the home, the court may order a spouse to pay alimony until the supported spouse's death or **remarriage**.

Length of Marriage: Effect on Alimony and Child Support: When a **marriage** was relatively short—three years or so is a good rule of thumb—and no children were born or **adopted**, courts often refuse to **award alimony** to the spouse with the lower income. If there are children under school age, however, alimony may be awarded to the parent given **physical custody** because the court wants to enable the **custodial parent** to care full time for the child.

Child support is a different matter altogether, because parents are obligated to support their children regardless of the length of the marriage. State law determines the extent of that obligation.

Lesbian Lifestyle: See *Gay or Lesbian Lifestyle: Effect on Custody.*

Liabilities: See *Debts.*

Libel: See *Complaint.*

Lien: A lien is a charge on **property** as security for payment of a **debt**. If the person to whom the debt is owed (the creditor) has a lien on an item of property, he sometimes has the right to have the property sold in order to get the proceeds to pay the debt. Other times, the lien only gives the creditor the rights to payment when the debtor voluntarily sells the property.

Lifestyle and Social Factors: Effect on Custody and Visitation: The way each parent lives can be an important factor when a court decides which parent is entitled to **physical custody** and what **visitation** rights are appropriate. In any given case, the judge may consider one parent's lifestyle more in the **best interest of the child** than the other's. The main elements courts tend to consider when examining a parent's lifestyle are: family stability, occupation, type of home maintained, interest and hobbies, sexual history, religious practices, and income.

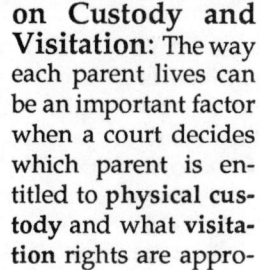

Changes in custody or visitation **orders** may be obtained if substantial changes in a parent's lifestyle threatens or harms the child. If, for example, a **custodial parent** begins working at night and leaving a 9-year-old child alone, the other parent may request a change in custody. Similarly, if a **non-custodial parent** begins drinking heavily or taking drugs, the custodial parent may file a **request for modification** of the visitation order (asking, for example, that visits occur when the parent is sober, or in the presence of another adult).

What constitutes a lifestyle sufficiently detrimental to warrant a change in custody or visitation rights varies tremendously depending on the state and the particular judge deciding the case. For instance, **cohabitation** by a parent may be ignored in one place, but not another. Similarly, a lesbian parent may be denied custody by one judge, while another may decide that her sexual orientation is irrelevant.

Limitation of Action: See *Statute of Limitation.*

Limited Divorce: See *Legal Separation.*

Lis Pendens: Lis pendens means pending lawsuit. A lis pendens notice is a document filed in the public records of the county where particular **real property** is located stating that a pending lawsuit may affect the **title** to the property. Because nobody wants to buy real estate if its ownership is in dispute, a lis pendens notice effectively ties up the property until the case is resolved. Lis pendens notices are often filed in **divorce** actions when there is disagreement about selling or dividing the **family home**.

Litigation: Litigation is the process of bringing and pursuing a lawsuit. It includes preparing and filing **court papers**, **motions**, and **briefs**, and conducting **discovery**, **hearings**, **trials** and **appeals**.

Litigation often proceeds much like trench warfare; initial court papers define the **parties'** legal positions as trenches define battlefield positions. After the initial activity, lawyers sit back for several months or years and lob legal artillery at each other in the forms of discovery and motions until they grow tired of the warfare and begin **settlement** negotiations. If settlement is unsuccessful (90% of all lawsuits are settled without trial), the case goes to trial, and may be followed by a lengthy appeal.

Living Apart: When spouses no longer reside in the same dwelling, they are said to be living apart even if they occasionally have sexual relations with each other. In some states, living apart without intending to reunite changes the spouses' **property** rights. For example, some states consider property accumulated and **debts** incurred between living apart and **divorce** to be the **separate property** or debt of the person who accumulated or incurred it. If the couple lives apart for a trial period with the hope of **reconciliation**, however, even if they don't get back together, the **assets** and debts they accumulate or incur during the trial period remain jointly owned until they decide to permanently live apart or obtain a divorce or **legal separation**.

See also *Separation*.

Living in Sin: See *Cohabitation*.

Living Pattern: See *Established Living Pattern*.

Living Together: See *Cohabitation*.

Living Together Agreement: See *Cohabitation Agreement* and *Marvin v. Marvin*.

Long-Arm Statute: Long-arm statutes allow persons in one state to sue out-of-staters in the first state's courts, and **serve** the out-of-staters in their own states. The statutes got their nickname because they permit the state to reach out and bring out-of-staters into the state court as **defendants**. (If there is no long-arm statute, courts have **personal jurisdiction** only over persons who have been properly served with a **summons** and **complaint** within the state.) For a state court to have personal jurisdiction over an out-of-stater under a long-arm statute, the out-of-stater must have had certain kinds of connections (called significant contacts) with the particular state. Long-

arm statutes are used in **family law** disputes because **divorced** people often move around, and **child support, alimony** and **custody orders** need to be enforced in the state that issued the order in the first place.
See also *Service of Court Papers*.

EXAMPLE

Eve and Craig divorced in Arkansas; Craig was ordered to pay alimony. Craig moved to Missouri and made five payments but then stopped. Arkansas' long-arm statute will probably allow Eve to haul Craig into court in Arkansas in an effort to enforce the alimony order.

Longer Visitation Periods: As a child grows older, many courts allow a **non-custodial parent** longer **visitation** periods than when the child was younger, due to an older child's ability to better adjust psychologically to longer visits.

Loss of Consortium: Consortium is the relationship between a husband and wife, which include love, affection, fellowship and sexual companionship. If a third party interferes with that relationship (e.g., a neck injury disables the husband from having sexual intercourse), the spouse who loses elements of consortium can sue the third party on that ground. Although **cohabitating** and same-sex couples have argued that loss of consortium **statutes** should apply to their relationships as well, virtually no states have applied the law to them.

Loss of Income or Job: See *Decrease in Income*.

Loving v. Virginia: See *Miscegenation*.

Lump Sum Support: In a few states, a spouse may pay his total **alimony** (and occasionally **child support**) obligation at the time of the **divorce** by giving the other spouse a lump-sum payment equal to the total amount of future monthly payments. This is also called alimony in gross.
See also *Integrated Property Settlement Agreement* and *Periodic Support*.

Maiden Name: A woman's surname that has not come from the husband is her maiden name. Thus, the surname given to her at birth or acquired by any process other than **marriage** is her maiden name. A **divorcing** woman who took her husband's name at marriage has the option of returning to her maiden name, a former married name (if she has been married more than once), keeping her married name, or choosing something completely new. A woman's maiden name is not automatically changed by marriage; the change becomes effective only if the woman starts using her husband's surname.

See also *Change of Name*.

Maintenance: Maintenance is the term used for **alimony** in some states.

Maintenance Period: See *Length of Alimony*.

Majority: See *Age of Majority*.

Management and Control of Property: Most states provide that both spouses have equal management and control over all jointly owned **property**. This includes the power to buy it, sell it, give it away, or invest it. Until the mid 1970's, most states placed the management and control of jointly-owned property exclusively with the husband.

In most states today, certain property, usually **necessaries** of life, such as clothing, furniture and similar items, cannot be sold or disposed of without the consent of both spouses.

Each spouse has management and control over all his **separate property**, even necessaries of life.

Mandatory Deductions: Mandatory deductions are those amounts of money employers are legally required to withhold from employees' paychecks. The most common mandatory deductions are federal income tax, state income tax, mandatory **pension** contributions, mandatory union dues and social security contributions.

See also *Ability to Earn* and *Net Income*.

Marital Agreement: See *Agreement During Marriage*.

Marital Communication Privilege: In virtually all states, private conversations between husbands and wives are **privileged communications**. This means that courts cannot force one or the other to testify as to the contents of the conversations.

Marital Debts: See *Community Debts; Debts: Effect on Alimony and Child Support; Debts Incurred Between Separation and Divorce* and *Debts Incurred During Marriage*.

Marital Deduction: When a person dies leaving **property** worth more than $600,000, the federal government requires that taxes be paid on the excess unless the property is left to a surviving spouse. In that case, under a federal estate tax deduction known as the marital deduction, no taxes need be paid.

Marital Misconduct: The various traditional fault **grounds for divorce**, such as **adultery, constructive abandonment, cruelty** and **desertion**, are also generally referred to as "marital misconduct."

Marital Misconduct as Defense to Alimony: In twenty-two states, a spouse guilty of **marital misconduct** may either be barred from receiving or receive less than her full fair share of alimony.

See chart, **FACTORS IN SETTING AND TERMINATING ALIMONY,** under Alimony.

Marital Misconduct as Defense to Divorce: See *Comparative Rectitude; Defense to Divorce;* and *Fault Divorce*.

Marital Property: Most **property** accumulated by a **married** couple is called marital property. In **community property states**, marital property is called community property. The rules as to what constitutes marital property in non-community property states differ. Some states include all property and earnings during marriage. Others exclude gifts and **inheritances** from this general rule. Some states exclude certain types of property even if acquired during marriage, while others exclude **improvements to property** that existed before marriage.

Upon **divorce**, marital property in community property states is divided equally. In **equitable distribution** states, marital property is divided equitably (fairly). In practice, equitable means equal, or nearly so, unless the court believes it is fairer to **award** one spouse more. In Mississippi (the **common law property** state), marital property is divided according to who has legal **title to the property**, that is, who owns it.

See also *Separate Property*.

Marital Settlement Agreement: See *Divorce Agreement*.

Marital Status: Marital status is the term used to describe whether a person is single, married, divorced, separated or widowed.

Marital Termination Agreement: See *Divorce Agreement*.

Marriage: Marriage is the legal union of a man and a woman as husband and wife. Once two people become married to each other, their responsibilities and rights toward one another concerning property and support are defined by the laws of the state in which they live. A couple may be able to modify the rules set up by their state (see *agreement during marriage*). A marriage can only be terminated by a court granting a divorce or an annulment.

Marriage entails many legal rights and benefits, including the right to:
• file joint income tax returns with the IRS and state taxing authorities, and claim dependency deductions
• receive marital and dependency social security, disability, unemployment, veterans', pension and public assistance benefits
• receive a share of the deceased spouse's estate under intestate succession laws
• claim gift and estate tax benefits
• sue for wrongful death, loss of consortium, alienation of affection and criminal conversation
• receive family rates for insurance
• avoid the deportation of a non-citizen spouse
• enter hospital intensive care units, jails and other places where visitors are restricted to immediate family
• live in neighborhoods zoned "families only"
• make medical decisions about one's spouse in the event of disability
• claim the marital communication privilege.

RELATED TERMS

Age of Consent
Agreement Prior to Marriage
Blood Test Prior to Marriage
Breach of Promise to Marry
Cohabitation
Common Law Marriage
Debts Incurred During Marriage
Fraudulent Marriage
Illegitimate Children
Intact Family
Legal Separation
Length of Marriage
Maiden Name
Marital Property

> *Marriage Certificate*
> *Meretricious Relationship*
> *Out of State Marriage*
> *Proxy Marriage*
> *Putative Marriage*
> *Reconciliation*
> *Residency: Effect on Marriage and Divorce*
> *Same-Sex Marriage*
> *Sham Marriage*
> *Wedding*

Marriage Ceremony: See *Wedding*.

Marriage Certificate: In order for people to be legally **married**, most states require that a couple undergo a **wedding** with a judge, **justice of the peace**, court **clerk**, or religious official (e.g., priest, rabbi or minister) and then file a marriage certificate with the proper authorities, usually the county clerk. (Usually, whoever performs the wedding may file the marriage certificate for the couple.) The filing usually must be done within a few days (often five) after the ceremony.

See also *Common Law Marriage*.

Marriage Contract: See *Agreement During Marriage*.

Marriage of Convenience: A marriage of convenience is one where the couple is legally married, but only for appearances, rather than because of a romantic or sexual relationship. A marriage of convenience often occurs where one or both partners wants to appear married for professional or social reasons (such as a gay man or lesbian who has succeeded in a very traditional profession and the only obstacle to full acceptance is the failure to conform socially).

A marriage of convenience is a perfectly legal marriage.

See also *Sham Marriage*.

Marriage License: A marriage license is a piece of paper issued by local officials authorizing a couple to get married in a **wedding** and obtain a **marriage certificate**. Forty-five states require the couple to undergo **blood tests** before obtaining the license.

Marriage of Short Duration: See *Length of Marriage*.

Married Women's Property Acts: Married Women's Property Acts were 19th century **statutes** enacted throughout the United States and England granting to **married** women for the first time the right to own **property** in their own names.

Marvin v. Marvin: The ruling in the well-known 1976 California Supreme Court decision of *Marvin v. Marvin* (1976) 18 Cal.3d 660, affected **cohabitation** in California. The decision said that unmarried couples may make enforceable contracts with each other regarding **property** and **alimony**-like support, and that where there is no explicit contract but the actions of the parties make it appear as though there is an understanding, the court may "imply" a contract to exist and enforce it. The decision does not give cohabitating couples the property rights of **married** people, but rather allows them to have their contracts and understandings enforced in court. There is no minimum number of years that a cohabitating couple must live together in order to obtain these rights.

> **EXAMPLE**
>
> Let's look at the *Marvin* case itself. Michelle Triola (who called herself Michelle Marvin) lived with actor Lee Marvin for a number of years. She claimed that she gave up her own career in exchange for becoming Lee Marvin's homemaker and an agreement that she would be entitled to half his income. When the couple separated, Michelle sued Lee for a lot of money. No written contract was produced, but Michelle insisted that an oral agreement had been made. The California Supreme Court allowed her to proceed on the basis of the oral contract and on the "implied contract" theory. In the end, a jury **awarded** Michelle nothing because she was unable to prove the contract or that her worth as a homemaker was worth the money she claimed.

It is important to remember this decision in toto is followed by only a few states. (Most states have followed the express written and oral contract theories, but many have rejected the implied contract theory.) No court will apply the *Marvin* principle when the sole "services" provided by a person are sexual in nature. In fact, even in states which follow *Marvin*, courts do not recognize a contract which contains any mention of sex.

See also *Cohabitation Agreement; Common Law Marriage; Meretricious Relationship; Palimony; Putative Marriage; Putative Spouse;* and *Same-Sex Marriage*.

Material Change in Circumstance: See *Change in Circumstance*.

Material Evidence: See *Immaterial Evidence*.

Material Issue: Any issue which must be decided to resolve a particular dispute is termed a material issue. Conversely, an issue not necessary for resolution of a dispute is an immaterial issue. For instance, in a **custody** hearing between unmarried parents, **paternity** is a material issue which must be established before deciding custody. In a **bifurcated divorce**, however, where only the status of the **marriage** is being terminated and the other issues are being postponed, **child support**, **alimony**, **custody** and **property division** are immaterial issues for the **hearing** on the divorce.

Matured Pension: See *Pension/Retirement Benefits*.

Mediation: Mediation is a non-adversarial process where a neutral person (a mediator) meets with disputing persons (often **parties** to a lawsuit or a threatened lawsuit) to help them settle the dispute. The mediator, however, does not have the power to impose a solution on the parties.

Mediation is often used to help a **divorcing or divorced couple** work out their differences concerning **alimony, child support, custody, visitation** and **division of property**. Some lawyers and mental health professionals employ mediation as part of their practice. In about half the states, counseling and mediation services are associated with **family courts**. In some places, mediation is mandatory for certain issues. California, for example, has mandatory mediation whenever custody or visitation is disputed.

See also *Arbitration* and *Conciliation Service*.

Medical Emergencies: Medical emergencies that require large expenditures of money are the kind of temporary and catastrophic circumstances that may support a **temporary modification of alimony or child support**. If the child or the **custodial parent** suffers the emergency, the **non-custodial parent** may be required to temporarily increase payments (if he is able). Likewise, if the non-custodial parent is the one with the emergency, his duty to support may temporarily be eased by the court.

Mental Capacity: Mental capacity means the ability of a person to understand what she is doing and what consequences her actions may have. In order for a **marriage** to be valid, each spouse must have had, at the time of the **wedding**, sufficient mental capacity to understand the marital relationship into which she was entering. If it is later shown that one spouse did not have the capacity, the marriage may be **annulled** by a court.

Meretricious Relationship: Some courts, especially those in states where **fornication** is illegal, describe **cohabitation** arrangements as "meretricious," meaning "of an unlawful sexual nature."

Military Pensions: See *Pension/Retirement Benefits*.

Military Service: See *Active Military Service*.

Minor: A minor is a person under the **age of majority**. In almost every state, this means the person is less than 18 years of age. In a few other states, the age of majority is 17, 19, 20 or 21.

Minor Moving Out of House: Legal Effect: See *Emancipated Minor*.

Miscegenation: Miscegenation means the mixing of races. Miscegenation **statutes** prohibited people (mainly white people) from marrying people of different races. Typical was a statute that prohibited a white person from marrying a black person or Asian, but not prohibiting a black person from marrying an Asian. Miscegenation statutes were declared unconstitutional in 1967 by the

U.S. Supreme Court in *Loving v. Virginia*, 388 U.S. 1, and are not enforced in any state (although some states still have these laws on their books).

Mixing Property: See *Commingling*.

Modification: See *Modification Agreement; Request for Modification* and *Temporary Modification*.

Modification Agreement: When ex-spouses make an **agreement to modify alimony, child support, custody, or visitation** (either for an indefinite time or on a temporary basis), they normally put their understanding in writing and sign it. This is called a modification agreement. It is important that the modification agreement be approved by the court; otherwise, if one **party** breaks the modified agreement, the other party may not be able to get the court to enforce it. Courts usually approve modification agreements unless it appears that they are not in the **best interests of the child**.

Motions: A motion is a written request to the court. When a **party** asks the court to take some kind of action in the course of litigation, other than resolving the entire **case** at **trial**, the request is made in the form of a motion. Motions are often made before trials to resolve procedural and preliminary issues, and may be made after trials to enforce or modify **judgments**. Normally, one side submits a motion, the other side submits a written response, and the court holds a **hearing** at which the parties give brief oral arguments. (Some motions are considered only on the basis of the writings.) Then the court approves or denies the motion.

A **family law** case might involve any or all of these motions:
- for temporary **child support** and **custody**
- to exclude a party from the **family home**
- to compel **discovery** (for example, to make a party answer **deposition** questions);
- to postpone a hearing or trial
- for **sanctions**
- to exclude or include certain types of **evidence**
- or for a **new trial**.

Moving Away: See *Geographic Move: Effect on Custody and Visitation*.

On the east African coast, a groom pays cash to the bride's father, mother and sexual instructress. A bride brings a bed, mattress, cooking pots and crockery to the marriage.

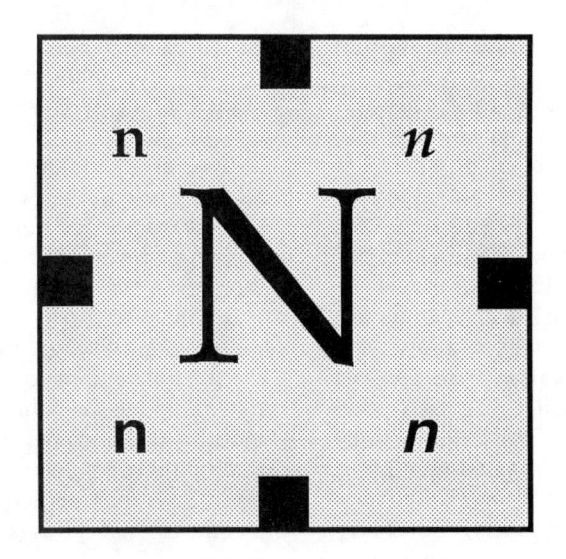

Name Change: See *Change of Name; Changing Child's Name* and *Maiden Name*.

Natural Parent: The biological parent of a child is sometimes referred to as the "natural parent." This term may fall into disuse, however, as **artificial insemination, surrogate motherhood** and **in vitro fertilization** techniques increase. This is because "natural parent" normally means legal parent (except when a child has been **adopted**), and the legal parent of a child conceived through artificial insemination, in vitro fertilization or a surrogate motherhood is not always certain.

Necessaries: Necessaries (also called necessities, necessities of life, or necessaries of life) are the articles needed to sustain life, such as food, clothing, medical care and shelter. In all states, the law requires men to provide necessaries for their wives and children; in many states, women must provide them for their spouses and offspring. When it comes to enforcing this obligation, however, courts have been notoriously reluctant to intervene as long as the couple is living together. The barest provision of food and shelter has been found sufficient under the law.

In some states, **debts** incurred by a spouse for necessaries are considered to be joint debts of the spouses even if the couple is **living apart** but not yet **divorced**. This means that in most states, creditors may sue either spouse for debts incurred for necessaries by either spouse.

Needs of Child: Normally, **child support** payments are based on the ability of a parent to provide support and the child's needs.

If a child's financial needs decrease after the level of support has been set, a decrease in child support may be ordered if the paying parent makes a **request for modification** to the court. This may occur, for example, if a child changes from private school to public school. If a child inherits a large sum of money, however, a court will not make the modification because state laws generally prohibit inherited money from being used for the child's day-to-day support. (Parents are obligated to support children; children are not required to support themselves.) Conversely, if a child's financial needs increase (for example, a sudden need for tutoring or medical care), an increase in child support may be **awarded** by a court if the parent who receives the payments can show **changed circumstance** and submits a request for modification to the court.

Negative Asset: See *Debt.*

Neglect of Child: See *Child Neglect.*

Nepotism: Originally, the term nepotism described the practice of government officials filling certain appointed public offices with their blood or marital relatives. In its broader sense, nepotism refers to the practice of giving a job to a person because she has a relative working there already. Some companies have anti-nepotism policies, which prohibit **married** people (or **cohabitating** couples) from working together.

Net Income: A person's net income is what remains after **mandatory deductions** such as income tax, **pension** deductions, mandatory union dues and social security contributions are subtracted. When a court sets **alimony** or **child support**, it does so on the basis of the **parties'** net incomes rather than their gross incomes (the amount received by the person before the deductions).

In most states, deductions for credit union payments, **wage attachments** and the like are not subtracted when calculating net income. Thus, if John makes $2,000 per month, and income tax, social security, unemployment insurance benefits and other government deductions reduce his income to $1,500, this is his net income. The fact that $300 more is withheld to pay a credit union loan does not further reduce his net income for the court's purposes. The reason for this rule is that the law accords support payments a higher priority than other types of debts, and would rather see other debts not paid than have a spouse or child go without adequate support.

New Support Obligation: When an ex-spouse paying **alimony** assumes a new legal support obligation (for example, **adopts**, **remarries** or has a child), the court may reduce the earlier alimony order if it would be a **hardship** to pay the prior alimony and meet the new obligation. On the other hand, if the new support obligation is voluntarily assumed (for example, helping to support stepchildren when there is no duty to do so), rather than required by law, a court is unlikely to order a reduction.

A parent paying **child support** may also attempt to reduce his payments after assuming a new legal support obligation. Many courts, however, do not look favorably upon parents who seek to reduce child support obligations in order to support second families.

New Trial: A **motion** for a new trial is a request following a **trial** to set the trial decision aside (i.e., act as though it never happened) and have another one. A motion for a new trial is made to the **trial judge** by the losing **party** to the lawsuit immediately after the trial is over. The party must show the judge that he made **errors** which seriously harmed the party (e.g., refusing to allow the party to present certain **admissible evidence**). As a practical matter, motions for new trials are infrequently granted because judges rarely decide something during a trial and then admit they made serious mistakes just a few days later. (The party may still **appeal** if her motion for a new trial is refused.)

"New trial" also refers to the additional trial held after a party appeals a **case** and the **appellate court remands** (sends back) the case to the trial judge to be redecided.

Nex Ex: Nex ex is Latin for do not exit. Nex ex **orders** are issued to prohibit a **party** from leaving a state or to prohibit someone from removing a child or **property** from a state.

Next Friend: When a child or an adult unable to legally care for himself wants to bring an **action** in court, a competent adult (often a parent, child or spouse) must usually bring the **case** for him as his next friend, as in "John Doe, a minor, through his next friend, Sally Doe, his mother."

See also *Guardian Ad Litem*.

Next of Kin: A person's next of kin is her closest blood relative (parent, child, or **sibling**). The term also refers to those people (including a spouse) who inherit under **intestate inheritance** laws when someone dies without a **will**.

No-Fault Divorce: No-fault divorce describes any **divorce** where the spouse suing for divorce does not have to accuse the other of wrongdoing. Rather, the spouse can simply state that the couple no longer gets along, or that the couple has been **living apart** for a specified period.

Until recently, the only way a person could get a divorce was to prove that the other spouse was guilty of **marital misconduct** and was at fault for the **marriage** not working (see *grounds for divorce*). Today, all states allow divorces regardless of who is at "fault." In 14 states, including California, Michigan, Oregon and Wisconsin, no-fault divorces have completely replaced **fault divorces**; in most states, however, both no-fault divorces and fault divorces can be obtained.

No-fault divorces are usually granted for reasons such as **incompatibility, irreconcilable difference,** or **irretrievable,** or **irreme-**

diable breakdown of the marriage. Also, some states allow **incurable insanity** as a basis for a no-fault divorce.

In 25 states, couples may obtain a no-fault divorce based on **separation**; the length of the separation required varies between six months and five years. In 12 states which have separation-based divorces, separation is the only no-fault ground for divorce.

See chart, **GROUNDS FOR DIVORCE** under *Grounds for Divorce*.

Non-Community Property States: See *Equitable Distribution States* and *Common Law Property*.

Non-Compliance with Child Support: See *Enforcement of Child Support*.

Non-Custodial Parent: When one parent is **awarded** sole **physical custody** of a child, the other parent is referred to as the non-custodial parent. Non-custodial parents almost always have some sort of **visitation** arrangement with the child. Where the parents have **joint physical custody** (i.e., the child spends near equal amounts of time with each parent), each is considered the **custodial parent** when the child is with that parent.

Non-Marital Partners: Non-marital partners are couples who are not married.

See *Agreement Prior to Marriage; Cohabitation; Cohabitation Agreement; Common Law Marriage; Co-Parent; Illegitimate Children; Marvin v. Marvin; Palimony; Paternity Action; Putative Marriage; Putative Spouse; Quasi-Marital Property;* and *Same-Sex Marriage*.

Non-Modifiable Alimony: In many states, **divorce agreements** or **decrees** may state that **alimony** amounts and periods are "non-modifiable," which means that they cannot be changed once they are established.

See also *Integrated Property Settlement Agreement; Extension of Alimony;* and *Permanent Alimony, Child Support, Custody, or Visitation*.

Non-Monetary Contributions to Marriage: Spouses make monetary and non-monetary contributions to the **marriage**. Monetary contributions tend to be in the form of **earnings** and benefits (and result in the acquisition of **assets**, such as furniture, car and a house). Non-monetary contributions include homemaking, child care, entertaining the working spouse's business associates, and working without a salary in a spouse's business.

Normally, when couples get **divorced**, only the monetary contribution is treated as having value and divided accordingly. Now, however, in over 35 states, when a couple divorces and their **property** is divided, the non-monetary contributions of a spouse are recognized to have monetary value. In some cases, the spouse who contributed the non-monetary services is compensated from the couple's property for the full value of the services. If that spouse's future earning capacity has been impaired by her absence from the income-earning world, she may be compensated by a large **alimony** award.

See also *Professional Degree or License*.

Non-Support: Non-support refers to the failure of a parent to support his children or the failure of a husband (in all states) or a wife (in some states) to support his or her spouse.

See also *Necessaries*.

Notary Public: A notary public is a public official who, depending on the state, has the power to acknowledge signatures, administer **oaths and affirmations**, take **depositions** and issue subpoenas in lawsuits (see *discovery*). Notaries public are most commonly used to acknowledge signatures, especially on **court papers** such as **affidavits**.

Although notaries public are public officials, most are people who work in private industry and take a state-administered test to become notaries public. Often, one or more employees of large institutions which process much paperwork (such as banks, insurance companies, and real estate brokers) and large law offices are notaries public. Also, many people who work at courthouses are notaries public.

Notice: A **party** to a lawsuit has the right to receive written notice that he is being sued or that a **hearing** will be held which might affect him in some way. Many rules have been developed to govern what notice needs to be given, and how and when it must be delivered. These are usually contained in **court rules** and rules of **civil procedure**.

EXAMPLE

Jane must give Tom written notice of a court hearing she has scheduled for the purpose of modifying **child support**; she can have the papers served on Tom by either mailing them to him (or to his attorney) or handing them to him personally.

See also *Service of Court Papers*.

Nunc Pro Tunc: Nunc pro tunc literally means "now for then." Occasionally, a court or **party** to a **divorce** forgets to file the papers necessary to obtain the final **decree** (after the **interlocutory judgment** has been granted), and the result is that the divorce never becomes final. If the oversight presents a problem (for example, one party has already **remarried**, or there is a tax advantage to being divorced earlier), the court may agree to issue a nunc pro tunc order, which grants the final divorce retroactive to the earlier date.

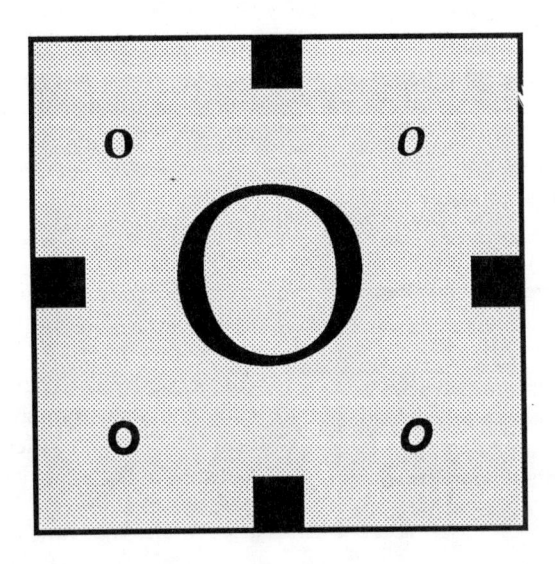

Oaths and Affirmations: When a person swears on the basis of a belief in God to tell the truth, it is called taking an oath. (Someone who doesn't want to swear to something may "affirm" it instead.)

An oath is typically administered to a witness at a **trial** or **deposition**. An **affidavit** is also signed under oath before a **notary public**. A **declaration** is a statement signed under oath (actually under penalty of perjury) but there the oath is self-administered. In some states, declarations may be used in place of affidavits.

Obligation to Support: See *Continuing Duty to Support.*

Open Adoption: An open adoption is an **adoption** where the birth mother remains in contact with the adoptive parents and the child throughout the child's life. In traditional adoptions, birth and **adoption records** are sealed by court **order**, and the child and adoptive parents may never know the mother's identity. Although open adoptions are not common, a growing number of **families** (especially where the adoptive parents are related to the birth mother) are choosing this route for a number of reasons, including:

• minimizing the birth mother's feelings of guilt and isolation

• reducing the likelihood that the birth mother will rescind the adoption

• minimizing the trauma to the child in

-129-

finding out that she was adopted
- maximizing the loving adult contacts the child has.

Operation of Law: "Operation of law" refers to the automatic application of a law to a particular situation.

EXAMPLE

Max is married to Erma, and they have two children. Max and Erma own a house (in **joint tenancy**) and miscellaneous furniture and fixtures around the house. There is also a family car, some stocks and bonds and other **assets** in Max's name. Max dies without a **will**. Max's **property** will therefore be distributed by operation of law under the **intestate succession** laws of his state: The house will automatically go to Erma because it is in joint tenancy. The rest of Max's property will pass by whatever scheme has been set up by his state legislature. Most likely, a portion of his property will pass to Erma and a portion to his children.

Opportunity: The actual opportunity of a person to have performed an act is called opportunity. In **family law**, a **plaintiff** seeking a **fault divorce** on the ground of **adultery** must prove (among other things) that his spouse had the opportunity to commit adultery. This opportunity may have been, for example, when the **defendant** and the **corespondent** attended a convention together or stayed at the same motel on the same night.

Order: An order is the decision rendered by a judge after a **hearing**. A **judgment** is a decision rendered after a **trial**. As part of the judgment, however, a court may "order" (i.e., require) a party to the lawsuit to do something, such as pay $500 a month in **child support**.

Order of Protection: See *Protective Order*.

Order to Show Cause Hearing: An order to show cause (sometimes referred to as an O.S.C.) is an **order** issued by a judge, requiring a person to appear in court at a **hearing** and tell the judge (i.e., "show cause") why the court shouldn't take a certain action. A person who does not show up can be held in **contempt of court**.

Many states allow a spouse or other person victimized by **domestic violence** to obtain a court order requiring the abuser to appear in court and show cause why the court should not issue a **temporary restraining order** prohibiting him from further harming the victims. The court can also issue an order requiring an abusive spouse to move out of the **family home**.

In some states, orders to show cause are the foundation of many other **family law** proceedings. When a couple **separates** or files for **divorce**, a **party** often needs the immediate intervention of a court to establish **alimony, child support, custody, visitation,** and other issues until the divorce becomes final. Many couples work out arrangements themselves. With other couples, one spouse proposes an arrangement and then requests an O.S.C. hearing (or in some states, a **preliminary hearing**) for the court to decide on the proposed arrangement. At the hearing, the other spouse has the opportunity to object and/or make his own proposals.

In family law, orders to show cause are also used when a party violates a court order, such as an order to pay alimony or child support. In this situation, the other party will ask the court to hold an O.S.C. hearing to determine whether the party who has violated the court order should be held in contempt of court.

Ordinance: An ordinance is a law enacted by a municipal body, such as a city council or county commission (sometimes called county council or county board of supervisors). Ordinances govern matters not already covered by state or federal laws such as **zoning**, safety, and building regulations.

Orphanage: An orphanage is a group home maintained for the care, **custody** and control of children who have no parents or **guardians**.
See also *Foster Home*.

Out of Control Children: See *Incorrigible Children* and *Juvenile Delinquent*.

In the Minho region of northwest Portugal, husbands are forbidden from washing, sewing and sweeping; wives cannot climb trees or prune vines.

Out of Country or Out of State Divorce: See *Dominican Republic Divorce; Foreign Divorce;* and *Uniform Divorce Recognition Act*.

Out of State Marriage: When a couple seeking a **divorce** was married in a state or country different from where they are seeking their divorce, the **marriage** is referred to as an out of state marriage.
See also *Quasi-Community Property*.

In West Germany, if a wife was declared solely or predominantly at fault in causing a divorce, the husband may petition a court to prohibit her from using his surname.

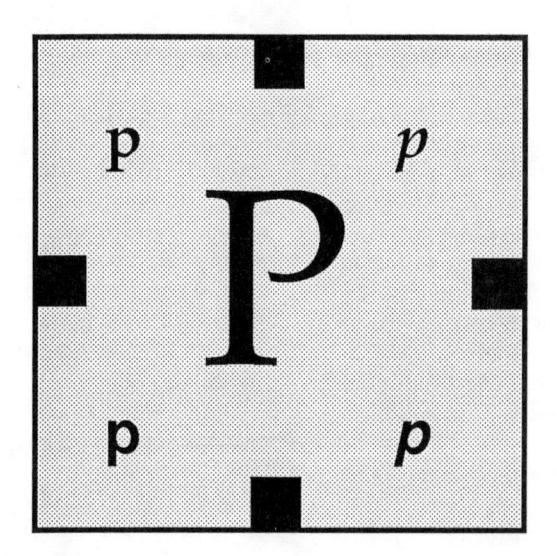

Palimony: Palimony isn't a legal term; it was coined by journalists to describe the division of **property** or **alimony**-like support given by one member of an unmarried couple to the other after they break up.

See also *Cohabitation; Cohabitation Agreement; Marvin v. Marvin;* and *San Sex Marriage.*

In Yugoslavia, cohabitating partners are entitled to receive support and to have their property divided when they break up.

Palmore v. Sidoti: *Palmore v. Sidoti*, 466 U.S. 429 (1984) is a United States Supreme Court decision in which the court ruled that it was unconstitutional for a court to consider race when making a **custody** decision. In *Palmore*, a white couple had **divorced**, and the mother had been awarded custody of their son. She **remarried** a black man and moved to a predominantly black neighborhood. The father filed a **request for modification of custody** based on the **changed circumstance** that the boy was now living with a black man in a black neighborhood. A Florida court granted the modification. The U.S. Supreme Court reversed that decision, ruling that societal stigma, especially a racial one, cannot be the basis for a custody decision.

Parens Patriae: Parens patriae is a Latin phrase meaning "parent of the country," which means that a state may act as the **guardian** of any child within its borders. Parents patriae is also used in a broader sense to describe a state's general obligation toward those who are unable to look after themselves, especially children, but also the mentally disabled. The concept was used by courts under traditional **common law** to provide their authority for making **custody** decisions and other decisions affecting **minors** and adults legally unable to care for themselves. Today, every state has adopted the **Uniform Child Custody Jurisdiction Act (UCCJA)** which explicitly defines the court's power in the area of child custody. Thus, courts today never use parens patriae power to make custody rulings.

Parent Locator Service: Parent locator services have been created by state and federal governments to assist a parent in locating her child's other parent in order to enforce **child support orders**. They also help parents locate missing children who may have been **childnapped** by the other parent. Many parent locator services are associated with district attorney or state's attorney offices.

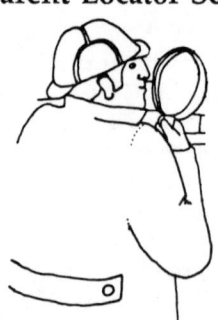

See also *Enforcement of Child Support*.

Parent Moving: See *Geographic Moves: Effect on Custody and Visitation*.

Parental Consent: See *Abortion* and *Age of Consent*.

Parental Contact: See *Visitation*.

Parental Control: Parental control is the right and responsibility a parent has to rear and nurture her child. If parental control is not being exercised, the child may be considered the victim of **child neglect**; if a parent is unable to control her child, the child may be considered **incorrigible**. If a **minor** becomes **emancipated**, he is no longer legally under parental control.

See also *Legal Custody*.

Parental Kidnapping Prevention Act (PKPA): The Parental Kidnapping Prevention Act (28 U.S.C. §1738A and 42 U.S.C. §§ 654, 663) is a federal **statute** enacted in 1980 to address **childnapping** by **non-custodial parents** and inconsistent child **custody** decisions made by state courts. The law provides for the maintenance of a federal **parent locator service**, penalties for kidnapping, and requires states to recognize and enforce the custody decisions of courts in other states, rather than make a second, and possibly inconsistent, decision.

See also *Uniform Child Custody Jurisdiction Act (UCCJA)*.

Parental Liability: Parental liability is the term used to refer to a parent's obligation to pay for damage done by negligent, intentional or criminal acts of his child. In 45 states, parents are responsible for all malicious or willful **property** damage done by their children; in 28 states, parents are liable for all malicious or willful personal injuries inflicted by their children. Eight states obligate parents only when their children have acted illegally. Hawaii and Louisiana hold parents responsible for all **torts** committed by their children. Only Minnesota, New Hampshire, Utah and Washington, D.C. do not hold parents liable at all. All parental liability laws limit the amount of liability to between $300 and $10,000, depending on the state.

Parental liability usually ends when the child reaches the **age of majority** and does not begin until the child reaches somewhere between eight and ten. (No one is liable for damage done by a child younger than eight or so unless the parent was grossly negligent—for example, giving the child a loaded gun.)

See chart, **PARENTAL LIABILITY LAWS.**

Partition: Partition means selling **real property** and dividing the proceeds among the joint owners. A partition **action** is a lawsuit brought by one owner of jointly owned real property to force its sale and split the proceeds in accordance with the state's **property** laws.

Partition actions are commonly brought by a **divorcing** spouse who wants to sell the **family home** when the other spouse doesn't want to. A request for partition may be refused if **custody, visitation** and **child support** have not yet been determined or if selling the home would not be in the **best interest of the child** who has been living there.

Party: A **plaintiff** or **defendant** in a lawsuit (or any person joined in a lawsuit, such as a **pension plan** administrator) is called a party. A party has the right to conduct **discovery** and receive **notice** of all proceedings connected with the lawsuit.

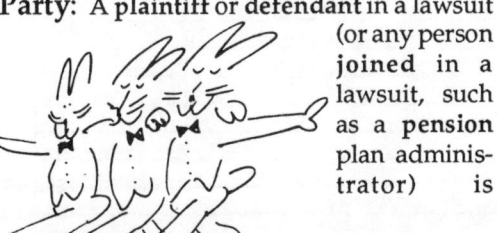

See also *Action* and *Case.*

Past Due Support: See *Arrearage.*

Paternity Action: A court suit filed to have a man declared the father of a child is called a paternity action (or a parentage action, in some states). It can be brought by either the mother or the father. If paternity is established, the court will probably order the father to pay **child support,** and grant him **visitation** rights if he wants them. Today, blood tests can affirmatively determine paternity with a 98% accuracy, and can rule out paternity with 100% accuracy.

Most paternity actions are initiated by welfare officials who provide **Aid to Families With Dependent Children (AFDC)** to the mother and are required by law to seek **reimbursement** from the father. The mother must cooperate in these proceedings; failure to do so can result in a reduction or loss of her AFDC grant.

Pendente Lite: Pendente lite literally means "pending the litigation." When the court makes an **order**, for example for temporary **alimony** or **child support**, which lasts only until the date of a **divorce trial** or until the **parties** to a lawsuit work out a settlement, it is a pendente lite order.

See also *Temporary Provisions for Alimony, Child Support, Custody, Visitation and Property Division.*

Pension/Retirement Benefits: A fund into which payments are made to provide an employee an income after retirement is

PARENTAL LIABILITY LAWS

Parental liability laws impose an obligation on parents to pay for damage done by their children. Four states impose no obligation. Nearly all states impose liability on parents for property damaged caused by their children's malicious or willful (deliberate) acts and many hold parents liable for personal injuries caused by their children's malicious or willful acts. A few states impose liability on parents for the property damage or personal injury caused by their children's illegal acts. And two states impose liability on parents for all property damage or personal injury caused by any tort (including negligent acts) committed by their children. Parental liability ceases in all states when the child reaches 18, except Nebraska (19) and Maine, South Carolina, Vermont and Wyoming (17). Parental liability usually doesn't apply with children under the age of eight, unless the parent was grossly negligent, for example, by giving the child a loaded gun.

State	None	All Torts	Malicious/Willful Property Damage	Illegal Property Damage	Malicious/Willful Personal Injury	Illegal Personal Injury
Alabama			•		•	
Alaska			•			
Arizona			•		•	
Arkansas			•			
California			•		•	
Colorado			•		•	
Connecticut			•		•	
Delaware			•			
Florida			•	•		
Georgia			•			
Hawaii		•				
Idaho			•			
Illinois			•		•	
Indiana			•		•	
Iowa				•		•
Kansas			•		•	
Kentucky			•			
Louisiana		•				
Maine			•		•	
Maryland			•	•	•	•
Massachusetts			•		•	
Michigan			•		•	•
Minnesota	•					
Mississippi			•			
Missouri			•		•	
Montana			•			

PARENTAL LIABILITY LAWS

State	None	All Torts	Malicious/ Willful Property Damage	Illegal Property Damage	Malicious/ Willful Personal Injury	Illegal Personal Injury
Nebraska			•		•	
Nevada			•		•	
New Hampshire	•					
New Jersey			•	•		
New Mexico			•		•	
New York			•	•(1)		
North Carolina			•			
North Dakota			•(2)		•(2)	
Ohio			•		•	
Oklahoma				•		•
Oregon			•		•	
Pennsylvania			•		•	
Rhode Island			•		•	
South Carolina			•	•		
South Dakota			•		•	
Tennessee			•		•	
Texas			•		•	
Utah	•					
Vermont			•			
Virginia			•			
Washington			•		•	
West Virginia			•			
Wisconsin			•		•	
Wyoming			•			
Washington, DC	•					

(1) To a house of worship or the articles inside.
(2) Arising only out of operation of an automobile.

termed a pension or retirement fund. The benefits the employee eventually receives are called pension or retirement payments. Because pensions are deferred employment benefits for work already done, in many **community property** and **equitable distribution states**, the portion of the pension earned during **marriage** is considered **marital property** and subject to division on **divorce**, especially if the pension has already vested.

When a pension has vested, the employee has the right to receive payments (i.e., it can't be taken away), even if he gets fired the next morning or quits the next month. Pensions vest after the employee works for a certain number of years. Many pensions don't vest until after the employee works 15 or 20 years. Other pensions vest gradually, that is, after five years the employee is entitled to a percentage of the pension (e.g., 25%); after ten years, he's entitled to more (e.g., 50%), and then after 15 or 20 years he's entitled to it all.

Once the pension vests, the employee may still have to wait before actually receiving the benefits. Usually, vested pensions do not pay out ("mature") until the worker reaches a certain age, such as 62 or 65. Some employees choose to continue to work even after the pension matures because the pension payments increase the longer the employee works past the maturity date.

Most federal retirement benefits (social security and railroad retirement pensions) always are the **separate property** of the spouse who earned them, no matter what state **property** distribution laws say. Military pensions, however, are subject to state property division laws when a couple divorces. Some states expressly define military pensions as separate property, therefore making them not divisible at divorce; other states define them as marital property, subject to division.

Periodic Support: Occasionally, **alimony** obligations are paid less frequently than monthly. This is called periodic support. Traditionally, periodic support was paid until the recipient died or remarried. Today, however, because alimony is usually paid for a fixed period, periodic support is more like **lump sum support** divided over a few periodic payments.

Permanent Alimony, Child Support, Custody, or Visitation: Permanent **alimony, child support, custody,** or **visitation** is intended to continue at the same payment rate indefinitely into the future or until a time specified in the court **order**.

In reality, however, all orders of child support, custody and visitation are subject to modification upon a showing of **changed circumstance**. Permanent alimony may also be modified, except when it is made nonmodifiable by agreement between the spouses or is part of an **integrated property settlement agreement**.

See also *Request for Modification*.

Permanent Separation: See *Separation*.

Personal Jurisdiction: Personal jurisdiction (also called "in personam jurisdiction") is the power a court has to make **orders** concerning an individual **defendant** in a lawsuit, as opposed to the power the court has to make decisions regarding the subject matter of the lawsuit (which is called **subject-matter jurisdiction**). For a court to obtain personal jurisdiction over a defendant, the defendant must be properly **served** with a **summons** (written **notice** of the lawsuit).

If the defendant lives out of state, the court can only exercise personal jurisdiction over him if the defendant has "minimum contacts" with the state. There is no set number or kind of contacts with a state that gives a court personal jurisdiction; each situation must be analyzed. Going into a state regularly to conduct business is usually sufficient for the court to obtain jurisdiction; sending **child support** payments to a state, without actually visiting the state, however, is not.

See also *Due Process; In Rem Jurisdiction; Jurisdiction;* and *Long-Arm Statute.*

EXAMPLE

Denise and Walter spent their entire married life in Colorado. Denise moved to New Mexico, established **residency**, and sued for divorce. If Walter has virtually no contacts with New Mexico, the New Mexico court has no personal jurisdiction over him. As a practical matter, this means the court may award Denise a **divorce**, but cannot make any decisions affecting the **division of property**, an award of **alimony** or **child support**, or a determination of **custody** and **visitation**. If, however, Walter and Denise spent five weeks every summer during their **marriage** in New Mexico, the court may rule that Walter's contacts with New Mexico are sufficient for there to be personal jurisdiction in New Mexico.

Personal Property: All **property** that is not classified as **real property** is called personal property. It includes such widely diverse items as money, stocks, furniture, cars, bank accounts, **pensions**, jewelry, oil paintings, and patents.

Personal Service: See *Service of Court Papers.*

Petition: See *Complaint.*

Petitioner: See *Plaintiff* and *Appellant.*

Pets: Effect of Divorce: Pets are a part of many **families**. In some **divorces**, spouses argue over who should keep the dogs, cats, rabbits and other pets. Some disagreements are so heated that the **parties** to the divorce cannot make the decision themselves. A growing number of judges (although still very few) are asked to make "custody" and "visitation" **orders** concerning the pets.

Divorce can also affect pets when a family breaks up and is forced to move to smaller living quarters. In this situation, there is often insufficient space for the pets, and they must be sold or given away.

Physical Custody: Physical custody is the right of a parent to have a child live with him. A parent to whom a court has granted physical custody is called the **custodial parent**. Some states recognize the concept of joint physical custody where the child spends approximately half the time in each parent's home.

See also *Birds' Nest Custody; Joint Custody;* and *Legal Custody.*

Physical Incapacity: In some states that allow **fault divorce**, lack of the physical capacity to engage in sexual intercourse is a **ground** for **annulment** or **divorce**, assuming the incapacity was not disclosed to the other spouse before the **marriage**.

Plaintiff: The person who initiates a lawsuit by filing a **complaint** is called the plaintiff. When the document that initiates a lawsuit is called a petition rather than a complaint, the initiating person is usually referred to as the petitioner rather than the plaintiff.

See also *Defendant.*

Pleadings: See *Court Papers.*

Points and Authorities: When a **party** to a lawsuit files a **motion** requesting the judge to rule on some matter, he must usually submit, along with his motion, a short written argument called Points and Authorities explaining why the law authorizes the judge to take the requested action. The term "points and authorities" comes from the fact that the legal discussion makes certain points followed by **citations** to legal authority (usually a court decision or **statute**) supporting each point.

See also *Brief.*

Polygamy: Polygamy is intentionally having more than two spouses at a time. (Intentionally having two spouses at once is called **bigamy**.) Polygamy, as well as bigamy, is a crime in every state. Bigamists and polygamists are usually prosecuted only when they have defrauded their spouses and when prosecutors find out about the multiple **marriages**, which they frequently don't.

Post-Marital or Post-Nuptial Agreement: See *Agreement During Marriage.*

Prayer: The part of a **complaint** which requests the court to grant some specific **judicial relief** (for example, a **divorce**, possession of the **family home**, **child support** or **custody**) is called a prayer or a prayer for relief.

Precedent: Precedent is a legal principle, created by a court decision, which provides an example or authority for judges deciding similar issues later. Generally, decisions of higher courts (within a particular system of courts) are mandatory precedent on lower courts within that system (i.e., the principle announced by a higher court must be followed in later cases). For example, the California Supreme Court decision that unmarried people who live together may enter into **cohabitation agreements** (*Marvin v. Marvin*), is binding on all **appellate courts** and **trial courts** in California (which are lower courts in relation to the California Supreme Court). Similarly, decisions of the U.S. Supreme Court (the highest court in the country) are binding on all other courts in the United States.

Decisions of lower courts are not binding on higher courts, although from time to time a higher court will adopt the reasoning and conclusion of a lower court. Decisions by courts of the same level (usually appellate courts) are considered persuasive authority. That is, they should always be carefully considered by the later court but need not be followed.

As a practical matter, courts can usually find precedent for any direction they want to go in deciding a particular **case**. Accordingly, precedent is used as often to justify a particular outcome in a case as it is to guide the decision.

Preference in Custody: See *Child's Preference in Custody*.

Preliminary Hearing: When a couple **separates** or files for **divorce**, a **party** often needs the immediate intervention of a court to establish **alimony, child support, custody,** and use of **property** (e.g., the car). Couples who are unable to work out arrangements themselves often request a **preliminary hearing** (also called a "temporary hearing") before the judge.

See also *Order to Show Cause Hearing* and *Temporary Provisions for Alimony, Child Support, Custody, Visitation and Property Division*.

Pre-Marital Agreement: See *Agreement Prior to Marriage* ar *Uniform Pre-Marital Agreement Act*.

Pre-Marital Sex: See *Fornication*.

Pre-Nuptial Agreement: See *Agreement Prior to Marriage* and *Uniform Pre-Marital Agreement Act*.

Presumption: A fact assumed to be true under the law is called a presumption. (For example, a criminal defendant is presumed to be innocent until the prosecuting attorney proves beyond a reasonable doubt that she is guilty.) Presumptions are used to relieve a **party** from having to actually prove the truth of the fact being presumed. Once a presumption is relied on by one party, however, the other party is normally allowed to offer **evidence** to disprove (rebut) the presumption. (The presumption is known as a "rebuttable presumption.") In essence, then, what a presumption really does is place the obligation of presenting evidence (see *burden of proof*) concerning a particular fact on a particular party.

The law does not allow some presumptions to be disproved, no matter how strong the evidence to the contrary. These are called "irrebuttable" or "conclusive" presumptions. The presumption that a child born to a **married** couple is considered the child of the husband is often irrebuttable (that is, you can't argue with it even if you can prove the husband isn't the father). A growing number of courts, however, have held irrebuttable presumptions to be unconstitutional (too unfair, and thus a denial of **due process**), especially in the area of **paternity**, because of blood tests which can exclude paternity with 100% accuracy.

Presumption of Decreased Need Caused by Cohabitation: In some states, an **alimony** recipient who begins **cohabiting** (in this context, living intimately with a person of the opposite sex) is automatically **presumed** to need less alimony than originally **awarded**. If the recipient objects, it is her burden to show that her needs have not decreased.

In a few states, cohabitation brings about a **termination of alimony**, if the paying spouse can show that the recipient spouse and new lover live together, share expenses, and are generally recognized as a couple.

See chart, **FACTORS IN SETTING AND TERMINATING ALIMONY** under Alimony.

Primary Residential Custody: See *Physical Custody*.

Primogeniture: Primogeniture laws were laws which gave first born sons the exclusive right to **inherit** their fathers' **property** (their mothers did not own property). These laws no longer exist in the United States.

Privacy, Right of: The right of privacy, although not expressly provided for in the United States Constitution, stems from the Bill of Rights (the first ten amendments to the constitution) as a whole. In the **family law** context, the right of privacy currently includes:
• the right to have an **abortion**
• the right to procreate
• the right to use **birth control** (see *Griswold v. Connecticut*)
• the right to view some kinds of legally "obscene" materials in one's home, free from government intrusion.

Because there is no express right of privacy, its scope can change depending on who is sitting on the U.S. Supreme Court. In addition, some state constitutions, such as California's, do contain an actual right of privacy, and thus add independent safeguards against intrusion by state governments.

Private Adoption: An **adoption** arranged privately between the birth mother and the adoptive parent(s) rather than through a public agency is termed a private (or independent) adoption. A court must approve a private adoption for it to be valid.

Privileged Communication: In judicial proceedings, the law allows people to refuse to disclose the contents of certain "privileged" conversations and writings. Communications between an attorney and client, husband and wife, clergyperson and penitent, and doctor and patient are all privileged. In a few states, the privilege extends to a psychotherapist and patient.

To qualify for privileged status, communications must generally be made in a private setting (i.e., in a context where confidentiality could reasonably be expected). The privilege is lost (waived) when all or part of the communication is disclosed to a third person.

These privileges are held by the client (but not the lawyer), the patient (but not the doctor or psychotherapist), the speaking (but not the spoken to) spouse and both the clergyperson and the penitent. The lawyer, doctor, psychotherapist and spoken to spouse, however, cannot reveal the communication without the other person's consent. The client, patient, speaking spouse, clergyperson and penitent may waive it (i.e., testify about the privileged conversation) and also may prevent the other person from disclosing the information.

EXAMPLE

Sandy has a budding marijuana brownie business which she operates out of her home. Sandy has told her husband Doug about her endeavors. All private conversations between them are privileged; that is, if Sandy is ever prosecuted for her business, she can prevent Doug from disclosing what he knows. If, however, Sandy told her friend about part of a conversation she and Doug had, the privilege has been waived (as to what she told the friend), and Doug can be forced to testify.

EXAMPLE

Sue and Martin are **divorcing**. When Martin first left Sue, he emptied out a joint bank account and placed that money in a separate account in another state. He refuses to tell Sue where the money is, but he has told his lawyer, Ann. The discussion between Martin and Ann is privileged, and unless Martin authorizes Ann to tell Sue where the money is, or unless Martin himself tells another person about his conversation with Ann, Ann cannot be forced to disclose the information.

Probate Court: Probate is the court process by which the **assets** of a deceased person are distributed, either by the terms of his **will** or by **intestate succession**. Most states have created special courts, or special divisions of the **trial courts**, to handle matters involving probating wills, estates, trusts and special **family law** matters like **guardianships**. These courts are often called probate courts; in some states, such as New York, they are called Surrogate's Courts.

Probation Department Investigation: When a child is suspected of being abused, neglected, or **incorrigible** (beyond his parents' control), or when an **adoption** or **guardianship** is pending, the court handling the matter will normally want the **family** environment investigated. The investigation usually consists of a series of visits to the home by a social worker who physically views the surroundings and talks to whomever is present. Most visits are scheduled; often, however, the social worker makes at least one unannounced visit. Depending on the state and kind of case, the investigation will be conducted by the juvenile probation department, the adult probation department, or the welfare department.

Pro Bono: When a lawyer takes a **case** for free or for a nominal fee, it is called taking the case "pro bono."

Process and Process Server: Any court document, carrying the court seal or **clerk's** signature, that must be properly **served** on (i.e., given to) the **party** or witness named in the document is called a process document or process. A subpoena (a document requiring the appearance of a person or the production of documents at a **hearing**) and a **summons** (notification of a lawsuit) are examples of court process. Rules as to who can serve process and how it must be done vary. Some states allow only sheriffs, marshals and constables to serve process. Other states also authorize registered process servers (often private investigators), and a few states allow service by anyone 18 or over who is not a party to the **case**.

See also *Accepting Service of Court Papers; Quashing Service of Process;* and *Service of Court Papers*.

Professional Degree or License: Some spouses financially, as well as emotionally support the other spouse through professional, graduate or trade school, and upon **divorce**, want a share in the value (increased earning capacity) of the other's degree or license. Courts in some states order the student-spouse to **reimburse** the other for the cost of support while the student was in school. Other states consider the efforts made helping a spouse through school in **awarding alimony**. New York and Washington courts have ruled that a professional degree or license acquired during the **marriage** constitutes **marital property** to be valued and divided upon divorce.

See also *Appraisal; Non-Monetary Contributions to Marriage;* and *Valuation of Property*.

Proof Of Service: A proof of service is a **court paper** filed by a **process server** as evidence that she **served** the witness or **party** to the lawsuit with the court papers she was instructed to serve.

See also *Service of Court Papers*.

Pro Per: Pro per (or pro se) means "for yourself" and refers to a **party** to a lawsuit who represents herself, rather than being represented by a lawyer.

Property: Virtually anything one can own is considered property. Generally, we think of items with monetary value as property, but valueless items can also constitute property.

Property is classified as either **real property** (basically, real estate) or **personal property** (everything else). It can also be characterized as tangible items (what you can see and touch, like furniture, houses, cars, cats, clothing, jewelry, record albums, photographs, bank accounts, and boats) and intangible items (like an interest in a future **pension** right, the right to receive royalties or benefits, and stock shares).

The item of property on the east African coast most valued is a coconut tree.

Most property accumulated by a couple during a **marriage** (including personal injury or worker's compensation awards in a few states) is called **marital property** which, in accordance with the state property laws, is divided upon **divorce**. In all states, a spouse may have **separate property** which is is not subject to division upon divorce. Property accumulated after **separation** is usually separate property, as are most government benefits, and property owned by a person before marriage or received as a gift or **inheritance**. In most states, a personal injury or worker's compensation award is considered the separate property of the spouse receiving it.

In many states, **debts** are also considered property (actually "negative" property) and are divisible at divorce.

RELATED TERMS

Agreement Before Marriage
Agreement During Marriage
Appraisal
Asset
Business Good Will
Business Value as Divisible Asset Upon Divorce
Characterization of Property Acquired During Marriage
Cohabitation Agreement
Commingling
Common Law Property
Community Debts
Community Estate
Community Property
Debts: Effect on Alimony and Child Support
Debts Incurred Before Marriage
Debts Incurred Between Separation and Divorce
Debts Incurred During Marriage
Division of Property
Divorce Agreement
Equitable Distribution
Equity
Family Living Expenses
Improvements to Property
Integrated Property Settlement Agreement
Joint Ownership
Joint Tenancy
Management and Control of Property
Marvin v. Marvin
Non-Monetary Contributions to Marriage
Professional Degree or License
Quasi-Community Property
Quasi-Marital Property
Reimbursement
Tax Refunds
Temporary Provisions for Alimony, Child Support, Custody, Visitation and Property Division
Tenancy by the Entirety
Tenancy in Common
Title to Property
Tracing of Funds
Transmutation Doctrine
Uniform Marriage and Divorce Act
Valuation of Property

Property Division: See *Division of Property*.

Property Settlement Agreement: See *Divorce Agreement*.

Pro Se: See *Pro Per*.

Protective Order: A protective order is any **order** issued by a court which is meant to protect a person from harm or harassment. A protective order is commonly used to protect a **party** or witness from unreasonable or invasive **discovery** requests (e.g., harassing questions in a **deposition**, or an unnecessary medical examination). Less often, a **temporary restraining order** issued to prohibit **domestic violence** is referred to as a protective order.

Provocation: Provocation is the inciting of another to do a certain act. In states which permit **fault divorce**, provocation may constitute a **defense to divorce**. For example, if the spouse suing for **divorce** claims that the other spouse abandoned her, her spouse might defend the suit on the ground that she provoked the abandonment.

Proxy Marriage: A proxy marriage is a **marriage** where someone is permitted to stand in for and represent an absent bride or groom at a **wedding**. Proxy marriages are usually resorted to only in extreme circumstances—for example, when one person is detained for an indefinite period in prison or in a foreign country.

Proxy marriages were not uncommon during World War II and the Korean War. States allowed women who discovered they were pregnant after their fiances had been sent overseas to have a friend or relative stand in for the groom. Today, only a few states allow proxy marriages.

Psychological Parent: An adult who is not legally responsible for the care, **custody** and support of a child, but who has established a significant emotional bond with the child such that termination of the contact between them would be detrimental to the child, is referred to by the courts in some states as the child's psychological parent. A few courts give psychological parents **visitation** rights with the children.

See also *Co-Parent*.

Public Adoption: See *Agency Adoption*.

Punitive Damages: Punitive damages are damages (money) **awarded** by a court to the prevailing **party** in a lawsuit to punish the other party for her behavior and set an example for others. Regular (compensatory) damages are awarded to compensate a party for loss he has suffered. Most **family law** cases do not include punitive damages because these **cases** mainly involve dividing **property**, deciding **child support** and **alimony**, awarding **custody**, or granting **adoptions**. A few family law cases, however, especially those for monetary compensation where there has been **domestic violence** or where one party has committed **fraud** against the other concerning **marital property**, may include punitive damage awards.

Putative Father: A putative father is the man named the father of a child born to unwed parents, but for whom **paternity** has not yet been established.

See also *Unwed Father* and *Unwed Mother*.

Putative Marriage: When two people reasonably and honestly think that they are married, but for some technical reason are not (e.g., the clergyperson who married them was not capable of performing a **marriage**), the couple is said to have a putative (meaning "reputed" or "supposed") marriage. In virtually all situations, the law treats putative marriages the same as any valid marriage. A putative marriage need not be "formalized," though the couple may do so by repeating the marriage ceremony.

To terminate a putative marriage, the couple must get a **divorce**, where the court will determine **alimony, child support, custody, visitation,** and the **division of property** as if the couple had been actually married.

See also *Common Law Marriage* and *Putative Spouse*.

Putative Spouse: A person who reasonably but erroneously thinks he is married is called a putative spouse. If one spouse believes the **marriage** is valid while the other knows it is not, the innocent or putative (meaning "reputed" or "supposed") spouse is entitled to the legal rights and privileges normally enjoyed by a regularly married spouse (e.g., the right to **alimony** or **property** division). The guilty spouse (the one who knew the marriage was not valid) may not have these same rights.

See also *Putative Marriage*.

In Poland, unless a couple prior to marriage elects that the children will bear their mother's surname, they must bear their father's.

Quashing Service of Process: When a person who has been **served** with **court papers** believes that the service was not made according to law, he can ask the court (by filing a **motion**) to invalidate or "quash" the service. If the motion is successful, service must be tried again. The reasons a court might quash service of process include improper service techniques (such as leaving the papers on a doorstep) or service outside the **jurisdiction** of the court.

See also *Service of Court Papers*.

Quasi-Community Property: Quasi means "like." Quasi-community property is a term used in only California and Arizona. It refers to the **property** accumulated by a **married** couple living in a non-community property state when the couple later moves to California or Arizona. (Property accumulated in another **community property** state during a marriage already is and remains **community property** when the couple moves to California or Arizona.)

At **divorce**, quasi-community property is treated exactly like community property.

EXAMPLE

Harold and Darlene married in Atlanta and bought a house, two boats, furniture and a car. Later, they moved to Tucson and got divorced. The Arizona courts will categorize the house, boats, furniture and car bought in Atlanta—which would have been community property had the couple been living in Arizona—as quasi-community property. It will be treated, for purposes of division, just like community property.

Quasi-community property rules operate a little differently when someone dies. **Personal property** (wherever situated) is treated like community property. **Real property**, however, is treated according to the laws of the state in which it is located.

EXAMPLE

Harold and Darlene married in Atlanta, bought and furnished a condo there and another in Tucson. After a few years in the southeast, they moved to Tucson and Harold died. In this situation, Arizona courts will treat the furnishings in the Atlanta condo, and the Tucson condo and its furnishings as quasi-community property. The Atlanta condo itself, however, will be distributed according to Georgia property laws.

Quasi-Marital Property: Quasi means "like." Quasi-marital property is the term used to describe any **assets, property** or **debts** accumulated during a **putative marriage.** In most states, quasi-marital property is treated the same as **marital property** for purposes of property division upon **divorce** or **separation,** and for property distribution upon the death without a **will** of one of the spouses.

Quitclaim Deed: See *Deeds.*

Race: Effect on Custody: See *Palmore v. Sidoti*.

Race: Effect on Marriage: See *Miscegenation*.

Real Estate: See *Real Property*.

A married woman in the Conja state of Ghana is given a plot in her husband's farm to plant beans, peppers and okra.

Real Property: Land and structures permanently attached to the land (houses, shed, pools, etc.) are referred to as real property or real estate. All other kinds of property are called **personal property**. Mobile homes are usually considered personal property unless they have been rendered immobile by being placed on a foundation. Crops are real property while they are growing and personal property after they have been harvested.
See also *Property*.

Reasonable Visitation: When a court determines the **visitation** rights of a **noncustodial** parent, it usually orders visitation at reasonable times and places, leaving it to the parents to work out a more precise schedule. If the parents are unable to do so, the court will impose specific terms (e.g., every other weekend). The reasonable times and places method allows the parents to exercise flexibility by taking into consideration both parents' and the child's schedules. For the reasonable times and places approach to succeed, however, the parents must cooperate and communicate with each other frequently. If the hostility between the parents is so severe that the constant contact between them may be of detriment to the child, they may be better off with a fixed visitation schedule.

Rebuttal: To rebut generally means to contest a statement or **evidence** presented by another. During a **trial**, the presentation of evidence by the **plaintiff** to contest the evidence presented by the **defendant** is called the rebuttal.

Reconciliation: Reconciliation, in the **family law** context, is the getting back together of a couple who have continuously lived apart for a period of time. Reconciliation requires more than occasional sex or living together; it requires that the couple actually intend to resume their **marriage**. If a judge determines that **parties** to a **divorce** have reconciled, a pending divorce **complaint** may be denied. If, however, an interlocutory judgment of divorce has been issued prior to the reconciliation, the judgment's terms concerning the **division of property** will remain in effect unless the spouses seek to have it set aside. Many states require a **waiting period** between the **interlocutory** and final judgments to give the parties an opportunity to reconcile. Once the divorce becomes final, however, the marriage cannot be reconciled (i.e., the couple must **remarry**).

See also *Debts Incurred Between Separation and Divorce.*

Recusal: Recusal is the process by which a judge voluntarily removes himself from hearing a particular **case** because of **bias**, conflict of interest, relation to a **party**, attorney or witness, or for any other reason.

Reduction of Alimony or Child Support: See *Request for Modification of Alimony, Child Support, Custody or Visitation.*

Rehabilitative Alimony: Rehabilitative **alimony** is alimony paid to an unemployed spouse on the condition that the spouse seek employment or training so she can become self-supporting. If the supported spouse has still not found employment at the time the alimony is to terminate, the court may grant an **extension of alimony** if it finds that the spouse was doing all she reasonably could under the circumstances to become self-supporting.

See also *Termination of Alimony.*

Reimbursement: Reimbursement is the right to be repaid for money paid out. This becomes a core concept when a couple **divorces**. This is because when a **marriage** is working, the spouses don't pay too much attention to **property** ownership laws. Money comes in and money goes out, and whether the money is **marital property** or **separate property** isn't important. If the marriage fails, however, whose money or property was spent by which spouse, and for what purpose, suddenly becomes important. One or both of the spouses will want the full benefit of the state's property ownership laws. Thus an accounting of money earned and money spent during the marriage will be necessary.

If during the marriage, one spouse contributed her separate property to marital property or to the other spouse's separate property, she may be entitled to reimbursement for the amount. Or, if one spouse paid a separate **debt** of the other, he may be reimbursed for the amount paid.

In a different context, reimbursement refers to the actions taken by local welfare departments that pay **Aid to Families with Dependent Children (AFDC)** to collect from the non-supporting parent, the money paid to the other parent and the children.

See also *Commingling; Debts Incurred Before Marriage; Debts Incurred Between Separation and Divorce; Debts Incurred During Marriage;* and *Tracing of Funds.*

Reimbursement Alimony: See *Professional Degree or License.*

Relative Income and Assets: When setting **child support**, a court normally considers the relative income and **assets** of both spouses. If the **custodial parent** earns more than the **non-custodial parent**, child support may be zero. In the real world, however, the custodial parent is usually the mother and normally has much less income than the non-custodial father. Accordingly, when courts consider the relative assets and income of the **parties**, they usually end up awarding child support to the custodial parent.

Relevancy: Relevancy is the logical connection between facts or statements, especially those offered as **evidence** in court. Before evidence is admitted during a **trial** or **hearing**, it must be shown to be relevant to the issues in the **case**. Thus, the fact that a spouse has three bank accounts is irrelevant to the issues in a **custody** hearing, but may be quite relevant in one distributing the **marital property**.

Remand: When an **appellate court** sends an appealed **case** back to the **trial court** for further action, the case is said to be remanded. This usually happens if the trial judge has made an error which requires a new **trial** or **hearing**. If, for example, a trial court refused to allow a **party** to introduce certain **evidence** (believing it to inadmissible under the **hearsay** rule), but the appellate court decided that the evidence should have been admitted and that the exclusion of the evidence was prejudicial to the party offering it (i.e., the result might have been different had the evidence been admitted), the appellate court would likely remand the case for **new trial** and order the evidence introduced.

See also *Appeal.*

Remarriage: Remarriage is a subsequent **marriage** by a once married person. In many states, a **divorced** person must wait a certain number of days (20 days to 18 months, depending on the state) after her divorce becomes final before marrying again.

See also *Entry of Judgment* and *Nunc Pro*

See also *Entry of Judgment* and *Nunc Pro Tunc*.

In West Germany, a woman must wait ten months after a divorce or annulment before remarrying unless she gives birth during the waiting period.

Remarriage: Effect On Alimony and Child Support: See *Additional Income from Remarriage*.

Request for Change in Alimony or Child Support: See *Request for Modification of Alimony, Child Support, Custody or Visitation*.

Request for Change in Custody or Visitation: See *Request for Modification of Alimony, Child Support, Custody or Visitation*.

Request for Default: See *Default Divorce*.

Request for Inspection: See *Discovery*.

Request for Modification of Alimony, Child Support, Custody or Visitation: When an ex-spouse or parent wants to change an existing **court** order affecting **alimony**, **child support**, **custody**, or **visitation**, he must file a **motion** requesting a modification of the order from the court that issued it, usually on the ground of **changed circumstance**.

Court approval is required for modification. If the **parties** agree on a modification, the court is likely to routinely approve it, as long as the child support included appears adequate. Parties may think that if they agree, getting court approval is not necessary, but if relations later sour, the absence of court approval may cause great difficulty in enforcing the modified agreement.

Request for Production of Documents: See *Discovery*.

Residency: Effect on Marriage and Divorce: To be a resident of a state is simply to live there; to be a domiciliary of a state is to live there intending to remain indefinitely (as opposed to being on vacation or temporary assignment). States require a spouse to be a domiciliary of a state before filing for a **divorce** there. Confusingly, this domiciliary requirement is often termed a residency requirement, making the two terms virtually synonymous in the real world. States do not require someone who wants to file for a divorce to prove that he is a domiciliary; instead, the state just looks to the fact that he is residing there as an indication that he plans to stay indefinitely.

Most states also require that someone live in the state for a certain period of time (often six months) before filing for divorce. This is called a durational residency requirement. No state has a residency requirement for getting married.

See also *Travel: Effect on Residency*.

See chart, **DURATIONAL RESIDENCY REQUIREMENTS**.

Residency of Minor: An unemancipated **minor** is considered to be a resident of the same state as her **custodial parent** or **guardian**. Emancipated minors are treated like adults and establish their residency by where they live and intend to remain.

Respondent: See *Appellee* and *Defendant*.

Responsible Parent: Under federal **child support** enforcement laws, a responsible parent is a parent legally obligated to provide support for an unemancipated **minor**.

Responsive Pleading: The term responsive pleading is used to describe any **court paper** filed by a **defendant** in direct response to the **complaint** or petition filed by the **plaintiff**. An **answer** is the typical responsive pleading. Others include various **motions**, such as a motion to **quash service of process** or a motion to dismiss the complaint.

Restraining Order: See *Temporary Restraining Order*.

Restricted Visitation: See *Supervised Visitation*.

Retirement Benefits: See *Pensions/Retirement Benefits*.

Retroactive Application of Laws: A **statute** passed by a legislature usually states that it shall only apply after a certain date. Occasionally, though, laws are made retroactive—that is, they apply to events that happened before the law was passed. (Criminal laws are never retroactive—the legislature cannot make a past act a crime.) If the statute itself doesn't indicate the date it is to become effective, courts normally interpret it to have future effect only.

EXAMPLE

Assume that the Minnesota legislature passes a law requiring a couple to undergo a blood test as a requirement of being married. The legislature intends that it apply to couples both planning to marry and already married. (Currently, Minnesota does not require **blood tests before marriage**.) Applying the law to already married couples is a retroactive application of the law. A married Minnesotan might challenge the law arguing that applying it to her is unconstitutional because she had no expectation of ever having to undergo a blood test as a requirement of being married in Minnesota.

Retroactive Modification of Alimony or Child Support: In theory, courts are supposed to refuse to retroactively modify an **alimony** or **child support**

DURATIONAL RESIDENCY REQUIREMENTS

The durational residency requirement is the length of time the plaintiff (or the couple when they are filing jointly) must live in a state before filing for divorce.

None	6 Weeks	60 Days	90 Days	6 Months or 180 Days	12 Months or 1 Year
Alaska	Idaho	Arkansas	Arizona	Alabama	Connecticut
South Dakota	Nevada	Kansas	Colorado	California	Iowa
Washington		Wyoming	Illinois	Delaware	Louisiana
			Missouri	Florida	Maryland
			Montana	Georgia	Massachusetts
			Utah	Hawaii	Michigan
				Indiana	Nebraska
				Kentucky	New Hampshire
				Maine	New Jersey
				Minnesota	New York
				Mississippi	Rhode Island
				New Mexico	South Carolina
				North Carolina	West Virginia
				North Dakota	
				Ohio	
				Oklahoma	
				Oregon	
				Pennsylvania	
				Tennessee	
				Texas	
				Vermont	
				Virginia	
				Wisconsin	
				Washington, DC	

obligation. This means if a person has been unable to pay support, he may petition the court for a reduction (see *request for modification)*, but even if the court reduces future payments, it should hold him liable for the full amount of support **due and owing**.

Unfortunately, however, many courts do not follow this rule. Although the courts will state that they refuse to make retroactive modifications, they frequently excuse payors from some of the **arrearages**. The courts' reasoning is that if the recipients survived the months (or years) without the support, they truly can get by without it.

EXAMPLE

Joe has a child support obligation of $300 per month. Joe is laid off of his job, and six months pass before he finds another one with comparable pay. Although Joe could seek a downwards **temporary modification** on the grounds of diminished income, he lets the matter slide and fails to pay any support during the six-month period. If Joe's ex-wife later brings Joe into court to collect the $1,800 **arrearage**, Joe's wife will argue that he should not be allowed to obtain a retroactive ruling excusing him from making the earlier payments.

Reversal: If an **appellate court** rules that a trial **court** or lower appellate court made errors that may have caused an incorrect outcome in a **case**, the appellate court can do a number of things, including:

- reverse (wipe out) the outcome and send the case back for a **new trial**, if the error occurred during **trial**
- substitute a new decision, if the error occurred at the first **appeal**
- or modify the outcome, for example reduce the amount of damages (see *actual damages* and *punitive damages).*

Revised Uniform Reciprocal Enforcement of Support Act (RURESA): This **uniform statute** (or its predecessor, the Uniform Reciprocal Enforcement of Support Act), is found in every state. It permits a parent who is owed **child support** to collect it by using the court in her state to enforce her child support **order** against the other parent living in another state. The court in the state where the recipient parent lives contacts a court in the other parent's state, which in turn requires the parent to pay. This procedure is free for the **party** seeking support.

As a practical matter, this procedure often falls short of its stated goals. District attorneys commonly give these **cases** low priority and often have large backlogs of pending RURESA cases. Also, when the party who owes the support is haled into court halfway across the country, judges often do not order payment of very much support. This is because they have very little information and only one parent before them, who is generally more convincing than the papers in the file which have been forwarded from the court in the state where the parent seeking the support lives.

Right of Privacy: See *Privacy, Right of.*

-157-

Right of Survivorship: See *Joint Tenancy*.

Roe v. Wade: See *Abortion*.

Rules of Court: See *Court Rules*.

Rules of Evidence: Rules of evidence (found in the **statutes** and **court rules** of each state) determine what **evidence** may be admitted into a **trial** or **hearing** and under what circumstances.

RELATED TERMS

Admissible Evidence
Admission
Authentication of Evidence
Character Evidence
Circumstantial Evidence
Expert Witness
Hearsay
Immaterial Evidence
Incompetent Evidence
Irrelevant Evidence
Privileged Communication
Relevancy

Ruling: Any decision made by a judge during the course of **litigation** is called a ruling. For example, if a court grants a request (**motion**) for temporary **child support** of $300 per month, that is a ruling. If a court grants a father **custody** after a **trial** on the custody issue, that is a ruling. Also, if a court sustains or overrules an objection to **evidence** raised during a trial, that is a ruling. The decision of an **appellate court** is also referred to as a ruling.

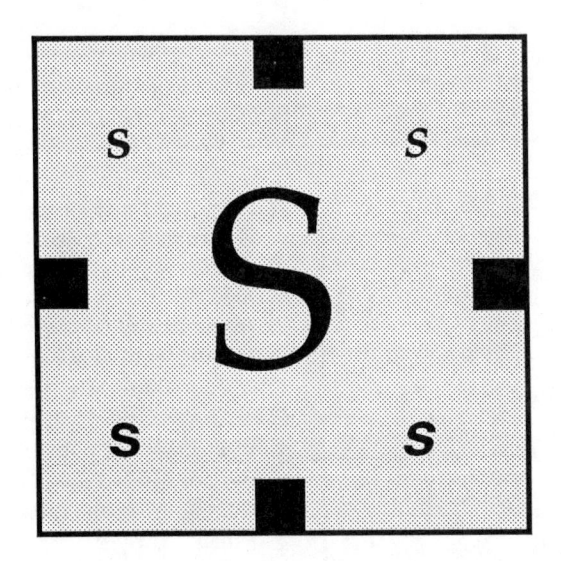

Same-Sex Marriage: All states restrict **marriages** to the union of one man and one woman. Same-sex couples, therefore, cannot marry. One same-sex couple was granted a marriage license and underwent a **wedding**, but state officials refused to recognize the marriage. Denying lesbian and gay couples the right to marry means they cannot obtain the legal and economic benefits of marriage, such as:

- filing joint income tax returns
- claiming dependency benefits
- **inheriting** from each other under state **intestate succession** laws (although they may leave each other **property** in their **wills**)
- and obtaining family rates for insurance, mortgage, loans and credit.

They are also denied the emotional and psychological benefits. To compensate, many lesbian and gay couples enter into **cohabitation agreements**, purchase property together, name each other as beneficiaries in wills and insurance policies, and participate in "union" ceremonies.

Sanctions: When a court concludes that a **party** to a lawsuit or an attorney has misused the legal process in some way, a penalty called a sanction may be imposed. Common sanctions are fines (to be paid to the other side or to the court), limitations on a party's ability to make certain arguments or to conduct **discovery**, and in extreme cases, a finding of **contempt of court**.

> **EXAMPLE**
>
> Nate has sued Lois for a breach of their **cohabitation agreement**. Lois scheduled Nate's deposition, but Nate did not appear, nor did he call to say he needed to reschedule or couldn't attend. As a result, Lois was out the money she paid the **court reporter** and her attorney. To recover it, she brings a **discovery motion**, asking the court to order Nate to appear for his deposition and also asking the court to impose sanctions against Nate in the amount of money his non-cooperation cost her.

Seduction Lawsuit: A seduction lawsuit is brought by a father against a man who has induced the father's unmarried daughter into having sexual intercourse by means of promises, bribes, etc. (but not force), regardless of whether the woman is a **minor** or an adult. Seduction suits are based on the notion that once an unmarried woman has had sexual intercourse, it is more difficult for her father to "marry her off." Seduction suits have been done away with in most states.

See also *Heart-Balm Lawsuits*.

Self-Supporting: See *Ability to be Self-Supporting* and *Emancipated Minor*.

Separate Maintenance: In some states, a spouse may obtain separate maintenance (**alimony**) from her husband while she lives apart from him, even though no **divorce** has been granted.

See also *Legal Separation*.

Separate Property: In all states, a married person is permitted to treat certain types of **earnings** and **assets** as his separate property. This means that the **property** can be disposed of (sold, given away, left in a **will**) without the consent of the other spouse, and upon **divorce** the property is not divided under the state's property distribution laws, but rather is kept by the spouse who owns it. By contrast, most property accumulated during **marriage** is called **marital property**. Marital property in most states is divided equally or equitably (fairly) upon divorce.

In the **community property states**, Arizona, California, Idaho, Louisiana, Nevada, New Mexico, Texas and Washington, and in Wisconsin (a modified community property state), the following is considered separate property:

• property accumulated by a spouse before marriage
• property accumulated during marriage with pre-marital earnings or with the proceeds of the sale of pre-marital property
• gifts directed to only one spouse, whenever received
• **inheritances**, whenever received
• and property acquired after permanent **separation**.

In the **equitable distribution states** (all the states not listed above except Mississippi), the laws usually define most earnings and property acquired during marriage as marital property. Some property is separate, however, including:

- property accumulated by a spouse before marriage
- gifts directed to only one spouse, whenever received
- and inheritances, whenever received.

In the **common law property state** (Mississippi), all property is the separate property of the acquiring spouse unless a document showing **title to property** indicates otherwise. This means that the court has no authority to divide that property on divorce.

Separation: There are five types of separation:

- **Legal separation** involves obtaining a court **order** of separation, usually instead of obtaining a **divorce**.
- **Living apart** is when spouses either no longer reside in the same dwelling, or do live in the same house but have ended virtually all relations. (A court usually considers a couple still living together separated if the couple intends to be separated, have stopped communicating, and have stopped sexual relations.)
- A trial separation is when a couple lives apart for a test period—that is, to decide whether to permanently go separate ways or to get back together (called **reconciliation**).
- A permanent separation is when a couple decides to split up. It may follow a trial separation, or may begin immediately when the couple starts living apart. In many states, all **assets** received and most **debts** incurred after permanent separation are the **separate property** or responsibility of the spouse incurring them.
- Separation may also be a basis for a no-fault divorce; the length of the separation required varies between six months and five years.

Separation Agreement: If a couple agrees to all the terms of a **legal separation**, or agrees to **live apart** for a lengthy period of time in contemplation of **divorce**, the parties often write and sign a separation agreement which settles the **property**, **custody**, **alimony** and **child support** issues between them. The agreement should be presented to the court for approval if it is part of a legal separation. The agreement becomes part of the legal separation **order** and does away with the necessity of having a **trial** on the issues covered by the agreement. It serves the same purpose as a divorce agreement except that the couple does not obtain a divorce at that time.

The term separation agreement is also used to refer to agreements made by couples living apart which are later incorporated into divorce agreements.

Separation from Bed and Board: See *Legal Separation*.

Sequestration: Sequestration is the taking of **property** by a government official to satisfy a **debt**, including **child support** or **alimony arrearages**. A person owed money must first obtain an **order** from the court entitling her to the money owed. (With child support or alimony, this often is done through an **order to show cause** or **contempt of court hearing**.) Once the person owed the debt has the court order, she presents it to a government official (usually a sheriff, marshal or constable), along with the identification of the property to be sequestered in order to satisfy the debt. The sheriff then takes the property from the debtor and delivers it to the person owed.

See also *Wage Attachment*.

Sequestration is also used in **trials** to mean that witnesses are excluded from the courtroom (sequestered) until it is their turn to testify, and in **jury trials** to mean that jury members are kept together (and not allowed to go home) while they are deliberating.

Serve: When a person has been provided with formal **notice** of the filing of a lawsuit (i.e., that he has been sued), of a court **hearing** or **trial**, or ordering him to attend a hearing, trial or **deposition**, he is said to have been served.

See *Service of Court Papers*.

Service by Mail: See *Service of Court Papers*.

Service by Publication: See *Service of Court Papers*.

Service of Court Papers: Service of court papers (also referred to as service of process or service) is the delivery of **court papers** to a **party**, witness, or other person who has a stake in the **case**. Every state has detailed laws spelling out just how the papers may be delivered, and by whom.

In most cases, including **divorces**, the first papers that must be served are the **summons** and **complaint**. These documents give the **defendant notice** that the lawsuit has been filed and what the **plaintiff** is seeking (for example, a divorce). The court cannot proceed unless the plaintiff properly serves the defendant with these papers. There are five major types of service:

• Personal service—When the person served is physically handed court papers notifying her that she has been sued, she is said to have been personally served. With almost all lawsuits, the complaint and summons must be personally served. If the defendant is not personally served, the court cannot take any action in the **case** (because there is no **personal jurisdiction**), unless the plaintiff can show that personal service was impossible.

• Service by mail—Once a party has been properly served with the complaint and summons, most future court papers in the lawsuit may be served on the parties by first-class mail. Most states require that someone other than a party to the **action** do the actual mailing and file a **proof of service** with the court.

• Service by publication—When the whereabouts of a defendant are unknown, or personal service within the state is impossible, a court may allow the defendant to be served with notice of the lawsuit by publishing the notice in a newspaper of general circulation. As a general matter, this type of service is only allowed in cases involving **property** and status (personal relationships affected by the law). Thus divorces and certain **adoptions** (status) and **partition** suits (property) may be allowed to proceed after service by publication.

- Nail and mail—Nail and mail service is the posting of the notice on the person's home and then mailing him a copy (hence nailing and mailing), and is often used in eviction lawsuits.

- Substituted service—In some states, substituted service is any method of service a court allows when personal service is impossible or impracticable (such as service by publication, mail, or nail and mail). In other states, such as California, substituted service is leaving the court papers with a responsible person at the defendant's home or business and then mailing the defendant a copy.

In most divorce cases, if a divorce is all that is being sought, service often can be made by mail or publication. If, however, **alimony**, **child support**, **custody**, **visitation** or a **division of property** is being sought in addition to the divorce itself, most states require personal service on the defendant. In either case, if the defendant's whereabouts are unknown, service by publication is often the only available method.

It is common in many states for the defendant to agree to voluntarily accept the papers. This means the papers are mailed to or left at her home, and she returns a signed and dated form to the plaintiff, acknowledging that she received the papers (this is called *accepting service of court papers*).

After the defendant has been served, she usually files an **answer** or other response. She must serve this on the plaintiff, and usually can serve it by mail because the plaintiff, by initiating the lawsuit, has already appeared in the case and consented to the court's **jurisdiction** (i.e., power) to hear the case.

Service of court papers on a witness (for example, service of a notice telling the witness that his **deposition** has been scheduled), must usually be done personally; service by mail or publication is almost never sufficient.

See also *Process and Process Server* and *Quashing Service of Process*.

Settlement Agreement: See *Divorce Agreement* and *Separation Agreement*.

Settlement Conference: Many states now require parties to family law disputes, and their attorneys, to meet before trial, with a judge to see if the matter can be settled. At these settlement conferences, each side makes offers and the judge comments on their validity and fairness. The judge has no official power to make the parties settle at this stage, but usually strongly encourages settlement by bluntly critiquing the parties' trial positions and indicating how the court is likely to rule on disputed issues during the trial.

Sever a Marriage: A divorce, dissolution, or annulment severs (ends) a marriage.

Severable: The word severable is used to describe something which can be divided or cut off from the rest and maintain its independent existence. Most divorce agreements contain "severability clauses" which state that in the event one clause in the agreement is held to be invalid (perhaps because a law prohibits that type of clause in a divorce agreement), the clause will be severed from the rest of the agreement, and the remaining portion will still be considered valid and enforced accordingly.

Severe Hardship: See *Hardship*.

In Holland, any non-Dutch person (without a criminal record) able to show a "serious, affective relationship" with a financially solvent Dutch citizen (of either sex) may enter into or remain in Holland for the duration of the relationship

Sham Marriage: When an American citizen marries a citizen of another country solely to make the foreign citizen a permanent resident of the United States, the **marriage** is called a sham marriage. (It is also called a "green-card" marriage because The United States Immigration and Naturalization Service (INS) issues green cards to permanent residents.)

These marriages are illegal because they are meant to defraud the INS. If the INS becomes aware of a sham marriage and takes action, the foreign citizen can be deported and the American citizen prosecuted and possibly fined or imprisoned. If, however, the couple live together, appear to the outside world to be married, and remain married for the period of time necessary for the foreign citizen to become a United States citizen, fraud will be difficult to prove and the couple usually can avoid INS involvement.

Shared Custody: See *Joint Custody*.

Shared Parental Responsibility: See *Joint Custody*.

Short Marriage: See *Length of Marriage*.

Shot-Gun Marriage: A marriage which results from an unmarried woman getting pregnant is sometimes referred to as a shotgun marriage.

Show Cause Hearing or Order: See *Order to Show Cause Hearing*.

Siblings: Siblings is the term used to refer to brothers and sisters, that is, people who, through biology or **adoption**, have the same parents. For legal purposes, such as **intestate succession** (**inheriting property** which a deceased person did not dispose of through a **will**), siblings generally include half-brothers and

-164-

half-sisters (people who have only one parent in common), but do not include stepbrothers and stepsisters (people who are not related biologically or through adoption, but whose parents are **married** to each other).

Single Father or Mother: A **divorced**, **separated**, widowed or **unwed father** or **mother** is often referred to as a single parent, or a single father or mother.

Single-Parent Adoption: See *Adoption*.

Social Factors: Effect on Custody and Visitation: See *Lifestyle and Social Factors: Effect on Custody and Visitation*.

Sodomy: Sodomy generally refers to any "unnatural" sexual intercourse. It usually means anal intercourse. Consensual sodomy is a crime in about half the states; most of these laws are interpreted as prohibiting homosexual sex. The United States Supreme Court upheld the constitutionality of state laws prohibiting homosexual sodomy in *Bowers v. Hardwick*, 106 S. Ct. 2841 (1986). Sodomy laws are often used to justify various forms of discrimination against lesbians and gay men, including the denial of child **custody** and the refusal to recognize **cohabitation agreements**. The rationale used by the courts includes:
• People who are criminals (that is, engage in the crime of sodomy) should not be allowed custody and
• If a state prohibits sodomy, the relationship covered by the agreement is illegal and therefore the agreement is unenforceable.

See also *Fornication*.

Soldiers and Sailors Civil Relief Act: See *Active Military Duty*.

Sole Custody: Sole custody means that only one parent (called the **custodial parent**) has **physical custody** and **legal custody** of a child, and the other parent (called the **non-custodial parent**) has **visitation** rights. In most states, one parent is **awarded** sole custody of the children, although, if there is more than one child, one parent may have sole custody of one child and the other parent sole custody of the other. In some situations, one parent is given sole physical custody, but legal custody is exercised jointly by the parents.
See also *Joint Custody*.

Special Equity: Special equity is a concept in **equitable distribution states** used in the **division of property** at **divorce**. A special equity **award** grants a non-owning spouse a share of her husband's **separate property** business when she has worked in his business but has not been paid or otherwise compensated for her work.

Specific Visitation Plan: See *Visitation Schedule*.

Sperm Banks: Sperm banks are private businesses to which men donate (or sell) their semen. The semen is bought by women, or doctors on their be-

-165-

half, who want to become pregnant by **artificial insemination**. Sperm banks have advantages over inseminations arranged through friends or acquaintances in that the banks obtain complete medical histories of the donors, often know where the donors are located should there be a need to contact them in the future, and allow women to proceed without knowing the identity of the donors. Most sperm banks will not reveal the identity of the donor to the woman unless the donor consented in advance and the woman requests the information.

Spousal Abuse: See *Domestic Violence*.

Spousal Rape: Under traditional common law, still followed in many states, a husband cannot be criminally prosecuted for rape of his wife (he can be prosecuted for assault and **battery** if he beats her). Some states, however, have recently changed their laws to define rape as any sexual act carried out without the consent of the other person, regardless of **marital status**. On the other side, a few states have extended the spousal rape exemption (i.e., no prosecution for the rape) to cohabitating partners.
See also *Battered Women's Shelters* and *Domestic Violence*.

Spousal Support: Spousal support is a modern term for **alimony**.

Spousals: Spousals is an old English term meaning the mutual promises of a man and a woman to **marry**.

Stable Living Pattern: See *Established Living Pattern*.

Standard of Living: When a court sets **alimony** or **child support**, it often considers the family's pre-**divorce** standard of living and attempts to continue this standard for both spouses and the children, if feasible. Mrs. Rockefeller, therefore, would be entitled to more alimony than most divorced spouses. If only one spouse worked outside the home, and in many **marriages** where both spouses worked outside the home, it is usually impossible to continue the same standard of living for both people after the spouses have gone their separate ways. Maintenance of the same standard of living is therefore more of a goal than a guarantee.

Standard of Proof: The amount of **evidence** which a **plaintiff** (or prosecuting attorney, in a criminal case) must present in a **trial** in order to win is called the standard of proof. Different **cases** require different standards of proof depending on what is at stake. The common standards are:
• Beyond a reasonable doubt (criminal cases)—for a criminal defendant to be convicted of a crime, the prosecutor must prove her case to the point that the jurors have no reasonable doubts in their minds that the defendant did whatever he is charged with having done.
• Clear and convincing evidence (civil cases involving the potential loss of important interests such as the **termination of parental rights**)—for a party to prove a case under this standard, she must show something more than it is more likely than not, but not as much as beyond a reasonable doubt. No legal scholar has ever been able to define "clear and convincing evidence" more precisely than that.

• Preponderance of the evidence (most civil cases including **fault divorces**)—preponderance of the evidence generally means that a party will win if she can show that it is more likely than not that her contention is true.

Standards for Custody: Many state **statutes** contain specific standards for **awarding custody** of minor children. These standards are guidelines for courts in determining the **best interests of the child**. The standards include:
- Age of the child
- Sex of the child
- **Child's preference** (if the child is above a certain age, usually about 12)
- Relationship of the child with the parent, **siblings**, any **stepparent**, and any other person(s) living in the home
- **Established living pattern** for the child concerning school, home, community, religious institution, etc.
- Mental and physical health of the child and parents (including any history of child abuse)
- and **lifestyle and other social factors** of the parents.

Status Offender: A child in trouble with juvenile authorities for an action that is not a crime is sometimes referred to as a status offender because, but for his status as a juvenile, he would not be involved in the legal system. That is, he has not committed any act that is criminal under the law.
See *Incorrigible Children* and *Juvenile Court*.

Statute: There are two major ways in which legal principles are developed in the United States. One is through **appellate court** decisions in individual **cases** (called **case law**). The other is through the passage of laws by voters and legislative bodies (called statutes). Under the United States and state constitutions, statutes are considered the primary source of law in the U.S., that is, legislatures make the law (statutes) and courts interpret the law (cases).
See also *Common Law; Legislative Intent; Ordinances; Retroactive Application of Laws;* and *Uniform Statutes*.

Statute of Limitation: A statute of limitation is a law that sets the deadline for filing a lawsuit in a particular kind of dispute. These deadlines vary depending on the state, the type of issues, and the circumstances of the **case**. A lawsuit filed after the deadline will be thrown out of court.
In California and Texas, for example, when one person breaches a written contract, the other person has four years to sue; this is called a four-year statute of limitation. A personal injury suit, such as an assault and **battery** case brought by the victim of **domestic violence**, must be brought within one year from the date of the injury in California and within two years in Texas.
There are no statutes of limitation for filing a **no-fault divorce**. Filing a **fault di-**

vorce, however, usually involves a time limitation; for example, an "innocent" spouse has only a set period of time after learning of her spouse's **adultery** (or **desertion** or **cruelty**) to file for divorce on this ground. Failure of one spouse to file the lawsuit within the time period may provide the other spouse with a **defense to the divorce**.

Statutory Rape: In all states, sexual intercourse with a woman (except by a husband with his wife) under the **age of consent** is irrebuttably **presumed** to be the rape of that woman. Her consent is irrelevant; she is presumed to be unable to consent to sexual intercourse until she reaches the age of consent. Depending on the state, the age of the man may determine the severity of the punishment. If he too, is very young, a court may view the situation as an experiment, rather than rape; young men, however, may very well may be prosecuted for rape.

In addition to statutory rape laws, most states have unlawful sex **statutes** that prohibit adults from engaging in sexual intercourse with **minors**. Unlawful sex statutes are usually misdemeanors (punishable by a fine, or a jail sentence not to exceed one year), whereas statutory rape is a felony (punishable by a jail sentence of a year or longer).

Stepbrother or Stepsister: See *Siblings*.

Stepparent: A stepparent is a person **married** to a man or woman who has a child. In general, the stepparent and stepchild have no legal relationship. This means, in most states, that there is no right of **inheritance** between a stepparent and a stepchild (absent a **will**) and no obligation to support nor any rights of **visitation** if the legal parent and the stepparent **divorce**.

See also *Siblings* and *Stepparent Adoption*.

Stepparent Adoption: A stepparent often wants to **adopt** her stepchild. Most states have special provisions making it relatively easy for a stepparent to adopt, if the child's **non-custodial parent** agrees, is missing, or has **abandoned the child**.

Sterilization: Sterilization is the process of rendering someone, through surgery, incapable of producing children. The most common methods for women are tying the Fallopian tubes or removing the uterus; the most common method for men is a vasectomy. Although most forms of sterilization are permanent, recent advances in medical science permit reversal under some circumstances. Involuntary court-ordered sterilization of mentally retarded people, people with severe emotional disturbances, epileptics and some prisoners is authorized today in a number of states and is quite controversial.

Stipulated Modification: See *Agreement to Modify Alimony, Child Support, Custody or Visitation*.

Stipulation: A stipulation is an agreement between **parties** to a lawsuit that a certain fact may be considered true or that a certain procedure may be followed in court. Most stipulations are put in writing, but it is usually not required.

> **EXAMPLE**
>
> Pedro and Maria are **divorcing**. During their **marriage** they bought a house, which they now agree is worth $140,000. They disagree, however, as to what portion is Maria's **separate property**, what portion is Pedro's separate property and what portion is **marital property**. At their **trial**, Pedro and Maria will stipulate that the house's value is $140,000, but not to who owns what portions.

Subject-Matter Jurisdiction: Subject-matter jurisdiction is the legal authority of a particular court to decide certain types of disputes. For example, a **family law** court has subject-matter jurisdiction over **divorces, paternity actions,** and often **adoptions,** but not over **bankruptcies** or criminal cases. Similarly, a bankruptcy court has subject-matter jurisdiction over bankruptcies but not over criminal cases or divorces. The subject matter jurisdiction of a court is set either by the state constitution or by the state **statutes.**

See also *In Rem Jurisdiction; Jurisdiction;* and *Personal Jurisdiction.*

Subpoenas and Subpoenas Duces Tecum: See *Discovery* and *Failure to Appear at Court Hearing.*

Substantial Change in Circumstance: See *Changed Circumstance.*

Substantive Law: Laws which define legal duties and rights are called the substance of the law, or substantive law. Substantive laws include the **standards for custody,** the **grounds for divorce** and the right to have an **abortion.** On the other hand, the body of laws which tells how to go to court and get **judicial relief** is generally called procedural law.

Substitute Marriage: See *Proxy Marriage.*

Substituted Service: See *Service of Court Papers*

Summary Proceeding: Certain court proceedings, such as the issuance of **temporary restraining orders** to stop **domestic violence,** occur very quickly, without the usual **notice** and waiting periods, because of the urgent nature of the problem. These proceedings are often called summary proceedings because of their speedy nature.

Summons: A paper issued by a court informing a person that a **complaint** has been filed against her (i.e., that she has been sued) is called a summons. The **plaintiff** must have the defendant **served** with the complaint and the summons in order for the court to obtain **personal jurisdiction** over her. The summons tells her that she is being sued, by whom, for what, and that she must file a response with the court within a certain time or she will lose.

See also *Service of Court Papers.*

Supervised Visitation: When a **non-custodial parent** has a history of violent or destructive behavior, especially toward her child, the court often requires that **visitation** between that parent and the child be supervised. This means that an adult (other than the **custodial parent**) must be present at all times during the visit. The adult may be known or unknown to the child, and may be someone agreed upon by the parents or appointed by the court. No matter how the adult is chosen, he must be approved by the court ordering the supervised visitation.

Support: See *Alimony* and *Child Support*.

Surrogate Mother: A surrogate mother is a woman who is paid to bear a child for someone else. Most surrogate mothers are impregnated with the semen of a man. A few others have already fertilized eggs of other women implanted in their wombs. In either case, upon the birth of the child, the surrogate mother relinquishes all rights in and responsibilities for the child and turns the child over to either the man (in the former case), or the man and/or the woman (in the latter situation).

The most common scenario with surrogate motherhood is where a woman is unable to bear children; her husband's semen is used to impregnate another woman who acts as the surrogate mother. After the child is born, the man's wife formally **adopts** the child.

Surrogate motherhood is a very new area of law. The best known surrogate motherhood **case** is the New Jersey *Baby M.* case, where the surrogate mother changed her mind after the baby was born and decided that she wanted to keep the baby. The baby's father and his wife sued the surrogate mother to enforce the contract. The **trial court** declared the contract valid, terminated the surrogate mother's **parental rights**, and allowed the father's wife to **adopt** the baby. The New Jersey Supreme Court **reversed** that decision, ruled that surrogate motherhood contracts are unenforceable, and then treated the case like any other disputed **custody** case, **awarding** custody to the father and **visitation** rights to the surrogate mother.

In response to the *Baby M.* case, many states are considering legislation to regulate or prohibit surrogate motherhood arrangements.

Survivorship, Right of: See *Joint Tenancy*.

Suspension of Alimony or Child Support: See *Temporary Modification of Alimony or Child Support*.

Tax laws applicable to married couples in Sweden apply to cohabitating couples who were formerly married (to each other) or have a child together.

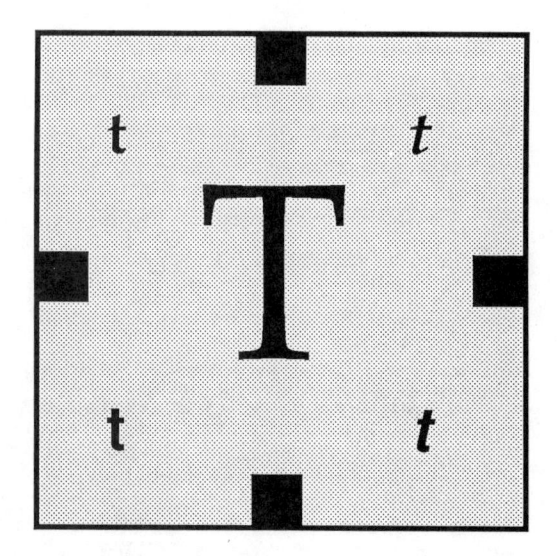

Tax Consequences of Alimony and Child Support: For federal income tax purposes, **alimony** paid under a court **order** is deductible by the payor and is taxable to the recipient. **Child support**, on the other hand, is tax-free to the recipient but not deductible by the payor.

Because many **non-custodial parents** have higher incomes than **custodial parents**, ex-spouses often agree to greater alimony and less child support because the resulting tax advantage to the payor will permit a larger total payment. In divorces where the payor pays **family support** (combined alimony and child support), the payments are treated like child support (neither deductible nor taxable) unless there is a court order expressly stating which portion is toward alimony and which is toward child support.

The parent who provides more than 50% of the child's support is permitted to claim the child as a deduction on his federal income tax return. If that person is unmarried he may use the **head of household** filing category. The tax rate for the head of household category is higher than that for married persons filing jointly, but lower than that for single persons. Head of household status thus provides an advantage for unmarried parents. Divorced spouses with similar incomes often fight over who will be entitled to use the head of household category. When the parents' incomes differ substantially, however, a common arrangement is for the parent with the greater income to pay high child support in exchange for taking the head of household deduction.

Tax Refund: Because a tax refund is considered **property** to be divided upon **divorce**, one issue which must be determined by divorcing spouses (or by the court if they can't agree) is who will be entitled to any tax refund received after the divorce.

In **community property** states, tax refunds are divided equally; in **equitable distribution states**, they are divided equitably (fairly), which usually means equally or near equally. In Mississippi (**common law property** state), they are divided in proportion to the spouses' incomes.

Temporary Disability: Effect on Alimony and Child Support: See *Disability*.

Temporary Hearing: See *Preliminary Hearing*.

Temporary Loss of Job: Effect on Alimony and Child Support: See *Temporary Modification of Alimony or Child Support*.

Temporary Modification of Alimony or Child Support: When the **needs of a** child or an ex-spouse receiving **alimony** change temporarily, or if the payor's **ability to pay** is temporarily impaired by illness, loss of job, or other condition, a court may modify an existing alimony or **child support order** for a specific period of time to account for the temporary condition. At the end of the set period, the temporary modification terminates and the alimony or child support reverts to the prior terms unless an order for **permanent alimony or child support** is obtained. Although desirable, a temporary modification of alimony or child support is not easy to obtain, as it often requires the filing of many **court papers**.

Temporary Modification of Custody or Visitation: When a **custodial parent** will be temporarily out of state, hospitalized, or otherwise unable to care for the child, she may request that a court make a temporary modification of **custody**, giving the other parent custody for the time of the incapacity, but restoring custody to her when the incapacity ends.

Where the custodial parent will be temporarily unavailable to care for the child, and there is no other parent to have custody, the custodial parent should name someone to act as **guardian** of the child for the temporary period.

Temporary Provisions for Alimony, Child Support, Custody, Visitation and Property Division: When a couple **separates** or files for **divorce**, the spouses often need the immediate intervention of a court to establish **alimony, child support, custody, visitation,** who drives the car, who pays the bills, who lives in the house, etc. pending the divorce proceedings. Either spouse may request a preliminary hearing before the judge to have these issues resolved. The orders made in these preliminary hearings are often, but not necessarily, what the interlocutory or final judgment will include.

EXAMPLE

Ken and Kim have separated; they have three teenaged children, own a house, a station wagon and a sports car. Ken is a psychotherapist who works out of the home, and Kim is a television reporter. Because Ken's practice is in the home, he stayed there with the kids and Kim moved in temporarily with a friend. Kim wants use of the house, but Ken has changed the locks. Kim filed a motion with the court requesting a preliminary hearing on the issues of use of the house, use of the cars and custody. (Neither Kim nor Ken wants alimony because their incomes are nearly identical.) At the hearing, the court is likely to grant Ken use of the home (because of his professional needs) and the station wagon (because he's got the kids), but will require him to allow Kim access to the house. If the kids were younger, or if Kim worked part-time, the court might have been more inclined to grant her use of the home and to order Ken to set up his practice elsewhere. When the court later makes the permanent orders (at the trial or when asked to review the couple's **divorce agreement**), it is likely to make these temporary provisions permanent unless the situation has changed or the **parties** agree to something different.

Temporary Restraining Order (TRO): When one spouse threatens to harm the other or wrongfully take the children or **property**, a court has the power, without holding a formal **hearing**, to temporarily order the wrongdoer not to take any further action until the court has had more time to fully consider the situation. This **order** is called a temporary restraining order (TRO). A TRO is usually issued after one party makes a request for an **ex parte** hearing (ex parte means that only the party asking for the TRO appears before the judge). Once the TRO is issued, the court holds a second hearing, where the other side can tell his story and the court can decide whether the TRO should be made permanent in the form of an **injunction**.

Although a piece of paper will often not stop an enraged spouse from acting violent, the police are more willing to intervene if the victim has a TRO. In some states, where **domestic violence** is involved, courts issue temporary restraining orders against live-in lovers as well as spouses.

See also *Childnapping*.

Tenancy by the Entirety: Tenancy by the entirety is a way married couples can hold **title to property** in some states. Tenancy by the entirety is very similar to **joint tenancy**; upon the death of one of the spouses, the **property** automatically passes to the surviving spouse, regardless of **will** provisions to the contrary. Unlike joint tenancy, however, one person cannot unilaterally sever the tenancy by the entirety.

Tenancy in Common: Tenancy in common is a way for any two or more people to hold **title to property** together. Each co-owner has an "undivided interest" in the **property** which means that no owner holds a particular part of the property and all co-owners have the right to use all the property. Each owner is free to sell or give away his interest. On his death, his interest passes through his will or by **intestate succession** if he had no will.

Tenancy in common differs from **joint tenancy** and **tenancy by the entirety** where the property passes automatically to the surviving co-owners on one own's death, regardless of any will provision. Tenancy in common is a more appropriate form of title than joint tenancy when co-owners do not have a close personal relationship, such as when individuals are all willed a home and find themselves joint owners.

Tender Years Doctrine: In the past, most states provided that **custody** of children of tender years (about five and under), had to be **awarded** to the mother when parents **divorced**. This rule has been rejected in most states, or relegated to the role of tie-breaker when both parents request custody, are fit to have custody and the children are preschool age. In many areas, the trend in this situation is toward **joint custody**.

Termination of Alimony: Alimony usually ends automatically when the recipient **remarries**, when either ex-spouse dies, or when a condition set out by the court **order** occurs (for example, **ability to be self-supporting**, or **cohabitation**). Alimony may also end at a specific date set by the court's alimony order. If **periodic payments** are part of a **divorce agreement** or an **integrated property settlement agreement**, however, the alimony may continue even after the recipient remarries. When the recipient has not remarried, and no condition or date set for the alimony to expire has occurred, termination of alimony can only be by court order.

See also *Non-Modifiable Alimony* and *Request for Modification of Alimony, Child Support, Custody or Visitation.*

Termination of Child Support: Child support terminates only when a child reaches the **age of majority**, goes on **active military duty**, is **adopted**, or is declared **emancipated** under state law. Otherwise, a parent has a **continuing duty to support** his child.

See also *Request for Modification of Alimony, Child Support, Custody or Visitation.*

Termination of Parental Rights: Parental rights are rights to exercise **parental control** and **custody** of a child. When a child is placed up for **adoption**, the biological parents' rights are terminated. (If a child is adopted by her **stepparent**, only the **noncustodial** parent's rights are terminated.)

If a court finds a parent **unfit**, or places a child in a **foster home**, parental rights may be temporarily suspended while the parent tries to rehabilitate herself. If the rehabilitation succeeds, parental rights may be restored.

Test-Tube Babies: See *In Vitro Fertilization*.

Title States: See *Common Law Property States*.

Title to Property: The owner of a piece of **real property** is said to have title to it. Title is proof of ownership. A **deed** is evidence of title to real property; some kinds of **personal property** (car, boat, R.V., motorcycle, and stocks) have title documents as well. Deeds and other title documents specify how the owners hold title to their property. Common methods of taking title include **joint tenancy, tenancy by the entirety, tenancy in common, community property,** and **separate** title.

In all states except **community property states**, **property** ownership upon death is determined by who holds title to the property (if property is the type that carries title). In community property states, each spouse owns one-half of all community property. When one spouse dies, the other spouse automatically keeps his half of each item of community property. The deceased spouse's half goes either to whomever is named in a **will**, or to the surviving spouse if there is no will provision.

In the case of **divorce**, all states but Mississippi ignore whose name is on the title if the property was acquired in the course of the **marriage**, and divide the property between the spouses under **community property** or **equitable distribution** principles. In Mississippi, the name on the title document governs who owns the property at divorce.

Tort: A tort is an act that injures someone in some way, and for which the injured person may sue the wrongdoer for damages. Legally, torts are called "civil wrongs," as opposed to criminal ones (though some acts, like battery may be both torts and crimes; the wrongdoer may face both civil and criminal penalties). Common torts are negligence (e.g., running a red light when driving and rear-ending another car), intentional (or negligent) infliction of emotional distress, defamation, invasion of privacy, false arrest and trespass.

Many states prohibit one family member from suing another for tortious acts. Other states allow **intrafamilial tort suits**, especially when there is evidence of **domestic violence**.

See also *Actual Damages* and *Punitive Damages*.

Tracing of Funds: In **community property states**, when one spouse's **separate property** is combined (commingled) with **community property**, the mixed **assets** are presumed to be community property. Upon **divorce**, community property is divided equally, while each spouse keeps his own separate property. The owner of the separate property, however, may be able to overcome the presumption of community property created by the commingling by establishing the separate source of the funds. This is called tracing the funds. Tracing usually involves carefully analysis of bank, credit union and other fund deposits and withdrawals.

See also *Reimbursement*.

EXAMPLE

Jim and Leslie live in Idaho, a **community property state**. They deposited their paychecks (community property) into a bank account which usually had a balance of about $2,000 to pay the household bills. Leslie also deposited into the account, $5,000 in proceeds from the sale of a boat she owned before marrying Jim (her separate property). Four thousand dollars from the account was then used to buy exercise equipment for the house. Jim and Leslie divorce, and Jim claims that half the the equipment is his. Leslie says it's all hers.

There are two ways Leslie can prove her position. First, she can show that at the time the exercise equipment was bought, there was an excess of her separate property deposits over her separate property expenses (for example, a student loan she incurred before marrying Jim) in the account (this must be done by reconstructing each separate property deposit and expenditure from the account) and then showing that the excess was used to buy the equipment. Second, she can show that other than the equipment, they only used the commingled funds to pay for household expenses; the law presumes that household expenses are paid for from the community portion, leaving the separate property portion to pay for the exercise equipment.

Transition Period: The period of time between **divorce** and when a spouse receiving **alimony** is to become self-supporting is often called the transition period.

Transmutation Doctrine: In community property states, when **property** is changed from **separate property** to **community property**, or vice versa, the change is called a transmutation. Property can be automatically transmuted, as when it is **commingled**, or changed by an **agreement** during marriage.

See also *Reimbursement* and *Tracing of Funds*.

Transportation of Children: One issue which must be decided when arranging **custody** and **visitation** is who will be responsible for transporting the children to and from the **non-custodial parent**. Often, the time and cost involved is shared, or if the parents live far from each other, the parent in better economic condition may be required to pay more of the cost. Transportation of children for visitation purposes is a commonly disputed issue after the **divorce** and should not be overlooked when the parents draft their **divorce agreement**.

Travel: Effect on Residency: Travel for any length of time does not affect residency for the purpose of obtaining a **divorce**. Thus, if Henry moved to New Hampshire from

Florida, lived there for several years, and then took a leisurely trip around the world, he could still return to New Hampshire and file for divorce based on his prior established residency.

See also *Residency: Effect on Marriage and Divorce*.

Trial: The phase of **litigation** where **evidence** is introduced by the **parties** and contested issues of fact are resolved by a judge or jury is called the trial. Virtually all **family law** trials are held without juries.

In a trial before a judge only, the parties usually begin with the presentation of evidence, although in some cases the **plaintiff** and **defendant** make opening statements. After the plaintiff finishes presenting his evidence, the defendant presents her case. After the defendant concludes her presentation, the plaintiff may **rebut** the defendant's case. Rarely are **closing arguments** made (as they are in **jury trials**). The judge often takes the case under submission (i.e., takes between a few hours and a few weeks) to consider the evidence and reach a decision.

In jury trials, the jury is selected by the parties through a process called voir dire, where the judge or parties ask jurors questions in order to determine their **biases** and opinions. (Each side gets to reject a certain number of potential jurors.) After the jury is chosen and sworn in, the parties give opening arguments, present their evidence, and give closing arguments. The jury then deliberates; when it reaches a decision, it returns to the courtroom and announces the verdict.

Trial Court: The trial court is the court in which a lawsuit is filed, and where a **trial** is held. Over 90% of all civil (as opposed to criminal) lawsuits, however, are settled by the parties without a trial.

See also *Appellate Court*.

Trial Separation: See *Living Apart* and *Separation*.

The model community property jurisdictions are California, France, Mexico, Quebec, South Africa and the Soviet Union.

Unadoptable Children: Agencies often have a hard time finding **adoptive** parents for older children (above age five), minority children, and children with special needs, such as abused or neglected children, children with physical and mental disabilities, or underprivileged children. These children are sometimes referred to as "unadoptable." As more single, lesbian and gay people seek to adopt, however, more children with special needs may be adopted. This is because single, lesbian and gay people have traditionally been prohibited from adopting and are often more flexible than **married** couples about adopting older, disabled, or underprivileged children.

Uncontested Divorce: See *Default Divorce.*

Uncontested Hearing: See *Contested Hearing.*

Uncontested Modification: See *Agreement to Modify Alimony, Child Support, Custody or Visitation.*

Under-Age Children: See *Age of Consent; Age of Majority; Emancipated Minor* and *Minor.*

Underpayment of Support: See *Arrearage.*

Unfitness of Parent: If a parent's lifestyle is found to be detrimental to a child, a court may declare that parent unfit to have any contact—including **supervised visitation**—with her child. What constitutes unfitness depends on many issues, including the social, psychological and sexual behavior of the parent. Unfitness is an extreme determination. It often leads to a **termination of parental rights**, and usually involves abuse or severe neglect.

Uniform Child Custody Jurisdiction Act (UCCJA): All states and the District of Columbia have enacted a **statute** called the Uniform Child Custody Jurisdiction Act, which sets standards for when a court may make a **custody** determination and when a court must defer to an existing determination from another state. In general, a state may make a custody decision about a child if (in order of preference):

• The state is the child's home state—this means the child has resided in the state for the six previous months, or was residing in the state but is absent because a parent has removed the child from or retained the child outside of the state

• There are significant connections with and substantial evidence in (such as teachers, doctors, grandparents, etc.) the state concerning the child's care, protection, training and personal relationships

• The child is in the state and either has been abandoned or is in danger of being abused or neglected if sent back to the other state

• and No other state can meet one of the above three tests, or a state can meet at least one of the tests but has declined to make a custody decision.

If a state cannot meet one of these tests, even if the child is present in the state, the courts of that state cannot make a custody **award**. Also, a parent who has wrongfully removed or retained a child in order to create a "home state" or "significant connections" will be denied custody. In the event more than one state meets the above standards, the law contemplates that only one state awards custody. This means that once the first state makes a custody award, another state can neither make another "initial" award nor modify the existing order.

Having the same law in all states helps achieve consistency in the treatment of custody **decrees**. It also helps solve many of the problems created by **childnapping** or disagreements over custody between parents living in different states.

EXAMPLE

Sam and Diane met and **married** in Missouri. They moved to Delaware where their child (Sam Jr.) was born. Sam, Diane and Junior lived in Delaware until Junior was 10. At that time, Sam took Junior to Missouri in an effort to **divorce** Diane and raise Junior himself. When Sam went to court in Missouri and requested custody, his request was denied because Delaware is Junior's "home state," the state with which he has "significant connections" and Sam removed Junior from Delaware in an effort to create "home state" jurisdiction in Missouri. (Diane should go to court in Delaware and request custody, even though Junior is in Missouri.)

See also *Parental Kidnapping Prevention Act (PKPA)*.

Uniform Desertion and Non-Support Act: This uniform statute has been adopted in a few states. It requires all husbands to support their wives and their children under the age of 16, and makes failure to provide such support a crime.

Uniform Divorce Recognition Act: The Uniform Divorce Recognition Act has been passed by a few states. This uniform statute provides that if both members of a married couple are residing within the state, and then the couple obtains a divorce from another state, the state in which the couple resides will not recognize or enforce the foreign divorce. This means that if a married couple lives in Ohio and gets divorced in South Dakota, Ohio will not consider the divorce valid. Having an invalid divorce can have many effects, including changing the filing status on state and federal income tax returns, altering the disposition of property on death, and in rare cases, leading to prosecution for bigamy where a spouse, knowing she has an invalid divorce, remarries.

See also *Dominican Republic Divorce*.

Uniform Gifts to Minors Act: See *Uniform Transfers to Minors Act*.

Uniform Marital Property Act: The Uniform Marital Property Act provides for division of property at divorce, in a manner nearly identical to the method used in community property states. This uniform statute has been enacted only in Wisconsin.

Uniform Marriage and Divorce Act (UMDA): The Uniform Marriage and Divorce Act (UMDA) is an extensive uniform statute which provides standards governing marriage, divorce, property distribution, alimony, child support and custody. It has been adopted by approximately ten states. The major provisions:

- Eliminate fault divorces (the only ground permitted is irretrievable breakdown, defined as either living apart for 180 days, or a serious marital discord adversely affecting the attitude of one or both spouses toward the marriage).
- Provide for equitable distribution of property for non-community property states; factors to include in making an equitable distribution are:
  - length of marriage and any prior marriages
  - agreement before marriage
  - age, health, station, occupation, income, vocational skills, employability, property and debts of each spouse
  - needs of the parties, including any future opportunities to acquire assets
  - who has custody
  - any economic misconduct
  - and whether the property distribution is in lieu of, or in addition to, alimony.
- Provide factors for distributing community property; the factors are:
  - non-monetary contributions to the marriage
  - value of property distributed to each spouse
  - length of marriage
  - and any other economic circumstances including the need to award the family home to the custodial parent.

- Award alimony only if the supported spouse both lacks property to provide for reasonable needs, and is unable to support herself through employment or is a custodial parent unable to seek employment outside the home.
- Base child support on:
  - resources of the child and the custodial parent
  - standard of living the child enjoyed before the divorce
  - physical, emotional and educational needs of the child
  - and resources and needs of the **noncustodial parent**.
- Base custody on:
  - parents' and child's **preferences**
  - relationship of child with parents, **siblings**, and others affecting child
  - stability of home, school and community environments
  - and mental and physical health of all involved.

Uniform Parentage Act: The Uniform Parentage Act is a **uniform statute** which gives courts procedures and standards for determining the paternity of a child in a contested **paternity action**. It has been enacted in nearly 20 states. The major provisions of the Uniform Parentage Act:

- Declare the **marital status** of the parents irrelevant.
- Provide a **presumption** of paternity in a man if:
  - he and the mother were married when the child was born or the the child was born within 300 days of the end of the **marriage**
  - he and the mother attempted to marry before the child's birth
  - he and the mother married or attempted to marry after the child's birth, and
    - Δ he acknowledged paternity in writing
    - Δ he consented to be on and is on the child's **birth certificate**
    - Δ or he is obligated to pay **child support** under a written promise or court order.
  - he has taken the minor child into his home and openly holds the child out as his
  - or he has acknowledged that he is the father.
- Declare that a child born to a married woman via **artificial insemination** is the child of her husband, not the donor.
- Allow a court to order the child, mother, and **putative father** to undergo blood tests
- and allow the following as **admissible evidence:**
  - instances of sexual intercourse
  - statistical probability of parentage, and medical and anthropological evidence, presented by an **expert witnesses**
  - and blood tests.

Uniform Pre-Marital Agreement Act: This act has been adopted in Alaska, California, Hawaii, Maine, Montana, North Carolina, North Dakota, Oregon, Rhode Island, Texas and Virginia. It provides legal guidelines for people who wish to make **agreements prior to marriage** regarding ownership, **management and control of property**; property disposition on **separation, divorce** and death; alimony; wills; and life **insurance** beneficiaries. The **statute** expressly prohibits couples from including provisions concerning **child support**. Pre-marital agreements are permitted in states that haven't adopted this **uniform statute**, but are subject to different guidelines in those states.

Uniform Reciprocal Enforcement of Support Act (URESA): See *Revised Uniform Reciprocal Enforcement of Support Act (RURESA)*.

Uniform Statutes: Uniform laws, such as the **Uniform Child Custody Jurisdiction Act**, the **Uniform Pre-marital Agreement Act**, and others, are model laws proposed by a national group of judges, lawyers and law professors called the Uniform Law Commissioners. The commissioners propose the laws; states are free to enact or reject them.

Topics covered by uniform laws are often ones where there is much interstate activity, such as **marriage**, **divorce**, **paternity**, **custody** and **child support** and in which consistency, predictability and uniformity are desirable. Some uniform laws have been passed by all states (e.g., the **Uniform Child Custody Jurisdiction Act**) whereas others have only been enacted by a few (e.g., the **Uniform Divorce Recognition Act**). Clearly, the central goal of uniformity is well served only if a significant number of states enact a given uniform law.

Uniform Transfers to Minors Act: This act was initially called the Uniform Gifts to Minors Act, and as the Uniform Gifts to Minors Act was adopted in all 50 states. It was then changed to the Uniform Transfers to Minors Act and has been adopted in many, but not all states. (The other states still follow the Uniform Gifts to Minors Act.) Both laws allow a person who makes a gift of substantial value to a child to select a "custodian" of the gift. The custodian has the authority to invest and manage the **property**. The custodian must manage the property wisely (invest it or use it to support the child) and must turn it over to the child when she reaches the **age of majority**. (California allows the donor to delay the custodian's turning the property over to the child before she reaches an age up to 25.)

Unwed Father: An unmarried man who impregnates a woman is referred to as an unwed father. Unwed fathers have a few rights concerning their children. For example, an unwed father does not have the right to require the mother of the child to obtain his consent, or even notify him, before she undergoes an **abortion**. If the mother decides to bear and keep the child, however, the unwed father will be required to pay **child support** if a court determines or he acknowledges that he's the father; in addition, he may seek **custody** or **visitation**.

If the mother of the child decides to place the child up for **adoption**, or if she has **married** and her husband (i.e., the child's **stepparent**) wants to adopt, the court must terminate the **parental rights** of the unwed father before granting the adoption. The unwed father may oppose the termination of his rights and the adoption. Whether his opposition will succeed depends on his relationship with the child. If he lived with the mother and helped raise the child, he has a greater chance of succeeding than if he neither visited nor supported the child. If the child to be adopted is a new born (and thus the unwed father has had no opportunity to create a relationship with the child), 20 states allow the father to prevent the adoption and obtain custody. In some of the remaining states, the father has no right to prevent the adoption; other states decide the question case by case.

If an unwed father is a **minor**, and moves out of his parents' home and raises the child, he is often considered **emancipated**.

See also *Aid to Families with Dependent Children; Paternity; Uniform Parentage Act;* and *Unwed Mother*.

Unwed Mother: An unmarried woman who becomes pregnant is often referred to as an unwed mother. Unwed mothers have virtually all the same rights as do **married** women who become pregnant—they cannot be denied the right to have an **abortion**; they cannot be required to obtain the father's consent before having an abortion; and they may raise the child or place the child up for **adoption**. An unwed mother who is under the **age of consent**, however, may be required to notify, or obtain the consent of, her parents or a court before having an abortion.

If an unwed mother is a **minor**, and moves out of her parents' home and raises the child, she is often considered **emancipated**.

See also *Aid to Families with Dependent Children; Child Support; Paternity; Uniform Parentage Act;* and *Unwed Father*.

One ground for divorce in Mexico is a husband's suggestion that his wife engage in prostitution.

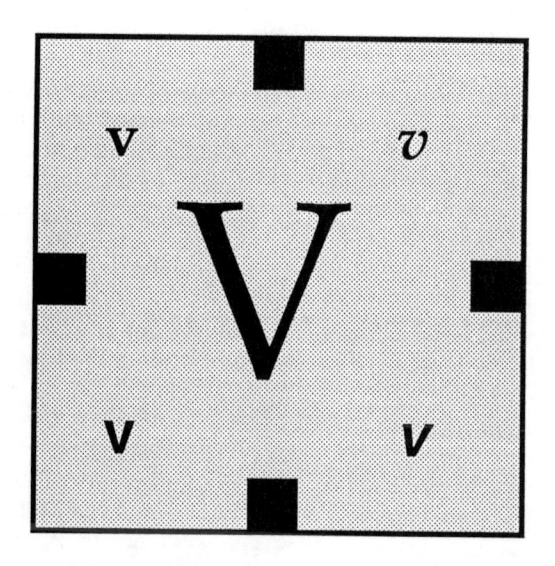

Vacated Judgment or Opinion: When an **appellate court** replaces a decision issued by a **trial court** or lower appellate court with its own opinion or **judgment**, the higher court usually declares the lower court's opinion or judgment vacated. A vacated opinion or judgment is considered to have never existed and cannot be used as **precedent**.

Valuation of Property: Valuation of property is the process of determining its monetary worth. The valuation of some or all of a couple's **marital property** is often necessary in preparing a **divorce agreement** and is always necessary when there is a **trial** to determine the **division of property**. Commonly, appraisers are required to accurately evaluate rare, unique, and valuable property.

See also *Appraisal*.

Venue: Venue is the legally proper place where a particular **case** should be filed or handled. Every state has rules determining the proper venue for different types of lawsuits. For example, the venue for a **paternity** suit might be the county where the mother or the man alleged to be the father (**putative father**) lives; the suit couldn't be brought in an unrelated county at the other end of the state.

See also *Forum; Forum Non Conveniens;* and *Jurisdiction*.

Vested Pension: See *Pension/Retirement Benefits*.

Village of Belle Terre v. Boraas: See *Zoning*.

Vinculo Matrimonii: Vinculo matrimonii is a Latin term literally meaning "from the chains of matrimony," and which has come to mean a complete **divorce,** as opposed to a **legal separation.**

Visitation: When one parent is **awarded** sole **physical custody** of the child, the other parent is awarded the right to see the child regularly, called visitation rights, unless the court believes visitation would be so detrimental to the child that the **non-custodial** parent should be prohibited from seeing the child.

RELATED TERMS
Agreement to Modify Alimony, Child Support, Custody or Visitation
Best Interests of the Child
Changed Circumstance
Custodial Parent
Custody
Destabilized Household
Established Living Pattern
Gay or Lesbian Lifestyle: Effect on Custody and Visitation
Geographic Move: Effect on Custody
Grandparents' Rights
Lifestyle and Social Factors: Effect on Custody and Visitation
Modification Agreement
Permanent Alimony, Child Support, Custody or Visitation
Reasonable Times and Places for Visitation
Request for Modification of Alimony, Child Support, Custody or Visitation
Sole Custody
Supervised Visitation
Temporary Modification of Custody or Visitation
Temporary Provision for Alimony, Child Support, Custody or Visitation
Transportation of Children
Visitation Schedule

Visitation Schedule: Some times courts ordering **custody** and **visitation** for children set up schedules, including the times and places for visitation with the **non-custodial parent** (such as every other weekend, Tuesday and Thursday evenings, etc.). In other cases, the court orders **reasonable visitation,** leaving the parents to work out the details.

Void Marriage: A void **marriage** is one that is invalid at the outset and cannot be made valid. The **parties** to a void marriage may go their separate ways without obtaining a **divorce** or an **annulment.** In virtually all states, **incestuous** marriages (e.g, between a brother and a sister) are void marriages. See also *Voidable Marriage*.

Voidable Marriage: A voidable marriage is one that is invalid at the outset, but can be made valid by some act of the couple. Parties to a voidable marriage must obtain an **annulment** or a **divorce** in order to have it declared invalid.

EXAMPLE

In some states, a marriage by a person under the **age of consent** is voidable, that is, if she or her parents object before she reaches the age of consent, the marriage may be legally terminated. If, however, neither she nor her parents object before she reaches the age of consent, her marriage becomes valid.

Voluntary Loss of Job: See *Ability to Earn*.

Divorce is not allowed in Ireland.

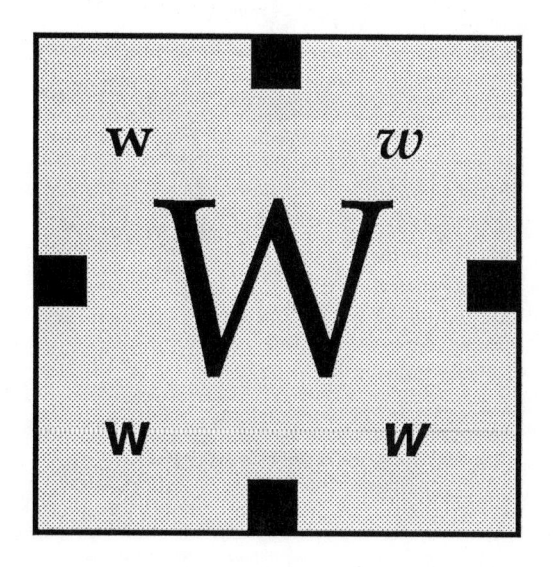

Wage Attachment: A wage attachment is a court **order** requiring an employer to deduct a certain amount of money from an employee's pay check each pay period in order to satisfy a **debt**. Wage attachments are often used to collect **alimony** or **child support arrearages** and to secure payment in the future. Under federal law, all states must provide (but, there is no requirement that it be used) some type of "automatic wage attachment" when a parent has been ordered to pay child support, even when there is no history of non-payment.

EXAMPLE—TEXAS

The automatic wage attachment law in Texas requires that when a judge makes a child support order (or modifies an existing one), he immediately notify the payor's employer that the payor's wages are being attached to pay her child support. This applies to parents who have a history of non-payment, or to parents who have faithfully paid for years without ever missing a payment, or to parents who are paying for the first time and have never had an opportunity to make—or miss—a payment. The theory behind the automatic wage attachment law in Texas is that no parent suffers the stigma of a "non-payor whose wages must be attached" if every parents' wages are attached.

> **EXAMPLE-CALIFORNIA**
>
> In California, the automatic wage attachment law requires that a judge making a child support order (or modifying an existing one) include a wage attachment provision in the order. The provision, however, does not become immediately effective. For the wage attachment to take effect, the payor must miss one month's payment. Then, the recipient files a **motion** for an **ex parte** court **hearing** (without notifying the payor); at the hearing, she tells the judge that the payor hasn't paid, and the judge orders the wage attachment effective.

Wage Garnishment: See *Wage Attachment.*

Waiting Period: See *Interlocutory and Final Judgment.*

Waiver of Fees: See *In Forma Pauperis.*

Ward: Any **minor** or adult who is unable to care for himself and is cared for by a court-appointed **guardian** is called a ward. The term ward also refers to a **delinquent child**, **dependent** child or incorrigible child over whom a **juvenile court** has assumed authority.

Wedding: Most states require a ceremony of some type for persons to be legally **married**. This ceremony, called a wedding, must be performed by a clergy member (priest, minister, rabbi) or other person (**justice of the peace**, judge, court **clerk**) given authority by law to perform weddings. The normal procedure for getting married is to obtain a **marriage license**, have the ceremony, and then file a **marriage certificate** with the county recorder within a few days after the ceremony. Usually, no special words are required as long as the bride and groom acknowledge their intention to marry each other; in fact, many people write their own ceremonies. Although it is customary to have witnesses, they are required only in some states.

See also *Common Law Marriage; Confidential Marriage;* and *Proxy Marriage.*

Welfare Department Investigation: See *Adoption; Agency Adoption; Child Neglect; Paternity Action;* and *Probation Department Investigation.*

Will: A will is a legal document in which a person (called the testator) states various intentions about what he wants done after his death. Will provisions must be carried out unless they are illegal or impossible. A will can accomplish many things, including:

• Name beneficiaries (people or organizations entitled to receive benefits) of the testator's **real property** and **personal property** (this is also called making bequests)

• Forgive **debts** owed to the person making the will

• Nominate a **guardian** of the testator's children in the event there is no other biological or **adoptive** parent to care for the children

• Create trusts in which property can be put and managed by a trustee until the person you leave the property to reaches a certain age or dies

• Name an executor of the will, that is, the person who will manage the testator's **property**, deal with the **probate court**, collect the testator's **assets** and distribute them as identified in the will after the testator dies

• and disinherit relatives (by not naming them in the will or by leaving them very little, such as $1.00).

Wrongful Death Action: A wrongful death action is a lawsuit brought by a survivor (someone who outlives another) of a deceased person. In such a lawsuit, the survivor claims that the deceased was killed due to the wrongful act of a third person (the **defendant**). Only a person who had a certain relationship with the deceased person (a parent, child or spouse usually) may sue for wrongful death. In nearly all states, **cohabitating** and **same-sex couples** are not allowed to sue for wrongful death.

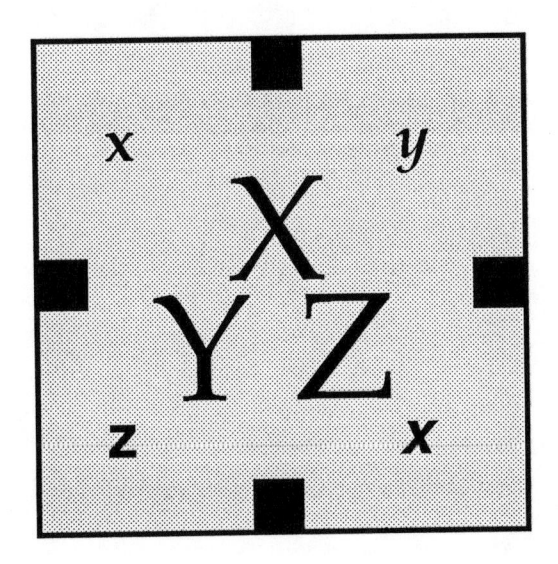

Xylophone: See *Property*.[*]

Youthful Offender: See *Delinquent Children; Incorrigible Children;* and *Juvenile Court*.

Zoning: Zoning laws divide a city or county into zones and specify what uses of land are allowed in each kind of zone. Usually, land is zoned for residential, commercial, agricultural, or industrial use, with sub-categories of those broad classifications.

Many towns have passed zoning **ordinances** restricting certain neighborhoods to **families** only. What constitutes a family under such laws varies. A family has been defined as "one or more persons related by blood, **adoption** or **marriage** or no more than two unrelated persons" (Belle Terre, New York) or "the spouse, parents, grandparents, grandchildren, children and **siblings** of the owner or tenant" (White Plains, New York). The Belle Terre ordinance was upheld as constitutional by the United States Supreme Court in *Village of Belle Terre v. Boraas*, 416 U.S. 1 (1974). That decision has allowed towns and cities to enact zoning laws restricting certain neighborhoods to certain types of families. Many towns and cities, including Denver, Colorado, have passed ordinances prohibiting unmarried couples from living in certain neighborhoods.

---

[*] We just needed an X.

self-help law books

BUSINESS & FINANCE

California Incorporator
By attorney Mancuso and Legisoft, Inc. About half of the small California corporations formed today are done without the services of a lawyer. This easy-to-use software program lets you do the paperwork with minimum effort. Just answer the questions on the screen, and *California Incorporator* will print out the 35-40 pages of documents you need to make your California corporation legal.
California Edition $129.00

How To Form Your Own Corporation
By attorney Mancuso. Provides all the forms, Bylaws, Articles, minutes of meeting, stock certificates and instructions necessary to form your small profit corporation. Includes a thorough discussion of the practical and legal aspects of incorporation, including the tax consequences.
California Edition $29.95
Texas Edition $21.95
New York Edition $19.95
Florida Edition $19.95

1988 Calcorp Update Package
Attorney Anthony Mancuso
This update package contains all the forms and instructions you need to modify your corporation's Articles of Incorporation so you can take advantage of new California laws.
$25.00

The Non-Profit Corporation Handbook
By attorney Mancuso. Includes all the forms, Bylaws, Articles, minutes, and instructions you need to form a non-profit corporation. Step-by-step instructions on how to choose a name, draft Articles and Bylaws, attain favorable tax status. Thorough information on federal tax exemptions, which groups outside of California will find particularly useful.
California only $24.95

The California Professional Corporation Handbook
By attorneys Mancuso and Honigsberg. In California a number of professions must fulfill special requirements when forming a corporation. Among them are lawyers, dentists, doctors and other health professionals, accountants and certain social workers. This book contains detailed information on the special requirements of every profession and all the forms and instructions necessary to form a professional corporation.
California only $29.95

Marketing Without Advertising
By Phillips and Rasberry. A creative and practical guide that shows small business people how to avoid wasting money on advertising. The authors, experienced business consultants, show how to implement an ongoing marketing plan to tell potential and current customers that yours is a quality business worth trusting, recommending and coming back to.
National Edition $14.00

Billpayers' Rights
By attorney Warner. Complete information on bankruptcy, student loans, wage attachments, dealing with bill collectors and collection agencies, credit cards, car repossessions, homesteads, child support and much more.
California only $14.95

Bankruptcy: Do-It-Yourself
By attorney Kosel. Tells you exactly what bankruptcy is all about and how it affects your credit rating, property and debts, with complete details on property you can keep under the state and federal exempt property rules. Shows you step-by-step how to do it yourself; comes with all necessary forms and instructions.
National Edition $17.95

The Partnership Book
By attorneys Clifford and Warner. When two or more people join to start a small business, one of the most basic needs is to establish a solid, legal partnership agreement. This book supplies a number of sample agreements which you can use as is. Buy-out clauses, unequal sharing of assets, and limited partnerships are all discussed in detail.
National Edition $18.95

Chapter 13: The Federal Plan to Repay Your Debts
By attorney Kosel. This book allows an individual to develop and carry out a feasible plan to pay most of his/her debts over a three-year period. Chapter 13 is an alternative to straight bankruptcy and yet it still means the end of creditor harassment, wage attachments and other collection efforts. Comes complete with all necessary forms and worksheets.
National Edition $17.95

Small Time Operator
By Kamoroff, C.P.A.. Shows you how to start and operate your small business, keep your books, pay your taxes and stay out of trouble. Comes complete with a year's supply of ledgers and worksheets designed especially for small businesses, and contains invaluable information on permits, licenses, financing, loans, insurance, bank accounts, etc. Published by Bell Springs.
National Edition $10.95

Start-Up Money: How to Finance Your Small Business
By Business Consultant McKeever. For anyone about to start a business or revamp an existing one, this book shows how to write a business plan, draft a loan package and find sources of small business finance.
National Edition $15.95

Getting Started as an Independent Paralegal (two audio cassette tapes)
By attorney Warner. In these two audiotapes, about three hours in all, Ralph Warner explains how to set up and run an independent paralegal business and how to market your services. He also discusses in detail how to avoid charges of unauthorized practice of law.
National 1st Edition $24.95

The Independent Paralegal's Handbook: How to Provide Legal Services Without Going to Jail
By attorney Warner. More and more nonlawyers are opening legal typing services to help people prepare their own papers for divorce, bankruptcy, incorporation, eviction, etc. Called independent paralegals, these legal pioneers pose much the same challenge to the legal establishment as midwives do to conventional medicine. Written by Nolo Press co-founder Ralph Warner, who established one of the first divorce typing services in 1973, this controversial book is sure to become the bible of the new movement aimed at delivering routine legal services to the public at a reasonable price.
National Edition $12.95

ESTATE PLANNING, WILLS & PROBATE

Plan Your Estate: Wills, Probate Avoidance, Trusts and Taxes
By attorney Clifford. Comprehensive information on making a will, alternatives to probate, planning to limit inheritance and estate taxes, living trusts, and providing for family and friends.
California Edition $17.95

Nolo's Simple Will Book
By attorney Clifford. This book will show you how to draft a will without a lawyer in any state except Louisiana. Covers all the basics, including what to do about children, whom you can designate to carry out your wishes, and how to comply with the technical legal requirements of each state. Includes examples and many alternative clauses from which to choose.
National Edition $14.95
with cassette $19.95

WillMaker
—a software/book package
By Legisoft. Use your computer to prepare and update your own valid will. A manual provides help in areas such as tax planning and probate avoidance. Runs on the Apple II family, IBM PC and compatibles, Commodore, Macintosh.
National Edition $59.95
Commodore Edition $39.95

How to Probate an Estate
By Nissley. Forms and instructions necessary to settle a California resident's estate after death. This book deals with joint tenancy and community property transfers as well as showing you how to actually probate an estate, step-by-step. The book is aimed at the executor, administrator or family member who will have the actual responsibility to settle the estate.
California Edition $24.95

FAMILY & FRIENDS

Family Law Dictionary
By attorneys Leonard and Elias. A national reference guide containing straightforward explanations and examples of an area of law which touches all of our lives. The book is extremely useful for people who want to know how the laws of marriage, divorce, cohabitation and having children affect them, and for legal practitioners in the area of family law.
National Edition $13.95

How to Do Your Own Divorce
By attorney Sherman. This is the original "do-your-own-law" book. It contains tear-out copies of all the court forms required for an uncontested dissolution, as well as instructions for certain special forms.
California Edition $14.95
Texas Edition $12.95

A Legal Guide for Lesbian/Gay Couples
By attorneys Curry and Clifford. Here is a book that deals specifically with legal matters of lesbian and gay couples: raising children (custody, support, living with a lover), buying property together, wills, etc. and comes complete with sample contracts and agreements.
National Edition $17.95

The Living Together Kit
By attorneys Ihara and Warner. A legal guide for unmarried couples with information about buying or sharing property, the Marvin decision, paternity statements, medical emergencies and tax consequences. Contains a sample will and Living Together Contract.
National Edition $17.95

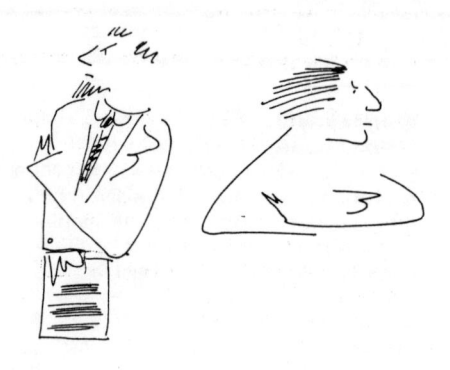

California Marriage and Divorce Law
By attorneys Ihara and Warner. This book contains invaluable information for married couples and those considering marriage or remarriage on community and separate property, names, debts, children, buying a house, etc. Includes prenuptial contracts, a simple will, probate avoidance information and an explanation of gift and inheritance taxes. Discusses "secret marriage" and "common law" marriage.
California only $15.95

Social Security, Medicare & Pensions: A Sourcebook for Older Americans
By attorney Matthews & Berman. The most comprehensive resource tool on the income, rights and benefits of Americans over 55. Includes detailed information on social security, retirement rights, Medicare, Medicaid, supplemental security income, private pensions, age discrimination, as well as a thorough explanation of social security legislation.
National Edition $14.95

How to Modify & Collect Child Support in California
By attorneys Matthews, Segal and Willis. California court awards for child support have radically increased in the last two years. This book contains the forms and instructions to obtain the benefits of this change without a lawyer and collect support directly from a person's wages or benefits, if necessary.
California only $17.95

How to Adopt Your Stepchild
By Zagone. Shows you how to prepare all the legal forms; includes information on how to get the consent of the natural parent and how to conduct an "abandonment" proceeding. Discusses appearing in court and making changes in birth certificates.
California only $19.95

The Power of Attorney Book
By attorney Clifford. Covers the process which allows you to arrange for someone else to protect your rights and property should you become incapable of doing so. Discusses the advantages and drawbacks and gives complete instructions for establishing a power of attorney yourself.
National Edition $17.95

How to Change Your Name
By attorneys Loeb and Brown. Changing one's name is a very simple procedure. Using this book, you can file the necessary papers yourself, saving $200 to $300 in attorney's fees. Comes complete with all forms and instructions for the court petition method or this simpler usage method.
California only $14.95

Your Family Records: How to Preserve Personal, Financial and Legal History
By Pladsen and attorney Clifford. Helps you organize and record all sorts of items that will affect you and your family when death or disability occur, e.g., where to find your will and deed to the house. Includes information about probate avoidance, joint ownership of property and genealogical research. Space is provided for financial and legal records.
National Edition $14.95

LANDLORD/TENANT

Tenants' Rights
By attorneys Moskovitz, Warner and Sherman. Discusses everything tenants need to know in order to protect themselves: getting deposits returned, breaking a lease, getting repairs made, using Small Claims Court, dealing with an unscrupulous landlord, forming a tenants' organization, etc. Sample Fair-to-Tenants lease, rental agreements, and unlawful detainer answer forms.
California Edition $14.95

The Landlord's Law Book: Rights and Responsibilities
By attorneys Brown and Warner. Now, for the first time, there is an accessible, easy to understand law book written specifically for landlords. Covers the areas of discrimination, insurance, tenants' privacy, leases, security deposits, rent control, liability, and rent with-holding.
California only $24.95

The Landlord's Law Book: Evictions
By attorney Brown. This is the most comprehensive manual available on how to do each step of an eviction, and the only one to deal with rent control cities and contested evictions including how to represent yourself in court if necessary. All the required forms, with directions on how to complete and file them, are included. Vol. 1 covers Rights and Responsibilities.
California only $24.95

Landlording
By Robinson (Express Press). Written for the conscientious landlord or landlady, this comprehensive guide discusses maintenance and repairs, getting good tenants, how to avoid evictions, record keeping and taxes.
National Edition $17.95

REAL ESTATE

All About Escrow
(Express Press) By Gadow. This book gives you a good understanding of what your escrow officer should be doing for you. Includes advice about inspections, financing, condominiums and cooperatives.
National Edition $12.95

The Deeds Book
By attorney Randolph. Adding or removing a name from a deed, giving up interest in community property at divorce, putting a house in joint tenancy to avoid probate, all these transactions require a change in the way title to real estate is held. This book shows you how to choose the right deed, fill it out and record it.
California Edition $15.95

Homebuyers: Lambs to the Slaughter
By attorney Bashinsky (Menasha Ridge Press). Written by a lawyer/broker, this book describes how sellers, agents, lenders and lawyers are out to fleece you, the buyer, and advises how to protect your interests.
National Edition $12.95

For Sale By Owner
By Devine. The average California home sold for $130,000 in 1986. That meant the average seller paid $7800 in broker's commissions. This book will show you how to sell your own home and save the money. All the background information and legal technicalities are included to help you do the job yourself and with confidence.
California Edition $24.95

Homestead Your House
By attorney Warner. Under the California Homestead Act, you can file a Declaration of Homestead and thus protect your home from being sold to satisfy most debts. This book explains this simple and inexpensive procedure and includes all the forms and instructions. Contains information on exemptions for mobile homes and houseboats.
California only $8.95

COPYRIGHTS & PATENTS

Legal Care for Your Software
By attorney Remer. Shows the software programmer how to protect his/her work through the use of trade secret, trademark, copyright, patent and, most especially, contractual laws and agreements. This book is full of forms and instructions that give programmers the hands-on information they need.
International Edition $29.95

Intellectual Property Law Dictionary
By attorney Elias. "Intellectual Property" includes ideas, creations and inventions. The Dictionary is designed for inventors, authors, programmers, journalists, scientists and business people who must understand how the law affects the ownership and control of new ideas and technologies. Divided into sections on: Trade Secrets, Copyrights, Trademarks, Patents and Contracts. More than a dictionary, it places terms in context as well as defines them.
National Edition $17.95

How to Copyright Software
By attorney Salone. Shows the serious programmer or software developer how to protect his or her programs through the legal device of copyright.
International Edition $24.95

Patent It Yourself
By attorney Pressman. Complete instructions on how to do a patent search and file for a patent in the U.S. Also covers how to choose the appropriate form of protection (copyright, trademark, trade secret, etc.), how to evaluate salability of inventions, patent prosecution, marketing, use of the patent, foreign filing, licensing, etc. Tear-out forms are included
National Edition $29.95

Inventor's Notebook
By Fred Grissom and attorney David Pressman. The best protection for your patent is adequate records. The Inventor's Notebook provides forms, instructions, references to relevant areas of patent law, a bibliography of legal and non-legal aids, and more. It helps you document the activities that are normally part of successful independent inventing.
National 1st Edition $19.95

RESEARCHING THE LAW

California Civil Code
(West Publishing) Statutes covering a wide variety of topics, rights and duties in the landlord/tenant relationship, marriage and divorce, contracts, transfers of real estate, consumer credit, power of attorney, and trusts.
California only $17.00

California Code of Civil Procedure
(West Publishing) Statutes governing most judicial and administrative procedures: unlawful detainer (eviction) proceedings, small claims actions, homestead procedures, wage garnishments, recording of liens, statutes of limitation, court procedures, arbitration, and appeals.
California only $17.00

Legal Research: How to Find and Understand the Law
By attorney Elias. A hands-on guide to unraveling the mysteries of the law library. For paralegals, law students, consumer activists, legal secretaries, business and media people. Shows exactly how to find laws relating to specific cases or legal questions, interpret statutes and regulations, find and research cases, understand case citations and Shepardize them.
National Edition $14.95

RULES & TOOLS

Make Your Own Contract
By attorney Elias. Provides tear-out contracts, with instructions, for non-commercial use. Covers lending money, selling or leasing personal property (e.g., cars, boats), leasing and storing items (with friends, neighbors), doing home repairs, and making deposits to hold personal property pending final payment. Includes an appendix listing all the contracts found in Nolo books.
National Edition $12.95

The Criminal Records Book
By attorney Siegel. Takes you step-by-step through the procedures available to get your records sealed, destroyed or changed. Detailed discussion on your criminal record what it is, how it can harm you, how to correct inaccuracies, marijuana possession records and juvenile court records.
California only $14.95

Everybody's Guide to Small Claims Court
By attorney Warner. Guides you step-by-step through the Small Claims procedure, providing practical information on how to evaluate your case, file and serve papers, prepare and present your case, and, most important, how to collect when you win. Separate chapters focus on common situations (landlord-tenant, automobile sales and repair, etc.).
National Edition $14.95
California Edition $14.95

Fight Your Ticket
By attorney Brown. A comprehensive manual on how to fight your traffic ticket. Radar, drunk driving, preparing for court, arguing your case to a judge, cross-examining witnesses are all covered.
California only $16.95

The People's Law Review
Edited by Warner. This is the first compendium of people's law resources ever published. Contains articles on mediation and the new "non-adversary" mediation centers, information on self-help law programs and centers (for tenants, artists, battered women, the disabled, etc.); and articles dealing with many common legal problems which show people how to do-it-themselves.
National Edition $8.95

How to Become a United States Citizen
By Sally Abel. Detailed explanation of the naturalization process. Includes step-by-step instructions from filing for naturalization to the final oath of allegiance. Includes a study guide on U.S. history and government. Text is written in both English and Spanish.
National Edition $12.95

Draft, Registration and The Law
By attorney Johnson. How it works, what to do, advice and strategies.
California only $9.95

JUST FOR FUN

Murder on the Air
By Ralph Warner and Toni Ihara. An unconventional murder mystery set in Berkeley, California. When a noted environmentalist and anti-nuclear activist is killed at a local radio station, the Berkeley violent crime squad swings into action. James Rivers, an unplugged lawyer, and Sara Tamura, Berkeley's first female murder squad detective, lead the chase. The action is fast, furious and fun. $5.95

29 Reasons Not to Go to Law School
By attorneys Ihara and Warner, with contributions by fellow lawyers and illustrations by Mari Stein. A humorous and irreverent look at the dubious pleasures of going to law school. 3rd Ed. $8.95

Poetic Justice
Edited by Jonathan & Edward Roth. A compendium of the funniest, meanest things ever said about lawyers with quotes from Lao-Tzu to Lenny Bruce. $8.95

nolo

self-help law books

ORDER FORM

Quantity	Title	Unit Price	Total

Prices subject to change

Subtotal _____

Tax (CA only): San Mateo, LA, & Bart Counties 6 1/2%
                   Santa Clara & Alameda 7%
                   All others 6%

Tax _____

Postage & Handling

No. of Books	Charge
1	$1.50
2-3	$2.00
4-5	$2.50

Over 5 add 5% of total before tax

Postage & Handling _____

Total _____

Please allow 3-5 weeks for delivery.
For faster service, add $1 for UPS delivery (no P.O. boxes, please).

Name _____

Address _____

_____

ORDERS: Credit card information or a check may be sent to:

Nolo Press
950 Parker St.
Berkeley CA 94710

Use your credit card and our **800 lines** for faster service:

ORDERS ONLY
(M-F 9-5 Pacific Time):

☐ VISA   ☐ Mastercard

_____ Exp. _____

Signature _____

Phone (   ) _____

US: 800-992-NOLO
Outside (415) area **CA:**   800-445-NOLO
Inside (415) area **CA:**   (415) 549-1976

For general information call: (415) 549-1976

☐ Please send me a catalogue